MasterClass in
Mathematics Education

MasterClass in Mathematics Education

International Perspectives on Teaching and Learning

Edited by Paul Andrews and Tim Rowland

MasterClass

BLOOMSBURY

LONDON · NEW DELHI · NEW YORK · SYDNEY

Bloomsbury Academic
An imprint of Bloomsbury Publishing Plc

50 Bedford Square	1385 Broadway
London	New York
WC1B 3DP	NY 10018
UK	USA

www.bloomsbury.com

Bloomsbury is a registered trademark of Bloomsbury Publishing Plc

First published 2014

© Paul Andrews, Tim Rowland and Contributors, 2014

British Library Cataloguing-in-Publication Data
A catalogue record for this book is available from the British Library.

ISBN: PB: 978-1-4411-7975-3
    HB: 978-1-4411-7235-8
  e-PDF: 978-1-4411-7608-0
  e-Pub: 978-1-4411-0333-8

Library of Congress Cataloging-in-Publication Data
Masterclass in mathematics education : international perspectives on teaching and learning / edited by Paul Andrews and Tim Rowland.
   pages cm. – (MasterClass)
 Includes bibliographical references and index.
  ISBN 978-1-4411-7235-8 (hardback) – ISBN 978-1-4411-7975-3 (pbk.) –
ISBN 978-1-4411-0333-8 – ISBN 978-1-4411-7608-0
  1. Mathematics–Study and teaching. 2. Effective teaching. I. Andrews, Paul (Paul R.)
editor of compilation. II. Rowland, Tim, 1945- editor of compilation. III. Title: Master class in mathematics education.
  QA11.2.M2679 2014
  510.71–dc23
                                             2013018696

Typeset by Newgen Imaging Systems Pvt Ltd, Chennai, India
Printed and bound in India

Contents

Notes on Contributors

Paul Andrews taught mathematics in three comprehensive schools in Telford, UK, before becoming a teacher educator at the Manchester Metropolitan University, UK, in 1990. He joined the Faculty of Education at the University of Cambridge, UK, in 1999 before becoming Professor of Mathematics Education at the University of Stockholm, Sweden, in 2013. His primary research interest lies in understanding how different European cultures' constructions of teaching and learning contribute to students' mathematics achievement.

Julia Anghileri was Head of Mathematics at Homerton College, and subsequently Senior Lecturer in the Faculty of Education at the University of Cambridge, UK. She gained an international reputation for her research into children's learning of arithmetic, notably in collaboration with Dutch researchers. She has published several books and been influential in the shaping of policy in England.

Richard Barwell is Associate Professor at the Faculty of Education, University of Ottawa, Canada. His research includes work on language, multilingualism and discourse analysis in Mathematics Education. He has worked in the United Kingdom, Pakistan and Canada.

Daniel Chazan is Professor and Director of the Center for Mathematics Education at the University of Maryland, USA. He studies the teaching of mathematics in compulsory high school settings as a practice carried out by individuals with their own identities and knowledge, embedded inside societal institutions, within a society with particular kinds of structure.

Fien Depaepe is a Post-Doctoral Researcher at the Center of Educational Policy, Innovation and Teacher Training at the KU Leuven, Belgium. Her main research interests are in the domains of Mathematics Education and teacher training.

Paul Ernest is Emeritus Professor at the University of Exeter, UK. His research questions the nature of mathematics and its relation to teaching, learning and society. His books include *The Philosophy of Mathematics Education* (Routledge/Falmer 1991) and *Social Constructivism as a Philosophy of Mathematics* (SUNY Press 1998). He edits the *Philosophy of Mathematics Education Journal*.

Angel Gutiérrez is Professor of Mathematics Education at the Universidad de Valencia, Spain. He teaches Mathematics Education to prospective primary and secondary school teachers, and Mathematics Education research to masters students. His research specializes in geometry education, including the teaching and learning of proof, use of dynamic geometry software, role of visualization, curriculum design and mathematically talented students in primary schools.

Jeremy Hodgen is Professor of Mathematics Education at King's College London, UK. Previously, he taught mathematics in secondary and primary schools. He has a wide range of research interests including assessment, the teaching and learning of algebra and multiplicative reasoning and international comparisons in Mathematics Education.

Eva Jablonka is Professor of Mathematics Education at King's College, London, UK. Her previous position was at Luleå University of Technology, Sweden. Her research interests include mathematical modelling, mathematical literacy, comparative classroom studies and sociological theorizing. Her most recent work has focused on the emergence of disparity in achievement in classrooms and on students in transition from school to university.

Stephen Lerman was a Secondary Teacher of Mathematics in the United Kingdom and in Israel, finally as a Head of Mathematics in a London comprehensive school, before completing a Ph.D. and moving into mathematics teacher education and research. He is a former President of the International Group for the Psychology of Mathematics Education (PME) and Chair of the British Society for Research into Learning Mathematics (BSRLM). He is now Emeritus Professor at London South Bank University, UK.

Dave Pratt is Professor of Mathematics Education at the Institute of Education, University of London, UK. He taught mathematics in secondary schools before moving to teacher education and research in Mathematics Education, initially at the University of Warwick, UK. Pratt's research has focused on the relationship between the design of digital resources and students' mathematical thinking, including research on students' probabilistic thinking.

Sebastian Rezat is Professor of Mathematics Education at the University of Paderborn, Germany. One of his main research interests is in instruments for teaching and learning mathematics, with a special focus on mathematics textbooks and their use by teachers and students.

Tim Rowland is Professor of Mathematics Education at the University of East Anglia, UK, Emeritus Reader in Mathematics Education at the University of Cambridge, UK, Vice President of PME, and Chair of the Joint Mathematical Council of the United Kingdom. He taught mathematics in two secondary schools before moving to teacher education and research in Mathematics Education. His current research focuses on mathematics teacher knowledge.

Kenneth Ruthven taught in schools in Scotland and England, before joining the Faculty of Education at the University of Cambridge, UK, where he is now Professor of Education and Director of Research. His research focuses on curriculum, pedagogy and assessment, especially in school mathematics, and particularly in respect of the complex and contested process of adaptation to technological innovation.

Rudolf Straesser (or Sträßer) is Emeritus Professor of Didactics of Mathematics at the Justus-Liebig University of Giessen, Germany. He previously worked at universities in Bielefeld and Kassel, Germany; Klagenfurt, Austria; and Luleå, Sweden. His present interests are in vocational contexts of mathematics, and the use of instruments (such as textbooks and computer software, especially for geometry) in Mathematics Education.

Andreas J. Stylianides is a Lecturer in Mathematics Education at the University of Cambridge, UK. Previously, he held fellowships at the Universities of California-Berkeley, USA, and Oxford, UK. His research focuses on the study and design of classroom environments that can support the learning of mathematics as a sense-making activity, with particular attention to mathematical reasoning, proving, problem solving and algebraic thinking.

Günter Törner is Professor in Mathematics (Algebra, Discrete Mathematics) at the University of Duisburg-Essen, Germany. Since 1975 he has also engaged in secondary teacher education. Günter has a wide range of research interests in Mathematics Education: his most recent work has focused on beliefs, affect and continuous professional development. He is Chair of the Committee of Education of the European Mathematical Society (EMS).

Marja van den Heuvel-Panhuizen is Professor of Mathematics Education at the Freudenthal Institute for Science and Mathematics Education at the Science Faculty and the Faculty of Social and Behavioural Sciences of Utrecht University, the Netherlands. Her research focuses on Mathematics Education in the primary school, special education and early childhood. She has a particular interest in assessment in Mathematics Education.

Wim Van Dooren is Assistant Professor at the Centre for Instructional Psychology and Technology at KU Leuven, Belgium. His current research focuses on mathematical (word) problem solving, rational number understanding, statistical reasoning, and the tension between intuitive and analytic thinking.

Lieven Verschaffel is Professor in Educational Sciences at the Center for Instructional Psychology and Technology at the KU Leuven, Belgium. His main research interests are mathematical problem solving, learning and teaching, especially in the domain of elementary mathematics.

Ngai-Ying Wong is Professor at the Chinese University of Hong Kong, Hong Kong. He taught mathematics in a secondary school for nine years before moving to teacher education. His research interests include Confucian Heritage Culture Learners' phenomenon, beliefs and values in Mathematics Education.

Series Editor's Foreword

Simply reading the introduction will demonstrate that this is no ordinary book about mathematics education. The editors, both eminent in the field, immediately pose sets of questions intended to engage the reader in 'thinking differently' about mathematics education. The volume is imbued with a sense of energy, purpose and academic curiosity about the 'young and developing research field' that is mathematics education.

Taking an international perspective, the volume is organized into three sections: broad educational issues, such as assessment; curriculum matters specific to mathematics, such as geometry or proof; and comparative and cultural matters. The chapters within these sections are organized around core readings, with 21 authors, all very well known in mathematics education, offering critical engagement with the research and ideas of those readings. Such an elegant approach not only introduces the reader to both seminal and newly emerging texts, but also models ways of thinking through and about mathematics education. As educators, the reader will emerge with a comprehensive overview of the field, and access to some of the most stimulating minds researching in mathematics education today.

This is no 'pre-digested thinking' text: readers have an active part to play. Ernest's 'What Is Mathematics and Why Learn It?' for example, immediately challenges any fixed preconceptions the reader might have, with the statement 'there is controversy both about what mathematics is, and the purposes of teaching and learning it.' The editors' own individual chapters similarly ask readers to 'think differently'. Rowland's 'Mathematics Teacher Knowledge' explores 'complex relationship between what a teacher knows and how this knowledge relates to their professional role', analysing not only knowledge bases but also demonstrating the importance for the educator in knowing about the nature of mathematical and professional knowledge; Andrews' 'European Mathematics Curricula and Classroom Practices' is an examination of the cultural construction of school mathematics in England, France, Germany and Russia, and demands that mathematics education be understood through a cultural lens, with the provocative claim that 'interactions of the idealized, received and intended curricula confirm the extent to which teachers are products of the cultures in which they are raised and work.' No bland claims here. Each chapter invited the reader to be a participant in the making of knowledge in mathematics education. In exploring the volume, mathematics educators can choose to follow themes in their reading, or read the sections sequentially. As the editors point out, 'in practice, the "Mathematics Education web" of interconnections will fall into place irrespective of the order in which the chapters are addressed.'

But the editors have yet further purposes in the design of this volume. They are clear that part of the function of the book is to set the reader on a wider journey of enquiry, and to deepen and extend the knowledge networks of mathematics education; indeed, for students 'to see themselves as members of a Mathematics Education research community, or communities'. This volume is designed to be a conversation: the reader's role is to take active part in the fascinating dialogues so carefully crafted for them by the authors and the editors.

It is my pleasure to include this excellent book in the MasterClass Series.

Sue Brindley, Senior Lecturer in Education
University of Cambridge, UK

Preface

Paul Andrews and Tim Rowland

Introducing mathematics education

This book is an introduction to the area of human activity, and the field of research, which is now generally called Mathematics Education, though it has also been called Mathematical Education. It is often mistaken for, or identified with, Mathematics; but it is not the same activity, and it has a different purpose and literature. Many, if not most, of the women and men who teach mathematics, from kindergarten to university, become curious about this work, and begin to ask themselves questions. Why is it that many learners find particular mathematics topics difficult to grasp, including topics that never caused them (the teacher) any trouble? Can we understand how students learn? How can we help them to learn better? Do computers help or hinder mathematics learning? What kind of education and training best equips people to teach mathematics? Why are students in some countries particularly successful at learning mathematics? Do teachers in one country enact their professional roles differently from teachers in another, and are such differences significant in respect of learning outcomes? Does where students live alter the nature of the mathematics they are offered at school? Of course, anyone can have an opinion about such matters, but opinions differ, and are inevitably based on personal experience and preference. Such opinions and prejudices are not a good basis for either educational policy or teaching practice. Attempts to look for answers in more responsible, systematic ways intensified in the second half of the twentieth century, originating in two overlapping expert groups in the first instance: mathematicians and psychologists. The first group, typified by Brian Griffiths and Geoffrey Howson in the United Kingdom and Hans Freudenthal in the Netherlands, turned their attention to curricula and practices in schools (mainly secondary), and applied their deep understanding of mathematics to the improvement of teaching (or 'instruction'). This route to Mathematics Education research remains the norm in much of Europe and elsewhere. The second group, represented by Richard Skemp in the United Kingdom and Efraim Fischbein in Israel, brought the concepts and methods of experimental psychology to their efforts to understand and explain how mathematical concepts are learned, and the obstacles that can inhibit learning. In fact, the development of mathematical thinking is a major theme in mainstream psychological research, and one can identify this line of investigation much earlier in the influential work of William Brownell in the United States, and Jean Piaget in Switzerland. In any case, one could say that the founding (by Freudenthal) of the journal *Educational Studies in Mathematics* in 1968 unequivocally marked the establishment of Mathematics Education as an independent research discipline. In the same year, the first UK Professor of Mathematics Education was appointed (Geoffrey Matthews at Chelsea College, now King's College, London). The first annual conference of the International Group for the Psychology of Mathematics Education (PME) took place in 1977, and the British Society for the Psychology of Learning Mathematics (BSPLM) was formed in 1978. The privileging of psychology (along with mathematics) in the names of both is significant. But this was a time when there were also rapid and significant advances in social theory (exemplified by Stephen Lerman in his chapter) and research methods in the social sciences, and these were soon embraced by Mathematics Education researchers. In particular, qualitative Social Science research methods involving interviews and case studies, for example, were valued for the explanatory insights that they gave to findings emerging from statistical analyses. Similarly, discourse analytic methods from linguistics were harnessed for more principled scrutiny of interviews and classroom interactions (see the chapter by Richard Barwell, this volume). Elsewhere, questions, concepts and methods from philosophical and historical research were surfacing in Mathematics Education research: Paul Ernest, one of the contributors to this book, was a key player in initiating this particular movement. In this way, Mathematics Education research expanded, irrevocably, beyond its origins in mathematics and psychology. The knowledge base underpinning the discipline of Mathematics Education is now highly eclectic, and interactions between different theoretical proponents have stimulated many fruitful interdisciplinary research projects. Appropriately, the 'P' in BSPLM was replaced by 'R' in 1985: the British Society for Research into Learning Mathematics.

Purpose and organization of the book

The purpose of this book is to introduce readers to some of the wealth of literature in what, compared with mathematics itself, is still a young and developing research field. As the series title indicates, we anticipate that the majority of our readers will be graduate students enrolled for masters courses in Mathematics Education (M.Ed., MA, M.Sc., M.Phil., etc.), in the United Kingdom or elsewhere. Our experience suggests that many of these readers will go on to doctoral study in Mathematics Education and a career in educational research, while others will be teachers studying part time, intending to develop their career in teaching. The book is also suitable for final year undergraduates in mathematics or Mathematics Education, and for teaching professionals in pre-service and in-service mathematics teacher education. In other words the book is intended to be accessible to anyone interested in developing a deep understanding of issues concerned with teaching and learning mathematics. From the outset, it has been our intention that this book, like our teaching in Cambridge and elsewhere, should be truly international in its approach. Therefore, we have avoided narrow UK-centric, parochial perspectives on global issues in Mathematics Education, when there is so much to be learned from viewing them with the fresh perspectives afforded by insights from other countries and alternative cultures. Of course, trends, events and research findings in the United Kingdom feature in some chapters, but usually to point to truths and human tendencies that transcend national boundaries.

An explanation of our approach to the structure and organization of the book will be helpful. First, we commissioned 21 colleagues from around the world to write the 17 main chapters, each of which addresses a significant, reasonably discrete and well-researched theme in the field. Such is the range of Mathematics Education research that we are acutely aware of themes that have had to be omitted from the list of chapter titles, although many are considered at points throughout the book. Each one of the international team of contributors is recognized as a leading researcher in Mathematics Education, and an expert in the topic that they address. Although we prescribed the basic format of each chapter in order to achieve some consistency, it will be apparent that these authors are individuals, each with their own emphasis and style. Importantly, characteristics of the national, regional and research culture in which they are embedded can be detected in their writing, and we decided against 'ironing out' these differences in order to achieve bland uniformity. We have organized the chapters into three main parts, addressing respectively: broad educational issues, such as assessment; curriculum matters specific to mathematics, such as geometry or proof; and comparative and cultural matters that enrich our appreciation of the field and develop our critical awareness of local practices, habits and dispositions. There would be some logic to reading the sections in order; however, in practice, the 'Mathematics Education web' of interconnections will fall into place irrespective of the order in which the chapters are addressed.

Second, each chapter mirrors an approach to masters-level teaching adopted in the well-established Mathematics Education programme with which we have been associated for many years, at the University of Cambridge. We could have asked each of the authors to write an introduction to their topic, with some additional recommended reading. Instead, the approach has been to base each chapter on three or four core texts – mainly journal articles or book chapters. Each author (or author team), in consultation with us, chose their own core readings. We then asked them to include some commentary and/or exposition of the readings, and to set them in the broader context of ideas and methods to which they belong. This 'core readings' expectation potentially involves some more reading, either (ideally) in advance, or after reading the chapter, but this has three possible benefits. It broadens readers' knowledge base in the relevant topic; it illustrates how another expert might respond to or critique the core texts; finally, perhaps most importantly, it supports readers in their encounters with some challenging leading-edge research literature. This last point is important because it models the way in which you will, or could, progress further after reading the book. Indeed, each chapter includes a short list of Further Readings for those who want to know more, perhaps in preparation for a research project or to inform professional decision making of some kind.

You will find the core texts displayed and listed at the beginning of each chapter: some, if not all, should be accessible in your university or department library. Better still, you will be able to access many of them online though your library's individual journal or publisher package subscriptions. You will benefit most from these core readings, and the chapters in this book, if you have the opportunity to discuss them with others, in ad hoc or organized seminar groups, perhaps in the presence of a graduate student or lecturer able to bring further knowledge, experience or wisdom to the discussion.

Mathematics education: People and communities

Whereas the 'greats' of mathematics (with a few exceptions) such as Euclid, Wang Xiaotong, Euler and Gauss are inevitably remote, 'historical' figures, most of the men and women who created the field of Mathematics Education (and continue to create it) are people who inhabit and share our time and space. These women and men are researchers whom you might meet at one of the many 'maths ed' conferences around the world, or at a seminar near you. One or more of them might be among your 'professors'. If someone's work interests you as you engage with the book, we would encourage you to get a sense of the author as a person: through online searches and perhaps by attending a talk given by them. With this in mind, you will find brief biographical notes on the 21 contributors at the beginning of this book.

We would encourage students of Mathematics Education, and especially graduate students, to see themselves as members of a Mathematics Education research community, or communities. As well as following sessions for your taught course at the university, you can begin to participate in such communities by attending optional research seminars. If your own university does not have a regular programme of seminars in Mathematics Education, you will be welcomed as a visitor at those which do. Alternatively, or in addition, join your national learned society for research in Mathematics Education (BSRLM in the United Kingdom, Mathematics Education Research Group of Australasia (MERGA) in Australasia, National Council of Teachers of Mathematics (NCTM) in the United States, etc.) and attend its meetings. If you find these activities stimulating and inclusive, then international conferences, such as the biennial conferences of the European Society for Research in Mathematics Education (CERME) may come later.

We conclude with the wish that engaging in the study of Mathematics Education may bring you as much fascination and satisfaction as it has given, and continues to give, to us.

Part I

Issues in Mathematics Education

What Is Mathematics, and Why Learn It?

Paul Ernest

Core readings

The Core readings addressed in this chapter are as follows:

Ernest, P., 2000. Why teach mathematics? In S. Bramall and J. White, eds, *Why learn maths?* London: Institute of Education, 1–14.

Hersh, R., 1995. Fresh breezes in the philosophy of mathematics. *American Mathematical Monthly*, 102 (7), 589–94.

Thompson, A. G., 1984. The relationship between teachers' conceptions of mathematics and mathematics teaching to instructional practice. *Educational Studies in Mathematics*, 15, 105–27.

Introduction

This chapter considers what mathematics is, why we should teach it, and some of the less obvious outcomes of teachers' beliefs about such matters, in terms of their classroom practices and public perceptions of mathematics. One of the surprising things that comes to light is that there is controversy both about what mathematics is, and the purposes of teaching and learning it. The chapter is overtly philosophical in its style and content, bringing to the surface the question of whether the philosophy of mathematics has any direct relevance to the teaching and learning of mathematics. Some well-known mathematicians have argued that there is a direct link, even if it is not always visible. René Thom (1973, p. 204) wrote, 'In fact, whether one wishes it or not, all mathematical pedagogy, even if scarcely coherent, rests on a philosophy of mathematics.' Reuben Hersh (1979, p. 34), whose ideas are referred to frequently in this chapter says 'The issue, then, is not, What is the best way to teach? but, What is mathematics really all about? . . . Controversies about . . . teaching cannot be resolved without confronting problems about the nature of mathematics.' In the next section I set out some answers to some of these questions.

What is mathematics? Answers from the philosophy of mathematics

Platonism and traditional absolutist views

A simple answer to the question 'What is mathematics?' is that it is a body of knowledge. So a further question is: 'How do we know the propositions of mathematics are true?' Different schools in the philosophy of mathematics have tried to establish programmes to demonstrate and safeguard the certainty of mathematics. What they wanted to do was to establish that mathematical knowledge is absolutely secure objective knowledge, the position known as Absolutism. The three main schools in modern philosophy of mathematics are Intuitionism, Logicism and Formalism. Each of them tried to apply the same overall strategy called foundationalism. This means finding a subset of true mathematical assumptions – the foundation – and then deriving the rest of mathematical knowledge from it. If they could do this, then they would have demonstrated that all mathematical knowledge is true and beyond any doubt.

Intuitionism argued that individuals intuit some shared basic truths about numbers and geometry, and a restricted logic can derive most of the rest of mathematical knowledge from this basis (leaving out the infinite set theory that had led to contradictions and problems). However, Intuitionism could not explain why everyone's intuitive, subjective truths should be the same, to give the necessary and agreed starting point. Also they deliberately left out some of the most important modern developments in mathematics, like set theory, on which many other branches of mathematics depend. Overall, Intuitionism is regarded as a failure. Even if it had succeeded in its programme it would not have demonstrated the truth of some of the most interesting and important parts of modern mathematics.

Logicism argued that to safeguard mathematics, first, all mathematical concepts must be defined using logical ideas and, second, all mathematical truths should be derived from logical axioms. One of the great successes of modern mathematics was the successful definition of all mathematical concepts using just logic, but Logicism is acknowledged as having failed to derive mathematical truths from just logic, because additional starting points (mathematical axioms) are needed. Mathematics cannot be reduced to logic, and so the certainty of mathematics cannot be reduced to the certainty of logic, whether or not that itself is beyond all doubt.

Formalism had a programme to translate all mathematical theories into formal theories – effectively marks on paper, and rules to apply to these marks. To establish the certainty of mathematical knowledge, it was then necessary to show that these formal systems are safe and free from contradiction. However, this programme failed when Gödel showed, with his landmark incompleteness theorem in 1931, that formal theories are not only incomplete (they fail to capture all truths) but also that it is impossible to demonstrate that they are free from contradiction.

Thus these philosophies of mathematics all failed to secure the certainty of mathematical knowledge. Of the three schools sketched, Formalism remains the most popular, as any undergraduate mathematics student will attest. Mathematicians often claim that mathematics is a formal game played with symbols and marks on paper. This is no longer put forward as a way to safeguard the foundations of mathematics, but as a way to understand mathematics. However, typically accompanying this view is a belief in the reality of mathematical objects. In other words, mathematicians have access to a world of meaning populated by mathematical objects which give sense to the otherwise empty sign systems that make up formal mathematical theories.

This second belief, in the reality of mathematical objects, also provides a possible answer to another basic philosophical question about mathematics: 'What are the objects of mathematics?' Philosophical answers to this question go back to Plato: the view that mathematical objects are real, that they exist in an objective and superhuman realm, is called Platonism. An outstanding question for Platonism remains: 'How can mathematicians and others access this objective realm to understand mathematical objects and grasp their relationships?' Nevertheless, Platonism remains the most popular view about the nature of mathematical objects among mathematicians and philosophers. Belief in Platonism leads to the view that mathematical truths are discovered and not invented. The further reading (Ernest 1999) discusses this issue, and the controversies surrounding it. There is a large literature on the philosophy of mathematics discussing the issues and questions raised above. The book by Davis and Hersh (1980) provides a readable and non-technical introduction to these issues, and those by Friend (2007) and Bostock (2009) survey the different schools in the philosophy of mathematics. For a more detailed characterization and critique of absolutism see Ernest (1998).

Fallibilist perspectives on the nature of mathematics

An outcome of absolutism is a philosophically sanctioned image of mathematics as objective, fixed, pure, abstract and wholly logical, which is the traditional and often negative image of mathematics held by many persons. Because it represents the way many philosophers, mathematicians and teachers describe their subject, it lends support to a public myth of mathematics as cold, hard and inhuman. Although absolutist philosophies of mathematics can be defended as rational, they are often incorrectly associated with such negative beliefs about mathematics. I claim that in the interests of successful schooling and a scientifically literate populace, this connection should be severed. There is an extensive literature on the part that such views play in maintaining mathematics as a male domain, and in reducing women's participation in it (Walkerdine 1995). In addition, such an image of mathematics is often linked with negative attitudes to mathematics such as dislike, lack of confidence, poor self-efficacy views, even mathematical anxiety in extreme cases.

However, it also needs to be recognized that the absolutist image of mathematics is what attracts some students to its study. The perfect, unchanging, reliable path to truth and certainty is a beautiful and attractive feature of mathematics for those who do not feel excluded from it. For example, the philosopher Bertrand Russell was attracted by, and sought perfection in, the 'mathematics which should leave no room for doubts' (1959, p. 28).

In the second core reading, the mathematician and philosopher of mathematics Reuben Hersh (1995) challenges the absolutist and Platonist assumptions of traditional philosophies of mathematics, and offers a humanistic alternative: fallibilism. Most versions of fallibilism view mathematics as the outcome of social processes. Mathematical knowledge is understood to be fallible and eternally open to revision, both in terms of its proofs and its concepts. In contrast to absolutism, this more recent 'maverick' development in the philosophy of mathematics emphasizes the *practice* of mathematics, and its human side (Kitcher and Aspray 1988). This fallibilist position is espoused by a growing number of philosophers, mathematicians and educationists. Indeed, Hersh's (1995) article is a manifesto for a fallibilist philosophy of mathematics. In his seminal text, Imre Lakatos (1976) argues that there are ineliminable empirical elements to the development and justification of mathematics, and terms his highly influential version of fallibilism 'quasi-empiricism'.

Fallibilist views reject the notion that there is a unique, fixed and permanently enduring hierarchical structure comprising mathematical knowledge. Despite the rigour and precision of mathematical concepts and proofs, fallibilism holds that mathematical knowledge never attains a final, ultimate form. Fallibilism embraces the history and applications of mathematics, the practices of mathematicians and the place of mathematics in human culture, as legitimate philosophical concerns. In short, it fully admits the human face and basis of mathematics.

From a fallibilist perspective, mathematics is no longer seen as defined by a body of pure and abstract knowledge which exists in a superhuman, objective realm. Instead mathematics is associated with sets of social practices, each with its history, persons, institutions and social locations, symbolic forms, purposes and power relations. These practices include academic mathematics, school mathematics and ethnomathematics (culturally embedded informal mathematics). These practices are distinct, but intimately interrelated, because the symbolic productions of one practice are recontextualized and used in another.

Fallibilism remains a controversial philosophy of mathematics, and there are almost certainly more supporters of absolutism than of fallibilism. What is important for mathematics professionals is to know is that such a controversy exists, and that, as in many philosophical disputes, there are no right or wrong perspectives. So if you are an absolutist you ought to know that fallibilism is a respectable and rational philosophy of mathematics, even if you disagree. Likewise fallibilists, while rejecting the authoritarian absolutist popular image of mathematics, ought to acknowledge the legitimacy of absolutist philosophies of mathematics.

Views of the purposes of mathematics teaching

The core reading by Ernest explores ideas about the aims and goals of mathematics education, and different views about its purposes. The teaching and learning of mathematics are purposeful organized activities with guiding aims. A number of different accounts of such aims can be found in the literature, such as in Ernest (1991), Mellin-Olsen (1987) and Niss (1996). The entire book from which this core reading is drawn (Bramall and White 2000) is devoted to the aims and purposes of teaching and learning of mathematics, and it is essential reading for those seeking a more comprehensive understanding of the topic.

The aims of mathematics teaching are expressions of intent, and thus educational aims are the expression of the values, interests and even the ideologies of certain individuals or groups. Furthermore, the interests and ideologies of some such groups are often in conflict. In Ernest (1991) I distinguish five competing interest groups with distinct aims for mathematics education. These groups, together with some of their views, such as different views of the nature of mathematics, are summarized in Table 1.1.

Table 1.1 Five interest groups and their aims for mathematics teaching

Interest group	Social location	Mathematical aims	View of mathematics
Industrial trainers	Radical 'New Right' conservative politicians and petty bourgeois	Back-to-basics numeracy and social training in obedience (authoritarian)	Absolutist set of decontextualized but utilitarian truths and rules
Technological pragmatists	Meritocratic industry-centred industrialists, managers, 'New Labour' politicians	Useful mathematics to appropriate level and certification (industry-centred)	Unquestioned absolutist body of applicable knowledge
Old humanist mathematicians	Conservative mathematicians preserving rigour of proof and purity of mathematics	Transmit body of pure mathematical knowledge (mathematics-centred)	Absolutist body of structured pure knowledge
Progressive educators	Professionals, liberal educators, welfare state supporters	Creativity, self-realization through mathematics (child-centred)	Absolutist body of pure knowledge to be engaged with personally
Public educators	Democratic socialists and radical reformers concerned with social justice and inequality	Critical awareness and democratic citizenship via mathematics	Fallible knowledge socially constructed in diverse practices

Thus the different social groups have different political orientations, differing views of the nature of mathematics, and different aims for the teaching of mathematics. The respective aims of these five groups can be expanded as follows:

1. Acquiring basic mathematical skills and numeracy, and social training in obedience (authoritarian, basic skills-centred view).
2. Learning basic skills, and learning to solve practical problems with mathematics (industry and work-centred view).
3. Acquiring understanding and capability in advanced mathematics, with some appreciation of mathematics (pure mathematics-centred view).
4. Acquiring confidence, creativity and self-expression through mathematics (child-centred, progressivist view).
5. The empowerment of the learner as a highly numerate critical citizen (empowerment and social justice concerns).

These aims, and the groups to which they are attributed, can be seen at work through a number of alliances in the development of the 1988 English National Curriculum in mathematics, and they persist to this day. Aims 1 and 3 are conservative, and both supported the National Curriculum model, with the focus on lower elements of knowledge and skill, together with external testing partly achieving the basic skills-centred aim (1), and the higher elements of knowledge and skill directed at the pure mathematics-centred aim (3). These aims are directed at goods external to the students, and embody views of knowledge and skills as decontextualized. Such views can be seen to remain central to the policies of the Secretary of State for Education in 2013.

Aims 2 and 4 both supported the inclusion of a progressive, personal knowledge-application dimension which survived through most versions of the National Curriculum in mathematics, as the processes of 'Using and Applying Mathematics'. For aim 2 supporters, this is seen as the embodiment of practical skills in being able to apply mathematics to solve work-related problems with mathematics. For aim 4 supporters, this is seen as the embodiment of exploratory and creative self-realization through mathematical activity. However, the language of Using and Applying Mathematics in the English National Curriculum is clearly utilitarian and more overt references to progressive 'personal qualities' of students in early draft versions of the curriculum were expunged fairly rapidly. Aim 5 concerns the development of critical citizenship and empowerment for social change and equality through mathematics. This played no part in the development of the English National Curriculum, and is virtually absent from any curriculum development in mathematics education too. Thus, although progressives see mathematics within the context of the individual's experience, the notion that the individual is socially located in an unequal and unjust world plays no part.

A different perspective on the aims and purposes of the teaching and learning of mathematics emerges from the work of Askew et al. (1997). This team studied the beliefs of primary school teachers about the purposes of teaching mathematics. The researchers interviewed the teachers and observed their teaching practices. They found three belief orientations towards mathematics teaching. These orientations are termed Connectionist, Transmission and Discovery, summarized as follows: *Connectionist* beliefs value students' methods, and teaching with emphasis on establishing connections in mathematics; *Transmission* beliefs emphasize the primacy of teaching, with a view of mathematics as a collection of separate routines and procedures; *Discovery* beliefs emphasize the primacy of learning, with a view of mathematics as being discovered by students.

The researchers found that the classes of the teachers with a connectionist orientation made the greatest learning gains after six months of teaching. Thus teaching for connectedness – as located both within the teachers' beliefs and teaching practices – was seen to be the most effective. Traditional transmission beliefs and practices were not shown to be as effective (aims 1 and 2). More surprisingly – especially for those with a Progressive orientation – discovery beliefs and practices were equally ineffective (aim 4). The connectionist beliefs are closest to aim 3, with its emphasis on pure mathematics-centred instruction, focusing on deeper understanding and capability in mathematics. However, this teaching for interconnectedness includes attending to and valuing students' methods, as well as teaching with an emphasis on establishing connections in mathematics, and thus includes elements of aim 4.

The new emphasis on connectionism foregrounds a distinction between mathematical *capability* versus the *appreciation* of mathematics. Such distinction can be applied to the learning of English, for example. English language is primarily about English capability, the skills of reading and writing. However, the learning of English literature entails appreciating great novels, plays and poetry that are a prized part of culture. Do we have the same distinction in mathematics? Is school mathematics all about capability, that is, about 'doing', or could there be an appreciation element that is overlooked in most mandated school curricula? Mathematics is typically seen to be about solving problems, performing algorithms and procedures, computing solutions, and so on. Thus, the capability dimension of school mathematics is dominant and perhaps universal. Of course, given the major role that mathematics has in the curriculum, a large capability element is necessary, for unquestionably knowledge of mathematics as a language and an instrument requires being able to understand and apply it. But is capability enough? Would the development of mathematical appreciation be a worthwhile and justifiable goal for school mathematics? If so, what is mathematical appreciation?

Provisionally, the appreciation of mathematics includes the following elements of awareness (Ernest 2000):

- having a qualitative understanding of some of the big ideas of mathematics such as infinity, symmetry, structure, recursion, proof, chaos, randomness, and so on, and how they link different branches of mathematics;
- being able to understand the organization of mathematics, its main branches and concepts, and having a sense of their interconnections, interdependencies and the overall unity of mathematics;

- understanding that there are multiple views of the nature of mathematics and that there is controversy over its philosophical foundations;
- being aware of the extent to which mathematical thinking permeates everyday and shopfloor life and current affairs, even if it is not called mathematics;
- critically understanding the uses of mathematics in society: to be able to identify, interpret, evaluate and critique the mathematics embedded in social and political systems and claims, from advertisements to government and interest-group pronouncements;
- being aware of the historical development of mathematics, the social contexts of the origins of mathematical concepts, symbolism, theories and problems;
- having a sense of mathematics as a central element of culture, art and life, present and past, which permeates and underpins science, technology and all aspects of human culture.

In short, the appreciation of mathematics involves understanding and having an awareness of its nature and value, as well as understanding and being able to critique its social uses. The breadth of knowledge and understanding involved is potentially immense, but many learners leave school without ever having been exposed to, or thought about, several of these seven areas of appreciation. I believe that including this element in school mathematics would strengthen the teaching and learning of mathematics by making it more interesting and relevant to students' lives and interests. I explore these ideas more fully in the core reading (Ernest 2000).

The relationship between philosophies, aims and classroom practices

I have outlined some different perspectives concerning philosophies of mathematics and aims for teaching mathematics. This raises once again the question of the relationship between philosophies, aims and classroom practices. The third core reading (Thompson 1984) reports an early empirical investigation into this relationship: the article continues to be influential. The study was based on in-depth interviews with three teachers, and brings to light the divergence of opinions and practices between them. From a methodological perspective, the case-study approach adopted for the study gives insight into the complex relationship between teachers' beliefs, or conceptions, and their practices in ways that analyses of quantitative data could not. In this section I shall propose that the impact of beliefs and aims on the practice of teaching mathematics is mediated by *images* of mathematics.

Images of mathematics

I define an image of mathematics to be a representation that is either social or personal. Social images of mathematics are public representations including mass-media representations including films, cartoons, pictures, popular music, and so on; presentations and displays in school mathematics classrooms and the learning experiences in them; parent, peer or other narratives about mathematics; and representations of mathematics utilizing any other semiotic modes or means.

Personal images of mathematics draw on some form of mental picture, visual, verbal, narrative or other personal representation, originating from past experiences of mathematics, or from social talk or other social representations of mathematics, potentially comprising cognitive, affective and behavioural dimensions. The conception of mathematics represented in such images may vary across research mathematics and mathematicians, school mathematics and mathematical applications, everyday or otherwise. They include beliefs about mathematics and what was hitherto described as personal philosophies of mathematics.

Social and personal images of mathematics are intimately related, as personal images result from exposure to social images of mathematics including mathematics learning experiences in the classroom. Social images of mathematics are constructed by individuals or groups based on their own personal images, and these are represented and made public. However, both kinds of image may have implicit elements which individuals are unaware of or which are portrayed publicly without conscious deliberation.

Negative images of mathematics

A widespread public image of mathematics in the Anglophone West is that it is difficult, cold, abstract, theoretical, ultra-rational, but important and largely masculine. It also has the image of being remote and inaccessible to all but a few super-intelligent beings with 'mathematical minds' (Walkerdine 1995).

This negative popular image of mathematics sets it apart from the daily concerns of the public, despite the many social applications of mathematics referred to daily in the mass-media, from sports and weather to economic and social indicators. Numeracy, contextual mathematics, even ethnomathematics are widely perceived to be quite distinct from school/academic mathematics, and the latter is understood to be 'real' mathematics. Overall, this widespread public image of mathematics is largely a negative and remote one, alien to many persons' professional and personal concerns and their self-perceived abilities.

Let me now summarize the negative public image of mathematics. Mathematics is perceived to be rigid, fixed, logical, absolute, inhuman, cold, objective, pure, abstract, remote and ultra-rational. This description closely resembles a set of values termed 'separated' by Gilligan (1982). In her theory of values, Gilligan distinguishes 'separated' and 'connected' values positions. Applying her distinction to mathematics, we have:

- Separated values emphasizing rules, abstraction, objectification, impersonality, dispassionate reason, analysis, atomism and object-centredness. These are values that are associated with a view of mathematics as a product, a body of knowledge with the role of humans minimized or factored out.
- Connected values emphasizing relationships, connections, processes, empathy, caring, feelings and intuition, holism and human-centredness. These values foreground the role of human activity in mathematics.

By identifying what is perceived to be a negative image of mathematics with separated values there is the danger of slipping in a gratuitous value judgement. For while there is a strong consonance between separated values and an absolutist philosophy of mathematics, an absolutist image of mathematics can exist without the negative connotations I have described. As I noted earlier, the absolutist image of mathematics is what attracts some persons to it. Many love mathematics precisely because of its rationality and logicality based on rules, its abstraction and concerns with a pure, timeless, unchanging, superhuman realm, its purity, certainty and freedom from ambiguity. It is both consistent and common for teachers and mathematicians to hold an absolutist and separated view of mathematics as neutral and value-free, but to regard mathematics teaching as necessitating the adoption of humanistic, connected values. In my research on student teachers' attitudes and beliefs about mathematics I found a subgroup of mathematics specialists who combined absolutist conceptions of the subject with very positive attitudes to mathematics and its teaching (Ernest 2000). So to call their image of mathematics negative would be inappropriate and incorrect.

Nevertheless, for simplicity, I shall argue that when a philosophy of mathematics is used as the basis for an image of mathematics and is combined with separated values, the outcome is a separated image of mathematics, and that this is frequently if not universally associated with negative attitudes to mathematics.

A separated image of mathematics may be encouraged in school by giving students mainly unrelated routine mathematical tasks which involve the application of learnt procedures, and by stressing that every task has a unique, fixed and objectively right answer, coupled with disapproval and criticism of any failure to achieve this answer. This may not be what the mathematician recognizes as mathematics, but it promotes a separated conception of the subject, and is often accompanied by negative attitudes to mathematics.

Positive images of mathematics

Positive images of mathematics can also associate a wholly different set of characteristics with the subject. One widespread positive image is that mathematics is a dynamic, problem-driven and continually expanding field of human creation and invention. This view places most emphasis on mathematical activity, the doing of mathematics, and it accepts that there are many ways of solving any problem in mathematics. It views mathematics as approachable and accessible, human and personal, practical, concerned with processes of inquiry and understanding and creative and flexible uses of knowledge to solve problems. Part of the approachability of mathematics is that anyone should be able to solve problems and check answers, and that problems have multiple solution methods and multiple answers. This makes it accessible to all, and is the humanistic image promoted by progressive mathematics education.

Drawing together the separate parts in the above account the point I want to make is that there is a parallel between the absolutist philosophy of mathematics, separated values and the separated image of mathematics. Likewise, a second parallel exists between the fallibilist philosophy of mathematics, connected values and the connected humanistic image of mathematics. These could be represented as two vertical columns. However, the path of a teacher's thinking within these columns need not be entirely on one side or the other. There is the possibility of crossing over. An absolutist philosophy of mathematics combined with connected values can give rise to a connected image of school mathematics. A deep commitment to the ideals of progressive mathematics education can coexist with a belief in the objectivity and neutrality of mathematics. Conversely, a fallibilist philosophy could theoretically combine with separated values, resulting in a separated image of mathematics.

But images of mathematics can occur at three levels in the teaching process (so we could extend the columns down further). We need to distinguish between the teacher's intended image, the classroom image presented to students, and the learner's personal image of mathematics as a result of classroom and other experiences. These can differ, first, because of the constraints and opportunities afforded by the social context – turning plans into reality is subject to a variety of constraints and opportunities. Second, the image of mathematics represented in the classroom is filtered through student preconceptions, interpretations, attitudes and beliefs before adding to learners' own personal images of mathematics.

Because of the complexities involved, discontinuities between the three types of image of mathematics can arise. Empirical research has confirmed that teachers with very distinct personal philosophies of mathematics (absolutist and fallibilist) have been constrained by the social context of schooling to teach in a traditional, separated way (Lerman 1986). Similarly, because of their preconceptions, students might personally reinterpret or 'misconstrue' the image of mathematics presented to them in the classroom and maintain their own oppositely characterized image of mathematics. Thus, the way that ideas filter down the two 'columns' into practice is closer to the path of a ball in a pin-ball game than it is to the straight path of water in a waterfall.

Conclusion

In this chapter, I have shown that there are differing views of the nature of mathematics among academics, teachers, students and more widely, across society. There are also varied ideas about what are, or should be, the aims of teaching mathematics. I have also tried to show the complex relationships that exist between views of mathematics (philosophies or images of mathematics), aims of teaching mathematics, the outcomes in terms of student images, beliefs and attitudes, and student performances in mathematics. Because of these complexities, the final jump to measures of learning outcome is the most difficult to demonstrate. Although there is no simple mechanism at work, most researchers agree that teachers' and students' images, beliefs and attitudes to mathematics have a major impact on their performances and student learning outcomes in mathematics, and are vital contributing factors in the teaching and learning of mathematics (Askew et al. 1997; Thompson 1984).

Further reading

Askew, M., Brown, M., Rhodes, V., Johnson, D. and Wiliam, D., 1997. *Effective teachers of numeracy, final report*. London: King's College, University of London.

Davis, P. J. and Hersh, R., 1980. *The mathematical experience*. Boston, MA: Birkhauser.

Ernest, P., 1991. *The philosophy of mathematics education*, London: Routledge.

—, 1999. Is mathematics discovered or invented? *Philosophy of Mathematics Education Journal*, 12. Available at http://people.exeter.ac.uk/PErnest/pome12/article2.htm [accessed on 16 May 2013].

Additional references

Bostock, D., 2009. *Philosophy of mathematics: an introduction*. Chichester: Wiley.

Bramall, S. and White, J., eds, 2000. *Why learn maths?* London: Institute of Education.

Ernest, P., 1998. *Social constructivism as a philosophy of mathematics*. Albany, NY: SUNY Press.

Friend, M., 2007. *Introducing philosophy of mathematics*. Stocksfield: Acumen.

Gilligan, C., 1982. *In a different voice*. Cambridge, MA: Harvard University Press.

Hersh, R., 1979. Some proposals for reviving the philosophy of mathematics. *Advances in Mathematics*, 31, 31–50.

Kitcher, P. and Aspray, W., 1988, An opinionated introduction. In W. Aspray and P. Kitcher, eds, *History and philosophy of modern mathematics*. Minneapolis: University of Minnesota Press, 3–57.

Lakatos, I., 1976. *Proofs and refutations*. Cambridge: Cambridge University Press.

Lerman, S., 1986. Alternative views of the nature of mathematics and their possible influence on the teaching of mathematics. Unpublished Ph.D. Thesis. King's College, University of London.

Mellin-Olsen, S., 1987. *The politics of mathematics education*. Dordrecht, Netherlands: Reidel.

Niss, M., 1996. Goals of mathematics teaching. In A. J. Bishop, ed., *The international handbook of mathematics education*. Dordrecht, Netherlands: Kluwer, 11–47.

Russell, B., 1959. *My philosophical development*. London: George Allen and Unwin.

Thom, R., 1973. Modern mathematics: does it exist? In A. G. Howson, ed., *Developments in mathematical education*. Cambridge: Cambridge University Press, 194–209.

Walkerdine, V., 1995. *Counting girls out*. London: Routledge.

Learning and Knowing Mathematics

Stephen Lerman

Core readings

The Core readings addressed in this chapter are as follows:

Lerman, S., 2000. The social turn in mathematics education research. In J. Boaler, ed., *Multiple perspectives on mathematics teaching and learning*. Westport, CT: Ablex, 19–44.

Steffe, L. P., 2004. On the construction of learning trajectories of children: the case of commensurate fractions. *Mathematical Thinking and Learning* 6 (2), 129–62.

Lerman, S., 2001. Accounting for accounts of learning mathematics: reading the ZPD in videos and transcripts. In D. Clarke, ed., *Perspectives on meaning in mathematics and science classrooms*. Dordrecht, Netherlands: Kluwer, 53–74.

Cooper, B. and Dunne, M., 1998. Anyone for tennis? Social class differences in children's responses to national curriculum mathematics testing. *Sociological Review* 46 (1), 115–48.

Introduction

As researchers and teachers, mathematics education presents us with two very different discourses: the subject 'mathematics', with its precise grammar; and education, a weak grammar, open to a range of views and opinions and drawing on a range of other discourses, such as psychology, sociology, anthropology and others. By 'strong' and 'weak' grammars, terminology offered by Bernstein (2000), is meant the following: we can decide if a structure satisfies the laws of a Boolean algebra, for example, and we can agree with certainty and in a few moments perhaps. Meanings are precise and unambiguous: a strong grammar. To determine if a student *understands* some mathematics, however, based on what they produce verbally or in writing, depends on how one interprets 'understanding', and might lead us into days, if not years of discussion without reaching universal agreement. Education, then, exhibits a weak grammar.

Research in our field calls for a study of the options, in terms of what learning and knowing are, careful elaboration of how we might recognize learning and knowing according to the view(s) we have adopted, and some decisions regarding what information we will need in order to be able to call it evidence of learning or knowing. What we produce, in the end, is some form of text that reflects the researcher's interpretation of how the data function as evidence of knowing and learning mathematics according to the theoretical position adopted. Because we work with multiple options in educational research, in terms of what learning and knowing mean, and how it's recognized, researchers need to be precise about how they are working with these concepts and to be reflective and reflexive about those theories and how they are used in the research.

In this chapter, then, I will take three examples of theories of knowing and learning and research planned and carried out in which the authors have succeeded, in my view, in developing a coherent and justified account of why they have carried out their research in the way they have. I do not want to suggest that anyone can be neutral about different theories. Some things work for me and others do not. For instance, I do not find explanations of student learning expressed in terms of reflective abstraction to be convincing. In my research I would have to say why and give the reasons for the concepts I adopt instead. Subsequently, I should reflect on the outcomes of my research in terms of my assumptions and make them explicit to readers, and also how that research has been affected by my assumptions and how the findings affect me, in a reflexive manner. As both supervisor and examiner of doctoral students, as a reviewer of articles for publication in refereed journals and research bids for funding, I am one of the many gatekeepers to our community. I look for that coherence and justification, not for someone subscribing to the same views as me on theories of teaching and learning.

I will begin with a brief account of the range of theories of learning that are available to researchers by drawing on the first core reading (Lerman 2000), though the reading develops the account much further than can be done in this chapter (see also Lerman 2010). I will then look at each of the three exemplars, the other core readings, to show how the connection between the theoretical approaches adopted by the authors are translated into their research plans and the ways in which they interpret their findings. These three theoretical perspectives have been chosen from among the range because they are the most commonly adopted in the case of the first two, constructivism and socio-cultural theories, and because of the presence of intellectual resources to address what I consider to be one of the most important issues facing us, that of who fails in mathematics and why, in the case of the third.

Overview of theories of learning and knowing

Theories of what it is to know and to learn go back at least to Plato who, in the dialogue *The Meno*, shows Socrates extracting from a slave boy, by suitable questioning, the length of the diagonal of a unit square, which Plato wanted to be seen as a process of reminding the boy of knowledge that he had in his immortal soul before birth, rather than being taught, or even scaffolded, by Socrates. However, I will jump 2,300 years or so to Behaviourism to begin my brief account properly. This approach to learning, known also as associationism or reflexology, was dominant before Piaget and Vygotsky entered the scene, and formed the backdrop to the work of those two great thinkers who have so transformed our knowledge of child development. Both Piaget and Vygotsky, separately of course, argued for the inadequacy of behaviourism as an account of human learning and consciousness, but in very different ways. We can see also that features of behaviourism are still in evidence in teaching (rewards and punishments), and methods of training, as well as some behavioural modification therapies, such as overcoming (if that is what happens) fear of spiders, and hence it is appropriate to begin here.

Behaviourism is associated with psychologists such as Pavlov, Thorndike, Watson and Skinner and is based on their work in training animals. It is a materialist theory, meaning that it is based on the notion that actions of all kinds are reactions and responses to what is going on around the individual and can be observed. What is in the mind is a result of the internalization of what has been established as a response to something material. In other words it carries the assumption that there are no philosophical differences between publicly observable processes (such as actions) and privately observable processes (such as thinking and feeling). Behaviourism draws on the well known and still used tools of reinforcement and reward and punishment.

Both Piaget and Vygotsky considered behaviourism inadequate to explain any higher cognitive functions in humans. It might be considered to have something to say about basic aspects of learning, such as practising techniques in sport or learning multiplication tables. One can always allow pupils to use a multiplication table, but in the service of more complex tasks it is useful to know the answer to 6×7 without needing to think about it. But there are other elements of behaviourism present in teachers' strategies, the gold stars and smiley faces given for good work and detentions or extra homework when teachers are not satisfied. Such reinforcements are still essential tools of many teachers.

Behaviourism's view of learning is represented by a stimulus–response link, the appropriate response to a particular stimulus being established and reinforced as I mentioned earlier. Piaget severed the link by inserting the interpreting individual:

stimulus → interpreting individual → response

When any stimulus appears the individual responds to it from within her/his prior set of experiences and interprets that new stimulus in her/his private way. Thus Piaget placed the interpreting individual at the heart of his theories; the work of learning can only be carried out by the individual making sense of the world for her/himself. Thinking precedes language, which performs an organizing and externalizing function. These fundamental underlying focuses can be seen as emerging from Piaget's own early life experiences and his view of the world. Another person, parent or teacher, for example, cannot know the prior experiences and understandings of any individual, nor can they know whether that individual has, as a result of their interactions together, learnt what the teacher or parent wanted the learner to know. Learning takes place only when the individual reorganizes her/his conceptual framework; the child constructs her/his knowledge. Just following what a teacher has tried to convey will probably not lead to learning, only copying and then forgetting. It is important to add that Piaget's constructivism is a theory of learning, not of teaching. Teachers' actions, such as lecturing, or supporting, insisting on individual work or encouraging group collaboration, are not constructivist or anything else. This means that it is not sufficient for a teacher or a researcher to claim they are taking a constructivist approach to teaching. In relation to the focus of this book, research, the researcher must establish any theoretical connections between their interpretation of the teaching and a constructivist view of learning. Constructivist theory is the first that we will examine in the following section.

Vygotsky argued that the response to any stimulus is always mediated or interpreted, it is explained, and its use is elaborated: by a parent, by a sibling, by a peer, by a text and, of course, by teachers. Vygotsky considered that the materialist perspective of behaviourism was fundamentally correct and wanted to build on it, rather than oppose it completely, towards higher thinking. Thus mediation is Vygotsky's way of breaking the direction of the response to a stimulus. The response is mediated:

stimulus → mediation → response

We must note the Marxist roots of Vygotsky's approach. In the years after the Russian revolution of 1917 there was a flowering of the arts, the sciences, indeed of all social and cultural life in Russia. These developments were inspired by the desire to identify how Marxism might inform any particular field. In developmental psychology the story was the same, and Vygotsky's elaboration of how to develop a psychology that takes Marx's view of consciousness became the accepted psychological theory in the Soviet Union. Marx understood consciousness as produced by one's social and economic relations to the means of economic production which, for Vygotsky's concerns, became concentrated specifically on culture. With his theory of internalization, where '(e)very function in the child's cultural development appears twice: first, on the social level, and later, on the individual level' (Vygotsky 1978, p. 57), and his theory of Zones of Proximal Development, 'the distance between the actual developmental level as determined by independent problem solving and the level of potential development as determined under adult guidance or in collaboration with more capable peers' (Vygotsky 1978, p. 86), his cultural psychology becomes a materialist account of learning and knowing. The cultural–historical approach will be the second that we will examine.

The third approach is drawn from sociology: specifically sociology of education. In general, psychology has always been the intellectual field to which educators have turned for explanatory frameworks of learning and knowing. The strong correlation between socio-economic background and success or failure in education, and in mathematics in particular, cannot be explained in psychological terms however, except for Vygotskian psychology, as will be explained. Sociologists of education such as Pierre Bourdieu and Basil Bernstein have developed powerful explanatory constructs to show how education reproduces social class rather than challenging it. Such analyses are necessary prerequisites to determining action to bring about changes. We will examine work drawing on Bernstein's constructs in the third analysis.

Constructivist research on learning and knowing mathematics

In the 1980s a radical version of Piaget's constructivism became a rich source of research in mathematics education, particularly in the United States. The principles, as set out by Ernst von Glasersfeld (1990, pp. 22–3) are:

1. Knowledge is not passively received either through the senses or by way of communication. Knowledge is actively built up by the cognizing subject.
2. a. The function of cognition is adaptive in the biological sense of the term, tending towards fit or viability;
   b. Cognition serves the subject's organization of the experiential world, not the discovery of an onto-logical reality.

These principles constitute a theory of learning and, as I discussed earlier, to move from that to suggesting that particular ways of teaching are constructivist requires careful justification. I believe that Simon (1995) has best elaborated a notion of teaching which is compatible with supporting students' constructions of their own knowledge in what he calls hypothetical learning trajectories. All learning is by construction and that applies to the teacher too. Hence, the teacher learns by making a conjecture, a model of what a student knows, based on responses to questioning, observation, written answers, but most fruitfully in teaching experiments. These latter are situations in which students work on problems with the teacher or researcher, often one-to-one, or a researcher with a small group of students, who asks questions as the students work, both for explanation to help the teacher in modifying their model of the child's knowing and also to aid the student's construction of appropriate knowledge. It should be noted that teaching experiments assume a methodology rejecting objectivity: the researcher affects the research outcome intentionally and the responses and interpretations are the data.

Steffe's work in general, and the core reading in particular, makes very careful use of the teaching experiment, of using language rigorously in terms of constructivist learning theory. Hence, rather than speaking of the child's learning, of which the teacher cannot actually know, he speaks of the teacher's constructions of the conjectured student's constructions, and the teacher's strategies as following the hypothesized learning trajectory towards accepted mathematical concepts. That model of the child's trajectory is constantly changing as the teacher's model of the child's understanding, called by Steffe the second order model, where the child's is called the first order model, is adapted as further insights emerge into the possible thinking of the student.

The article looks at the learning trajectories of two fifth-grade students, Jason and Laura, as they engage in tasks to support their development of rational numbers and their schemes for partitioning wholes into specified fractional parts, en route to commensurate fractions, Steffe's preferred term for equivalent fractions. The task for the teacher is to construct an understanding of children's mathematics and how 'teachers can affect that mathematics' (p. 130). Both of these are the goals of the research; hence, the need for interactions within the teaching experiments. Steffe consistently uses the term 'bringing forth' when referring to students' learning. The teacher/researcher cannot know what the child constructs as the process is invisible, but the tasks, the teacher's interventions, and the interactions between researcher and student enable evidence of developing concepts to be brought out of the student that allows the researcher to modify the second order model of the child's learning. The goal of the teacher has to be to induce a perturbation (e.g. p. 139) in the student's conceptual system, since learning occurs when the individual reorganizes her/his conceptual system as a result of it being disturbed. Without that disequilibrium, any new encounter that might produce knowledge is just absorbed into the already existing framework, the process in the child's conceptual development that Piaget termed assimilation. Teachers, in the constructivist theoretical framework, try for the most part to induce accommodation in the child, Piaget's term for the need to construct a new schema.

To give an example of the detailed analysis and careful argument for the researcher's modification of his model of Laura's understanding, and hence for the teacher's choice of tasks that follow the hypothesized learning trajectory, we will examine one section of the research. On page 147 Steffe writes: 'In the teaching episode . . . two occasions arose in which it is possible to make a judgement concerning the operations Laura used to justify why $\frac{4}{12}$ is commensurate with $\frac{1}{3}$'. On the basis of the transcript that follows, Steffe argues that there is evidence that Laura did not know why 'the teacher insisted on referring to the $\frac{3}{15}$-stick[1] as $\frac{1}{15}$ she said "I don't know" when pushed by the teacher. This corroborates the belief that she couldn't yet engage in recursive partitioning operations.' In the previous protocol, when the task was about $\frac{4}{12}$ and $\frac{1}{3}$ Steffe claims that Laura's use of 'her concept of $\frac{1}{3}$ in reconstituting the $\frac{4}{12}$-stick as a $\frac{1}{3}$-stick . . . did not constitute an accommodation' (p. 149). On looking back, we read that Laura had constructed $\frac{4}{12}$ by repeatedly taking $\frac{1}{12}$ four times. When the software showed that the $\frac{4}{12}$-stick was $\frac{1}{3}$ both children said that they could see why. Laura constructed two copies of the $\frac{4}{12}$-stick and put all three together to show that the whole $\frac{12}{12}$-stick resulted. Jason gave a different explanation. On the basis of this transcript and the one on pages 147 and 148, Steffe argues that she had not accommodated the new concept and therefore was not working with commensurate fractions whereas Jason had. Steffe says that Laura had certainly experienced a perturbation when the $\frac{1}{3}$ appeared, as was evident in her gestures, and had repeated the $\frac{4}{12}$-stick three times to justify why $\frac{1}{3}$ had appeared, but it would only constitute an accommodation if subsequent activities showed her repeating what seemed to be new-found knowledge. This did not happen with the $\frac{3}{15}$-stick as $\frac{1}{5}$ in the later activity reported on pages 147 and 148. I have commented here on the researcher's assumptions, in building the second order models, of the different competences developed by the two students Laura and Jason, to emphasize the strong inferences implicit in the methodology.

The evidence is presented in the article for the researcher's construction of his model of Laura's learning trajectory and is available for readers to construct their own models that may be different. Equally one could re-examine the evidence from within a different theoretical approach to learning. The point is that Steffe's methodology, together with the data produced, the analysis carried out and the conclusions arrived at are completely consistent with the justified framework of constructivist theory of Laura's and Jason's learning and the researcher's learning about their learning, and in this the article and the research are exemplary.

Cultural–historical research on learning and knowing mathematics

Turning now to the third core reading, the chapter is drawn from a collection in which each chapter author was invited to examine rich data collected from science and mathematics classrooms in Australia by a team led by the editor of the book, David Clarke, and present an analysis according to their theoretical orientation. In looking for evidence to construct a socio-cultural account, Lerman chose a section of the videos that showed sufficient continuous talk in teacher–student interactions followed immediately by student–student interactions. The goal here was to give an account of the students' mathematical productions in terms of the interactions and not on hypothesized cognitive schemata.

In the Vygotskian approach, the Zone of Proximal Development (ZPD) is the mechanism through which learning happens. While research exemplifying learning focuses generally on curriculum subjects, learning needs to be examined in all the ways in which the zone functions. The task of the researcher, then, is to trace developments in students' learning to the activities of the teacher or other mediators. In this chapter, Lerman looks to two features of the teacher–student interactions as they appear in the student–student interactions in particular: the ways in which students are positioned by the teacher in terms of discourses of ability, and the manner in which they think about the problem in terms of the ways of doing mathematics shown them by the teacher. Methodologically, the theoretical orientation calls for a focus on what is said, written, gestured and otherwise presented by the actors and not for hypothesizing what might be going on in the students' minds. The teacher needs to hypothesize the student's knowing in order to devise an activity so that a ZPD might emerge (Meira and Lerman 2010); the researcher's job is to draw on the observable material in constructing an account of learning.

There are two places in the data where the teacher indicates how she perceives the students' relative abilities. The first is in the choice of students to be called to the front of the class for extra instruction. The student M is a permanent member of this group. On this occasion the second student D asks to join and the teacher agrees. But the students in the class will have been aware of the categorization of the students as the fast group and the others. The second way is in the post-lesson video-stimulated interview when the teacher says:

> And the fact that he's helping D_ with this is fantastic because it'll help M_ in the process . . . uh, you know, for someone like M_ it'd be quite easy for him to do that. Someone like D_ wouldn't have a hope. But uh it's good to see them working together helping each other out.

When the two students M and D begin working together we can assume that they are aware of their relative statuses in terms of teacher-evaluated ability and we can examine the transcript for evidence of the effect. Lerman argues that D's tendency to defer to M, as demonstrated both in their interaction in lines 1 to 4 (p. 63), and in D's copying of M's answer and erasing his own, as well as M's tendency to pay little attention to what D is saying, ignoring D's comment on lines 8 and 10, for example, but to pursue his instructing style of speech, are evidence of the effect of the ability discourse. As a consequence Lerman suggests a ZPD does not develop between the boys.

Furthermore, the teacher offers two different ways of working with the set problems: a substitution of numbers for letters, and equivalent algebraic fractions through cancelling of letters in common to numerator and denominator. D appears to take up one of the methods, cancelling, on lines 8 and 10, which is actually the more powerful, more general, of the two, whereas M takes up and insists on the other method, substitution of numbers, choosing digits 1 and 2. Again because they are not approaching the task, that of simplifying the ratio *ab:ab*, in the same way they talk across each other and a ZPD does not emerge.

The teacher actually notices this and in the post-lesson video-stimulated interview, though not in terms of the different methods each student takes up, says:

> I'm surprised that D did as well as he did. It's easy to sort of pigeonhole students into an area and think that they may struggle with or they shouldn't try but with M beside him he's got a lot further than I thought he would.

Finally it is important to note the reflective account given in the last paragraph of the chapter, where Lerman examines his prior assumptions and the ways they might have affected the research. Research is always an interpretation and the text that presents the outcome of any study is inevitably affected by the researcher/author, at least from interpretivist and post-positivist methodological positions in social science in general and in education in particular.

Sociological approaches to learning and knowing mathematics

The final approach, drawing on the fourth reading, uses sociological theories to provide intellectual resources to address success and failure as associated with social class backgrounds. Once again, the theoretical perspective and the research design and interpretation are exemplary in their consistency and coherence.

A naïve view of cognitive development, as the normal process of a normal person, given the absence of constraints, comes up short against the strong correlation between socio-economic background and failure at school. Other explanatory structures are needed to account for why children from disadvantaged backgrounds disproportionately fail to gain mathematical qualifications. Knowing mathematics is somehow related to social background in a much more profound way than usually understood. Marxist sociologists, such as Basil Bernstein and Pierre Bourdieu, take Marx's hypotheses on consciousness and develop theories to elaborate the implications for education and other social settings that can account for the reproductive effects of education: children from middle-class backgrounds succeed and those from working-class backgrounds are failed by schools.

Bernstein condenses the consequences of different positions in relation to power (social class) to the social distribution of what he calls the recognition and realization rules. The recognition rules refer to recognizing what context a question is set within, and realization rules are about the production of an answer that will be accepted as such. Children come to school having acquired these rules in the home, or not. It is entirely possible for the school to induct children into these rules if they have not been acquired, but for the most part teachers are not aware of the issue. Bernstein predicts, actually in the same way that Vygotsky predicted outcomes from experiments with peasants emerging from feudalism into organized (in the modernist sense) communities, that children from working-class backgrounds will not distinguish tasks on either side of the everyday and the 'esoteric', or purely mathematical, boundary. It should be noted that there can be other, cultural, reasons for children misreading rules. Bernstein develops the contrasting notions of visible and invisible pedagogies; in the latter, rules are not made explicit and may not be read appropriately by children from homes in which relations are more explicit.

Questions set in everyday contexts, although actually rather pseudo-everyday as can be seen in the examples in the article and as will be very familiar to mathematics teachers, are likely to be misrecognized by working-class children. This is generally very surprising to teachers and researchers. Setting tasks within the everyday is usually thought to help students from disadvantaged backgrounds because it is assumed that the familiar will motivate them and make the activity more real. Bourdieu explains the phenomenon similarly, as the response of 'children who do or do not employ the resource of their everyday knowledge in their test responses' (p. 142), according to their family's distance from a form of life that is determined predominantly by economic necessity.

We will look at one of the examples in the article, that of the tennis item. What is most important is to realize that the researchers this time are working with predictions, drawn from a theory, of what will happen when children whose social background has been identified, are chosen from across different social classes and asked to answer particular questions that should 'test' theories of children's ability to treat the boundary appropriately.

The children interviewed, who were from working-class or intermediate-class backgrounds, tended to draw on their everyday experience to answer the question, giving reasons such as the possible nationality of the children based on their names for selection of an everyday arrangement, resulting in just three possibilities. One can imagine the real-life scenario for making the choice of possible opponents by taking one name from each bag, after which it would not make sense to return the names to the bags. This scenario will mislead students who have not acquired the 'rules'. The interviewers' questions (p. 136) push the children to recognize what is being asked and they are then able to realize the appropriate response of nine possibilities, although they distinguish further between a response that indicates an abstract arrangement from one still rooted in a real-life procedure. The researchers say that the child's response style may mask their mathematical competence.

A significant element of the power of these sociological insights is the languages that Bernstein and Bourdieu have created, though this is also one of the often-mentioned difficulties: their concepts are precise and specific and require work to understand and engage with. The rigour of those languages, however, is precisely what makes them able to explain phenomena such as social class differences in performance. Cooper and Dunne (2000) expanded on their study in their later book.

Conclusion

In the three latter sections of this chapter I have examined three examples of research, the second to fourth core readings, each drawing on a perspective on learning and knowing mathematics. There are other theories, of course; I could have looked at gestalt, embodied cognition, situated cognition (Lave and Wenger 1991), activity theory, and others. I have chosen these three because they represent, I believe, major approaches being worked within the mathematics education research community and are exemplary in how the methodology and methods are appropriate to the theoretical perspective chosen. In this way, I hope researchers can gain insight into how we need to work with multiple theories of learning and knowing mathematics.

I want to add here that there are two further perspectives on researching education that I have also chosen not to address. They stand out from the other theories, those I have illustrated here and those I have not, because they do not see the need for adopting one theory but consider either that research should be designed according to the problem being raised, design research (Cobb et al. 2000), or because all human (and non-human) functioning is complex and layered, and calls for complexity theory (Davis and Sumara 2006) for researching learning and knowing. References to these within mathematics education are provided in the further reading recommendations.

Note

1 This refers to TIMA:Sticks, a computer tool designed by Steffe and colleagues for the teaching experiment. 'In TIMA:Sticks, a segment can be drawn using the mouse cursor, the segment can be marked using hash marks, marked parts can be pulled out of the whole stick (an operation that left the marked stick intact), copies of the pulled part can be made, and copies can be joined together to make another stick' (p. 131).

Further reading

Cobb, P., Yackel, E. and McClain, K., eds, 2000. *Symbolizing and communicating in mathematics classrooms: perspectives on discourse, tools, and instructional design.* Mahwah, NJ: Laurence Erlbaum.

Davis, B. and Sumara, D., 2006. *Complexity and education: inquiries into learning, teaching, and research.* Mahwah, NJ: Laurence Erlbaum.

Glasersfeld, E. von, 1991. *Radical constructivism in mathematics education (Mathematics Education Library).* Dordrecht, Netherlands: Kluwer.

Lave, J., 1988. *Cognition in practice: mind, mathematics and culture in everyday life.* Cambridge, UK: Cambridge University Press.

Lave, J. and Wenger, E., 1991. *Situated learning: legitimate peripheral participation.* New York: Cambridge University Press.

Morgan, C., Tsatsaroni, A. and Lerman, S., 2002. Mathematics teachers' positions and practices in discourses of assessment. *British Journal of Sociology of Education*, 23 (3), 443–59.

Additional references

Bernstein, B., 2000. *Pedagogy, symbolic control and identity. Theory, research, critique*, (rev. edn). New York: Rowman & Littlefield.

Cooper, B. and Dunne, M., 2000. *Assessing children's mathematical knowledge: social class, sex and problem-solving*. Buckingham, UK: Open University Press.

Glasersfeld, E. von, 1990. An exposition of constructivism: why some like it radical. In R. B. Davis, C. A. Maher and N. Noddings, eds, *Constructivist views on the teaching and learning of mathematics. Journal for Research in Mathematics Education Monograph*, 4, 19–29.

Lerman, S., 2010. Theories of mathematics education: is plurality a problem? In B. Sriraman and L. English, eds, *Theories of mathematics education*. New York: Springer, 99–110.

Meira, L. and Lerman, S., 2010. Zones of Proximal Development as fields for communication and dialogue. In C. Lightfoot and M. C. D. P. Lyra, eds, *Challenges and strategies for studying human development in cultural contexts*. Rome: Firera Publishing, 199–219.

Simon, M., 1995. Reconstructing mathematics pedagogy from a constructivist perspective. *Journal for research in learning mathematics*, 26, 114–45.

Vygotsky, L., 1978. *Mind in society: the development of higher psychological processes*. Cambridge, MA: Harvard University Press.

Improving Assessment in School Mathematics

3

Jeremy Hodgen and Marja van den Heuvel-Panhuizen

Core readings

The Core readings addressed in this chapter are as follows:

Van den Heuvel-Panhuizen, M. and Becker, J. P., 2003. Towards a didactical model for assessment design in mathematics education. In A. J. Bishop, K. Clements, C. Keitel, J. Kilpatrick and F. K. S. Leung, eds, *Second international handbook of mathematics education*. Dordrecht, Netherlands: Kluwer, 689–716.

Black, P. J. and Wiliam, D., 1998. Assessment and classroom learning. *Assessment in Education*, 5 (1), 7–73.

Morgan, C. and Watson, A., 2002. The interpretative nature of teachers' assessment of students' mathematics: issues for equity. *Journal for Research in Mathematics Education*, 33 (2), 78–110.

Black, P., Harrison, C., Hodgen, J., Marshall, B. and Serret, N., 2011. Can teachers' summative assessments produce dependable results and also enhance classroom learning? *Assessment in Education: Principles, Policy and Practice*, 18, 451–69.

Introduction

In recent years, there have been a number of critiques of the ways in which examinations appear to be skewing the teaching of mathematics and other subjects in the United Kingdom and elsewhere (e.g. Advisory Committee on Mathematics Education 2005; Stobart 2008). These critiques highlight the extent to which examinations have 'high-stakes' for students, teachers or schools, so that doing well in these examinations takes precedence over other aspects of learning. In particular, researchers and other commentators have highlighted how teaching tends to focus on what is tested in high-stakes examinations, which in turn tend towards a narrow focus on what is most easily assessed.

As elsewhere in education, there are many 'technical' terms and concepts used in the assessment literature. The definitions that we provide here are limited by space constraints, but extensive discussions may be found elsewhere (e.g. Black 1998). The two most important concepts are 'validity' and 'reliability'. Validity refers to whether an assessment measures what it claims to measure, whereas reliability refers to consistency and the extent to which repeating an assessment would produce the same result. In the first core reading, Van den Heuvel-Panhuizen and Becker (2003) address the issue of validity by examining how test items can be improved to place more emphasis on mathematical understanding and processes rather than routine methods and procedures. The authors argue that traditional approaches to assessment, mainly drawn from psychometrics, the discipline of psychological measurement, have limited the scope of mathematics tests by giving more weight to questions that are more 'objective' in having a straightforward correct answer.

Over the past decade, a key focus for research and practice has been on the distinction between 'summative' and 'formative' assessment. Summative refers to the assessment of what students have already learned. Thus, summative assessment covers a wide range of types of assessment from national examinations such as (in England) GCSEs and A-levels to end-of-year school tests. Summative assessment may be designed for several purposes, including the accountability of schools and teachers in providing education, the provision of information on how well a particular student is progressing, the certification that a student has achieved a certain level, or the evaluation of how effective a teaching unit has been. In contrast, formative assessment is focused on informing learning and teaching by providing feedback to students and teachers.

This summative/formative debate was partly initiated by the second core reading in which Black and Wiliam (1998) review the evidence supporting the efficacy of formative assessment. Although this article is not focused specifically on mathematics, it has nevertheless been very influential in mathematics education and indeed much of the evidence is drawn from studies in the context of mathematics education. However, we feel that this original review provides the most authoritative and comprehensive starting point on formative assessment.

In the third reading, Morgan and Watson (2002) warn that assessment by teachers is not without dangers. The authors address both reliability and validity by examining how and why teachers can arrive at quite different judgements in both ongoing classroom assessment and high-stakes assessments. These different judgements can then have implications for educational equity.

In everyday parlance, assessment is often naïvely considered simply in terms of tests and examinations. Proponents of alternative modes, such as interviews, tasks and coursework, argue that these can provide a more valid assessment of mathematical understandings, although these modes may seem difficult and costly. In the fourth reading, Black et al. (2011) examine how summative assessment, conducted by teachers and involving such alternative approaches, can be integrated within classroom practice and enhance learning.

Towards a didactical model for assessment design

Instruction and assessment are linked in two directions. In an ideal situation this reciprocal relationship is in balance: what is taught is assessed and what is assessed is taught. In order to achieve this balance, instruction and assessment should be epistemologically consistent, that is, the views of assessment should be in agreement with the views on learning and teaching and the goals as expressed in curricula. However, as Shepard (2000) has indicated, instruction and assessment are not always consonant. In particular, the standardized tests which mostly stem from the psychometric-based measurement tradition are more aligned with traditional curricula and a behaviourist view on learning and teaching than they are in agreement with 'reformed' curricula (with enhanced content and process objectives) and a constructivist view on learning (see the chapter by Lerman, this volume). Therefore, it was no surprise that from the very outset of the worldwide reform movement in mathematics education, there was a strong call for a new approach to assessment (e.g. Romberg et al. 1990) that would be in line with reform views on the goals of mathematics education, the ways of learning mathematics and the methods by which teachers can teach mathematics.

Van den Heuvel-Panhuizen and Becker (2003) argue that to get an assessment that can support and evaluate the current approach to learning and teaching of mathematics, the dominant *psychometric* model for assessment design should be extended with a *didactic* model of assessment design that is grounded in the didactics of mathematics, that is, the scientific discipline that investigates the what and the how of learning and teaching mathematics in particular. Such a didactic model for assessment design can ensure that assessment tasks are used that represent relevant goals of mathematics education, offering students the opportunity to show mathematical competences that are considered to be meaningful to learn, and providing teachers with the information they need for instructional decision making.

To illustrate how educational goals may be embedded in assessment tasks, two problems are discussed which each are about the measurement of area. In the Flag problem on the left of Figure 3.1, the question read by the teacher is: 'What do you think the size of the flag on the top of this apartment building is in reality?' In the problem on the right, which is from the US California Achievement Test (CAT), the question printed on the test sheet says: 'What is the area of the shape?' Both problems are meant for Grade 5.

The problem on the right is an example of an item as they can appear in a standardized test. In this problem the students are asked to determine the area of a rectangle. All the necessary information is given. The students are even told that the area can be found by carrying out multiplication and that the area can be expressed in square metres. This CAT problem differs remarkably from the Flag problem on the left. Because of all the missing information in this Flag problem, there are many opportunities for the students to show

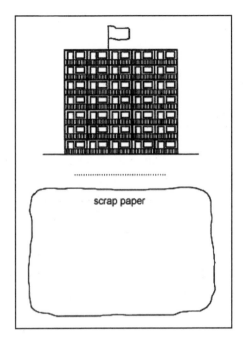 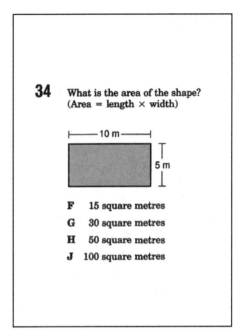

34 What is the area of the shape?
(Area = length × width)

F   15 square metres
G   30 square metres
H   50 square metres
J   100 square metres

Figure 3.1 Two contrasting assessment items

their mathematical understanding and skills. The problem does not only assess whether students can carry out a calculation to find the area of the flag, the problem also shows whether they can determine what is a suitable area unit, and can figure out the height and the width of the flag, for example, by using the size of a door as a reference.

From a psychometric perspective there are several reasons why this Flag problem is unlikely to be included in a standardized test: it is unclear what is actually assessed and the necessary data are not provided. Most importantly, there is not one 'correct' answer (and a 'correct' answer is dependent on the assumptions made and how 'reasonable' these assumptions are). This has implications for reliability in that objective scoring is not possible, since there are many potential 'correct' answers and deciding whether an answer is correct requires considerable judgement. However, many mathematics educators would judge the Flag problem to be appropriate for assessment because of its rich potential to provide a lot of information about the students' thinking, understanding and knowledge. Moreover, the problem is consistent with what many think is important for students to learn. Instead of writing out prescribed mechanical procedures, an opportunity is provided for students to apply flexibly their mathematical knowledge and understanding in a manner that makes sense to them in this particular problem situation.

In the remaining part of the Van den Heuvel-Panhuizen and Becker reading, the need for a different model for assessment design in mathematics education is further elaborated through a further critique of the psychometric model of assessment. The chapter concludes with a number of alternative assessment problems which provide students with a 'rich environment' to demonstrate the mathematics they know and which offer teachers detailed information about the mathematical thinking of their students which is necessary to adapt the instruction to their needs. Finally, the authors argue that standardized tests should not be abandoned, but that teachers (and researchers) need an additional and extended model for collecting data about students' achievement in mathematics.

The critiques of this broad approach within mathematics education have focused on the extent to which many of the problems actually used in mathematics are realistic and do require a broader mathematical understanding (e.g. Boaler 1993). In short, contextualized problems may require students to know more about the context than the inherent mathematics. Hence, Cooper and Dunne (2000) show that some groups, such as working-class children, girls and ethnic minorities, are disadvantaged by the contextualized problems used in national tests. A further issue with the didactic tasks is that the assessment requires considerable teacher judgement and can thus be both expensive and time-consuming. It is also worth noting that the discipline of psychometrics has begun to respond to Van den Heuvel-Panhuizen and Becker's critique by collaborating with reform-orientated researchers in mathematics education (e.g. Confrey et al. 2009).

Formative assessment and classroom learning

Black and Wiliam's (1998) article is a review of previous research on formative assessment. It sets out to establish the evidence base for the use of formative assessment. In doing so, they link it to research on motivation and pedagogy, thus redefining and clarifying the meaning of formative assessment. They define formative assessment as 'all those activities undertaken by teachers, and/or by their students, which provide information to be used as feedback to modify the teaching and learning activities in which they are engaged' (pp. 7–8). Clarifying the meaning of terms is clearly important in any research article. In this case, as the authors argue, it is particularly important, given the many and varied terms that are used to refer to similar ideas, including classroom evaluation, curriculum-based assessment, feedback and formative evaluation.

Reviews of research can be valuable in collating and synthesizing all the available evidence on a topic. However, such synthesis can be problematic in that research may draw on different methodological or epistemological traditions. There is also a problem of bias in that 'successful' studies are much more likely to be reported. In order to address these problems, Black and Wiliam adopt a methodological approach that contrasts sharply with the systematic approach to research reviews in which the field is very tightly defined, and a limited range of research methodologies are considered sufficiently rigorous for inclusion (see, for example, Harlen 2004). While the systematic approach is likely to provide more robust and rigorous findings for a mature field of research, Black and Wiliam's more eclectic approach allowed them to define and extend the meaning of formative assessment in what was, and to a large extent still is, a fragmentary field.

The review is based on 681 publications that provide evidence for the efficacy of or the nature of formative assessment. It takes as its starting point the two earlier reviews by Natriello (1987) and Crookes (1988) and largely considers studies published subsequent to these studies. Black and Wiliam describe their review method as 'eclectic' and the inclusion criteria as 'loosely rather than tightly drawn' (p. 7). They justify this approach through their discussion and sympathetic critique of the two earlier reviews in which they highlight difficulties in defining the field of 'formative assessment' research. A guiding criterion of Black and Wiliam's approach to selection is the 'ecological validity' of the studies considered, by which they mean the extent the results are applicable to normal classrooms. This relates to Black and Wiliam's central concern: the use of assessment to improve learning in general.

Systematic reviews often involve meta-analysis, which is a method of aggregating the results of quantitative studies (for a non-technical explanation, see Gorard and Taylor 2004). Black and Wiliam argue that for formative assessment such an approach was not 'possible or useful' because there was no commonly accepted definition of formative assessment, although they do cite the results of several such meta-analyses. As an alternative strategy, Black and Wiliam present the quantitative findings of research studies without aggregation while emphasizing the practical effects of the gains they describe to supplement what they term the 'dryness' of measures such as effect sizes (p. 17). For example, in order to map out the field, they initially describe eight research studies about formative assessment, all but one of which provide robust quantitative evidence for the effectiveness of formative assessment. While the evidence provided here and elsewhere in the article is certainly substantial, the studies described tackle formative assessment in different ways and in different contexts and this makes estimating the size and statistical significance effects of formative assessment difficult.

In the discussion of the eight studies, Black and Wiliam raise a number of issues that frame the review as a whole. First, formative assessment involves considerable changes to existing pedagogy and practice. Second, effective formative assessment appears to be strongly informed by theories of learning. In other words, in order to modify teaching, teachers need to have a framework of how learning progresses. Third, it is not sufficient simply to give feedback. Feedback needs to be used, which in turn means that, to be effective, feedback needs to be differentiated. Fourth, the role of students is central, but appears often to be ignored or taken for granted in much of the research. Finally, they note that student motivation and self-perceptions matter. Feedback made 'with the assumption that each student can and will succeed' is considerably more effective than feedback 'mentioning comparison with peers, with the assumption – albeit covert – that some students are not as able as others and so cannot expect full success' (p. 17). Some would argue that feedback is *the* key to formative assessment (see, for example, Hattie and Timperley 2007). However, Black and Wiliam argue that, while in comparison to other strategies feedback is effective, it does not always work. Ticks and crosses or a grade provide feedback, but the effect of this feedback might be, as in Butler's (1988) study, to prevent or even set back learning.

In addition to reviewing the elements of formative assessment that are effective, the article reviews the literature on effective teaching strategies. These include rich and meaningful tasks, the quality of discourse and questioning and the quality of feedback. However, terms such as quality, rich, meaningful, are somewhat vague and are, as the authors themselves observe, dependent both on the context and the students involved. Hence, Black and Wiliam conclude that there is an urgent need for research examining the implementation of formative assessment (see, Black et al. 2003, for a subsequent study that addressed this).

There are relatively few critiques of this article, which is somewhat surprising given the extent to which it is cited. Bennett (2011), for example, argues that formative assessment is not sufficiently well defined, and as a result the evidence for its efficacy is overstated (see also Higgins et al. 2011). In our view, Black and Wiliam would concur with the first point and, indeed, the lack of definition is a central thrust of their argument and subsequent work. With regard to the second point, the thrust of the review is that, *in Black and Wiliam's judgement*, although formative assessment was an immature field at the time of the review, it provided the most likely approach to improved learning outcomes (Black and Wiliam 2003). Another critique relates to the implementation of formative assessment. For example, in a case study of four schools, Smith and Gorard (2005) describe students' dissatisfaction with a 'no grades' approach, although the teachers appeared to misapply formative assessment by giving poorly directed feedback. Hodgen (2007) examines an expert mathematics teacher's attempt to use the dialogic techniques of formative assessment. While some evidence is found for changed practice, the strategies largely appear to have reinforced existing teacher-dominated patterns of talk, allowing limited opportunities for student talk. Implementation is certainly very difficult and, while formative assessment has been remarkably successful at least in terms of its widespread adoption by schools and policy makers across England, the strategy does not appear yet to have transformed education, nor has it produced the promised gains in attainment.

Interpretation in teachers' assessments

Teacher assessment is seen by some as a way of ameliorating the damaging effects of high-stakes assessment. However, the reliability, validity and objectivity of teachers judgements has been questioned (Borko et al. 1997). Morgan and Watson (2002) challenge the possibility of objective assessment and argue that interpretation is central to assessment. Like Van den Heuvel-Panhuizen and Becker (2003), they argue that interpretation allows mathematical understanding to be better assessed, but they show how teachers can arrive at radically different judgements based on very similar pieces of student work and thus caution that teachers should be sceptical of their own judgements.

The article is based on two empirical studies, each of which was conducted in England by one of the authors. Both studies considered a small number of cases of assessments by teachers, although in the article only one student from each of the original studies.

The first study, conducted by Watson, addresses the ongoing classroom assessments that teachers make and is most related to formative assessment. Watson's study involved students aged 11–12, who were at the time in their first term of secondary school. Data were collected over one term (about three months) and involved a regular weekly lesson observation in each class together with all the students' written work. The researcher adopts an insider stance and compares her assessment of the student with that of the teacher. Watson finds that the teacher's assessment and the researcher's were radically different. The teacher judged the student, Sandra, to be relatively strong in mental arithmetic, but relatively weak at mathematical thinking. The researcher, by contrast, took a diametrically opposite view and judged Sandra to be relatively weak at mental arithmetic and to have some strength in mathematical thinking. In part, this is due to the fact that they 'see' different evidence, with the researcher having more time and opportunity to observe Sandra using her fingers to work out the subtractions of relatively small numbers. She '*wanted* to appear good but was regularly making and hiding errors that were not appearing in her final written work' (p. 91). For the teacher, Sandra's social skills and enthusiasm for mental arithmetic obscured her weaknesses. In addition, the teacher was 'slow to change his opinion . . . even in the light of accumulating evidence' (p. 93).

The second study, conducted by Morgan, addresses the role of teacher assessment in tasks that contribute to a high-stakes examination. This study involved 11 experienced teachers assessing student 'texts' (written reports of a problem-solving or investigative task), who read and evaluated the work and were then interviewed using a 'think-aloud' approach. The authors focus on the teachers' judgements about one student, Steven, who had given an alternative, and unusual solution that was incomplete in that how Steven had produced it was only partially explained. The teachers formed different judgements based on different inferences about how the text represented the mathematics the student had actually done and different individual value systems about the relative importance of different aspects of mathematics.

In considering the implications for the promotion of more equitable assessment systems, Watson and Morgan argue that improved assessment tasks of the sort proposed in the first reading are necessary but not sufficient to ensure greater equity. They argue that in addition there is a need for increased professional dialogue about assessment judgements.

The strengths of the article by Watson and Morgan are in highlighting the potential flaws and biases in teachers' assessment judgements and how these can occur. However, while the authors raise the issue of values, they do not resolve it. They stress, for example, that the researcher's assessment is not 'better' or more objective than that of the teacher.

However, the authoritative voice of a journal article does not facilitate this stance and, as a result, the researchers' assessments do appear to be more valid. Moreover, the authors argue that classroom observation can lead to 'legitimately different' judgements about apparently straightforward tasks. This suggests a fundamental difficulty with teacher assessment that may be difficult to resolve through professional dialogue. One approach to addressing such difficulties is through the sampling of students' tasks, which the authors do not explicitly address. Making an assessment of a student's mathematical understanding on the basis of a sample of one task is a threat to both validity and reliability. In terms of validity, one task cannot represent mathematics as a whole, while, in terms of reliability, a student may perform particularly well or badly on the task. While one task is not sufficient, it is not clear how many tasks would be sufficient. It is also important that, as Van den Heuvel-Panhuizen and Becker argue, assessment tasks need to be carefully, and didactically, designed to provide sufficient evidence of mathematical thinking.

Quality and dependability in teachers' summative assessments

The final core reading, Black et al. (2011), is also concerned with the validity and reliability of teacher assessments. The aims were to investigate the strategies that could be adopted to enhance the teachers' summative judgements and whether such strategies can enable a positive relationship between summative and formative assessment practices.

The authors argue that the previous evidence suggests that, while teachers can produce assessments that are sufficiently valid and reliable for their intended purpose, this is dependent on favourable conditions (Harlen 2004). In order to investigate how such favourable conditions can be fostered, the authors conducted a collaborative study with eighteen teachers of English and mathematics, from three secondary schools. These teachers made summative judgements about their Year 8 classes (student age 12–13) over a two-year period. With the support of the researchers, the teachers assessed a broad range of classroom tasks creating portfolios of student work, which were then moderated by all the subject teachers.

The study found that in order to improve the quality of assessments, teachers needed to debate validity and what constitutes quality, although such deliberations were far from trivial. Indeed, the authors find that there are considerable obstacles to doing this within the current educational system. Teachers tended to view the process of making judgements as essentially a straightforward process and 'it was a surprise to some teachers to discover the wide differences between the judgments of colleagues about the same samples of work, as exposed at the moderation meetings' (p. 458). This, in Black et al.'s view, implies that the process of moderation is a crucial strategy not only in producing quality judgements but also in developing teachers' 'assessment literacy'. They also found differences between the two groups of teachers. The English teachers had more experience and more expertise than the mathematics teachers. In addition, the English teachers adopted a more holistic approach focused on the quality of a piece of work as a whole, whereas the mathematics teachers relied more heavily on mark scheme criteria.

The authors introduce two new terms both related to validity and reliability: 'quality' and 'dependability'. While these are valuable in emphasizing that there is a trade-off between validity and reliability in judging whether the assessment is fit for purpose, it is not clear that the introduction of new terminology is necessary or helpful. Moreover, the study required a significant input from the researchers in terms of professional development and guidance to the teachers, but does not address the question of how this could be provided in a cost-effective way on a wider scale.

Conclusion

In this chapter, we have focused on readings that seek to improve the assessment of mathematics through the design of better assessment and by promoting a greater role for teachers in assessment. All take a critical stance on the currently dominant assessment practices in mathematics education and all are concerned with issues of reliability and validity. Van den Heuvel-Panhuizen and Becker argue that assessment can be designed to better assess mathematical thinking and thus improve the validity. Black and Wiliam's review indicates the benefits of formative assessment, although it also highlights that there are many issues still to be addressed. Both Morgan and Watson and Black et al. examine assessment by teachers, and both indicate that achieving sufficiently reliable and valid judgements by teachers is not straightforward. Necessarily, in this short chapter, we have merely touched on some of the issues in the area, and the interested reader is directed to the suggestions for further reading. Black (1998) addresses the issue of assessment in its entirety, although from a generic rather than a specifically mathematical perspective. Ryan and Williams (2007) provide an analysis of English students' mathematical understandings and relate this to how students learn. Stobart (2008) provides an extended critique of the current assessment system. Finally, Wiliam (2007) examines the particular features of formative assessment in mathematics teaching (see also De Lange 2007; Hodgen and Wiliam 2006).

Further reading

Black, P., 1998. *Testing: friend or foe? The theory and practice of assessment and testing.* London: Falmer.

Ryan, J. and Williams, J., 2007. *Children's mathematics 4–15: learning from errors and misconceptions.* Buckingham: Open University Press.

Stobart, G., 2008. *Testing times: the uses and abuses of assessment.* London: Routledge.

Wiliam, D., 2007. Keeping learning on track: classroom assessment and the regulation of learning. In F. K. Lester, Junior, ed., *Second handbook of Research on mathematics teaching and learning.* Greenwich, CT: Information Age Publishing, 1051–98.

Additional references

Advisory Committee on Mathematics Education, 2005. *Assessment in 14–19 mathematics*. London: Royal Society.

Bennett, R. E., 2011. Formative assessment: a critical review. *Assessment in Education: Principles, Policy and Practice*, 18 (1), 5–25.

Black, P., 2009. Looking again at formative assessment. *Learning and Teaching Update*, 30, 3–5.

Black, P. J., Harrison, C., Lee, C., Marshall, B. and Wiliam, D., 2003. *Assessment for learning: putting it into practice*. Buckingham: Open University Press.

Boaler, J., 1993. The role of contexts in the mathematics classroom: do they make mathematics more real? *For the Learning of Mathematics*, 13 (2), 12–17.

Borko, H., Mayfield, V., Marion, S., Flexer, R. and Cumbo, K., 1997. Teachers' developing ideas and practices about mathematics performance assessment: successes, stumbling blocks, and implications for professional development. *Teaching and Teacher Education*, 13 (3), 259–78.

Butler, R., 1988. Enhancing and undermining intrinsic motivation: the effects of task-involving and ego-involving evaluation on interest and performance. *British Journal of Educational Psychology*, 58, 1–14.

Confrey, J., Maloney, A. P., Nguyen, K. H., Mojica, G. and Myers, M., 2009. Equipartitioning/splitting as a foundation of rational number reasoning using learning trajectories. In M. Tzekaki, M. Kaldrimidou and H. Sakonidis, eds, *Proceedings of the 33rd Conference of the International Group for the Psychology of Mathematics Education*, Vol. 1. Thessaloniki, Greece: PME, 345–52.

Cooper, B. and Dunne, M., 2000. *Assessing children's mathematical knowledge: social class, sex and problem-solving*. Buckingham: Open University Press.

Crookes, T. J., 1988. The impact of classroom evaluation practices on students. *Review of Educational Research*, 58, 438–81.

De Lange, J., 1999. *Framework for classroom assessment in mathematics*. Utrecht: Freudenthal Institute and National Center for Improving Student Learning and Achievement in Mathematics and Science.

—, 2007. Large-scale assessment and mathematics education. In F. K. Lester, Junior, ed., *Second handbook of research on mathematics teaching and learning: a project of the National Council of Teachers of Mathematics*, Vol. 2. Charlotte, NC: Information Age Publishing, pp. 1111–42.

Gorard, S. and Taylor, C., 2004. *Combining methods in educational and social research*. Buckingham: Open University Press.

Harlen, W., 2004. A systematic review of the evidence of reliability and validity of assessment by teachers used for summative purposes. *Research evidence in education library*. London: EPPI-Centre, Social Science Research Unit, Institute of Education.

Hattie, J. and Timperley, H., 2007. The power of feedback. *Review of Educational Research*, 77 (1), 81–112.

Higgins, S., Kokotsaki, D. and Coe, R., 2011. *Pupil premium toolkit: summary for schools spending the pupil premium*. Durham: Education Endowment Foundation/Sutton Trust/Durham University.

Hodgen, J., 2007. Formative assessment: tools for transforming school mathematics towards dialogic practice? In D. Pitta-Pantazi and G. Philippou, eds, *CERME 5: Fifth Congress of the European Society for Research in Mathematics Education, 22–26 February*. Larnaca, Cyprus: European Society for Research in Mathematics Education/Department of Education, University of Cyprus, 1886–95.

Hodgen, J. and Wiliam, D., 2006. *Mathematics inside the black box*. London: NFER-Nelson.

Natriello, G., 1987. The impact of evaluation processes on students. *Educational Psychologist*, 22 (2), 155–75.

Romberg, T. A., Zarinnia, E. A. and Collis, K. F., 1990. A new world view of assessment in mathematics. In G. Kulm, ed., *Assessing higher order thinking in mathematics*. Washington, DC: American Association for the Advancement of Science, 21–38.

Shepard, L. A., 2000. The role of assessment in a learning culture. *Educational Researcher*, 29 (7), 4–14.

Smith, E. and Gorard, S., 2005. 'They don't give us our marks': the role of formative feedback in student progress. *Assessment in Education: Principles, Policy and Practice*, 12 (1), 21–38.

Integrating New Technologies into School Mathematics

Kenneth Ruthven

4

Core readings

The Core readings addressed in this chapter are as follows:

Zevenbergen, R. and Lerman, S., 2008. Learning environments using interactive whiteboards: new learning spaces or reproduction of old technologies? *Mathematics Education Research Journal*, 20 (1), 108–26.

Ruthven, K., Deaney, R. and Hennessy, S., 2009. Using graphing software to teach about algebraic forms: a study of technology-supported practice in secondary-school mathematics. *Educational Studies in Mathematics*, 71 (3), 279–97.

Drijvers, P., Doorman, M., Boon, P., Reed, H. and Gravemeijer, K., 2010. The teacher and the tool: instrumental orchestrations in the technology-rich mathematics classroom. *Educational Studies in Mathematics*, 75 (2), 213–34.

Ruthven, K., Hennessy, S. and Deaney, R., 2008. Constructions of dynamic geometry: a study of the interpretative flexibility of educational software in classroom practice. *Computers & Education*, 51 (1), 297–317.

Introduction

The readings for this chapter focus on how the integration of digital technologies into mathematics teaching is shaped by wider practices, ideas and values. Around 30 years ago, Papert (1980) published *Mindstorms* at the crest of a wave of enthusiasm for the educational potential of emerging digital technologies. *Mindstorms* was a powerful expression of the idea that computer-based learning environments would transform the teaching of mathematics (in particular) and the practice of schooling (more generally). Whether these environments were of the exploratory form advocated by Papert or the tutorial form that was also acquiring currency at that time, it was widely assumed that, as interaction between student and computer moved to the heart of schooling, the (human) teacher would become more peripheral (Ruthven 1993). However, as new generations of digital technology came and went with surprisingly little impact on school mathematics, attention turned towards the ways in which educational institutions and individual teachers shape patterns of uptake and use. Indeed, it became clear that the situation of digital technologies could serve as a powerful exemplar for examining much broader questions about the circumstances under which schooling embraces innovation and the processes through which this takes place.

Studying integration into teaching of board technologies as a medium of classroom communication

It is about two centuries since the blackboard first came into use in schools, contributing to a transformation in the organization of classroom learning which took about a century to spread around the world (Villarreal and Borba 2010; Kidwell et al. 2008). The introduction of the blackboard created a medium for public inscription and whole-class communication. This supported a shift towards forms of classroom organization in which the teacher worked at the board with the class as a whole, not just with individual students or small groups in turn at their personal slates. The interactive whiteboard (IWB) represents the most recent step in this line of development. Designed to produce a convenient convergence between the ubiquitous black- or whiteboard and other audio-visual devices, the IWB also capitalizes on the interactivity of digital tools and the connectivity of digital networks.

The article by Zevenbergen and Lerman (2008) examines this generic presentation technology which has been customized for classroom use. In marked contrast to the more hesitant uptake by schools of many other forms of Information and Communications Technology (ICT), the IWB has been embraced unusually rapidly and readily over the course of the past decade by many systems, schools and teachers. The immediate research question posed in the article is an important practical one: what does classroom interaction in mathematics lessons look like when it is mediated by differing forms of new technology. To answer this question, the researchers use an explicit observational framework to describe patterns of teaching interaction in two samples of lessons. They compare lessons involving use of an IWB (which they term 'IWB lessons') with those employing other computer-based information and communication technologies (which they term 'ICT-based lessons'. There appear to have been no lessons in which both an IWB and some other form of ICT were used.)

Although relatively recently developed, the observational framework employed in this study – Productive Pedagogy (PP) – has already been quite widely used by other educational researchers. There are some important points to note about the PP framework. First, it has been developed to describe school pedagogy in general, and not specifically for mathematics as the subject under instruction, or for ICTs as mediators of teaching and learning. Second, it reflects a particular set of priorities and values as expressed in its four main facets, which seek to assess the intellectual quality, external relevance, student supportiveness and community inclusiveness of classroom exchanges.

The results that Zevenbergen and Lerman present identify differences which are particularly strong in terms of the student supportiveness of classroom interaction where trends consistently favour the 'ICT lessons' over the 'IWB lessons'. The article also reports that classroom observation of the 'IWB lessons' indicated that they were predominantly organized around whole-class teaching, with teacher-controlled use of the IWB typically underpinning a fast-paced introduction to the lesson, lasting between 5 and 15 minutes and emphasizing relatively low-level questioning.

There was, then, a marked difference between patterns of activity in the two types of lesson but this does not necessarily imply that 'the use of IWBs . . . actually reduces the quality of mathematical learning opportunities' (Zevenbergen and Lerman, p. 116). For example, if teachers were accustomed to following a pattern in which more teacher-directed whole-class lessons took their place alongside more student-centred small-group lessons then it would be natural for teachers to choose to make use of an IWB in a teacher-directed type of lesson as against other forms of ICT in a student-centred type, problematizing the causal relation implied in the quotation above. This was exactly the type of contrast between classroom use of graphing calculators as against other ICTs found in another study (Monaghan 2004). Nevertheless, the article is able to point to other studies which have found such differences in interaction patterns where similar types of lesson were being taught with and without IWBs.

This leads Zevenbergen and Lerman to seek to understand what considerations lie behind the patterns of teaching displayed in 'IWB lessons' by drawing on teachers' accounts of this aspect of their work. The main themes identified might be summarized as follows. First, IWBs and the resources associated with them are valued by teachers because of the economy of planning effort and the effective use of lesson time that they make possible: these considerations, of course, mirror those of efficiency and productivity that have underpinned the uptake of digital technologies in many other areas of work. Second, teachers value IWBs because of the way in which they help to hold the attention of students and to secure their engagement in whole-class teaching episodes: here, then, teachers perceive the new tool and its associated resources as supporting an established pedagogy.

This is in striking contrast to some of the claims made by advocates of the IWB concerning its transformative potential in matters of pedagogy. It is understandable, then, that Zevenbergen and Lerman conclude that 'technology is mediated by pedagogy' (p. 124) rather than the reverse. By and large, teachers have appropriated the IWB to facilitate – and accentuate certain characteristics of – an established instructional pedagogy. Inasmuch as there is this element of accentuation the IWB might be claimed to be 'amplifying' the effectiveness of an established form of practice rather than 'reorganizing' such practice to take new forms, in the terms introduced by Pea (1985). However, in terms of the PP conceptual framework, this greater efficiency in realizing an instructional pedagogy is considered a step backwards.

Zevenbergen and Lerman employ Engeström's widely referenced 'activity theory' (AT) to guide their analysis. This AT heuristic (Figure 4.1) provides a structure for analysing how some Subject (here a teacher of mathematics) acts in some context (notably that of their work). It focuses, first, on the combination of Object and Objective towards which the Subject's actions are directed (in this case, according to the article, an immediate object(ive) simply of making use of new technology, and ulterior object(ive)s of motivating pupils and supporting their learning). AT then identifies key Artefacts (such as, in this case, the IWB or the other forms of ICT) which mediate the Subject's actions towards these Object(ive)s.

This basic triadic scheme of Subject acting towards Object(ive) by means of Artefact (shown in the upper part of Figure 4.1) is then given a broader socio-cultural framing (shown in the lower part of Figure 4.1) in which this activity is located in relation to some wider Community (in this case, according to the article, 'stakeholders' including parents) with which are associated social Rules as well as norms for Division of Labour for such activity.

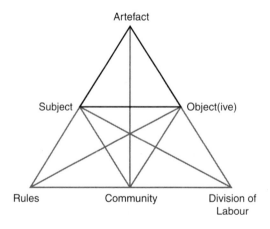

Figure 4.1 The interacting components of an activity system

Studying integration into teaching of graphing technologies as a medium for heuristic mathematics

Graph paper was introduced to school mathematics about a century ago through a reform movement which sought to capitalize on a range of practical forms of mathematics and their associated tools to develop a more heuristic pedagogy that built on student intuition and experiment (Brock and Price 1980; Ruthven 2008). Whereas many of the diverse technologies associated with this reform movement faded away, graph paper became successfully implanted in school mathematics. This success was due to four factors: *external currency* in wider mathematical practice beyond the school; *adoptive facility* of incorporation into existing classroom practice; and *educational advantage* of perceived benefits outweighing costs and concerns; but, perhaps above all, *disciplinary congruence* with an influential contemporary trend in scholarly mathematics which sought to give the mathematical idea of function a more central place (Ruthven 2008).

The modern successor to graph paper is the pixellated screen which (whether on a computer or calculator platform) facilitates interactive and adaptive styles of graphing, and affords sophisticated forms of graph manipulation and analysis, particularly those involving linkages between numeric data, symbolic expressions and graphic forms. Educationally customized forms of mathematical graphing software have become well established in secondary schools, even if their use tends to be restricted to those topics where graphing is central. In particular, it seems that, like their counterparts a century earlier, today's teachers value contemporary graphing technology for providing a medium to support their aspirations towards a more heuristic pedagogy.

The article by Ruthven et al. (2009) examines how teachers make use of mathematical graphing software. Like Zevenbergen and Lerman, they seek to analyse teaching practices and the considerations lying behind these practices. However, the two studies differ in their specific aims. Whereas Zevenbergen and Lerman are concerned to compare the quality of teaching across a typical range of lessons according to the type of technology in use, Ruthven et al. seek to identify the expertise that underpins the use of a particular technology to support what insiders to the profession judge to be quality teaching. Consequently, they study a selected sample identified through a staged process of professional recommendation.

Ruthven et al. use a previously developed 'practitioner model' (PM) of the ways in which teachers see ICTs as contributing to classroom teaching and learning to provide an organizing thematic framework. They report that teachers see the use of mathematical graphing software as increasing the efficiency and pace of lessons, as well as strengthening pupil engagement through increasing the variety and appeal of classroom activity and making graphing tasks more accessible. These parallel the considerations voiced by Zevenbergen and Lerman's teachers. However, Ruthven et al. add further contributions reported by teachers which include the contribution of mathematical graphing software to focusing attention on overarching issues and accentuating important features, to supporting processes of checking, trialling and refinement, and to fostering pupil independence and peer exchange. This last theme seems to link particularly to Zevenbergen and Lerman's finding that 'ICT lessons' featured patterns of classroom interaction that were relatively supportive to students.

However, Ruthven et al. consider the PM framework alone to be inadequate to describe teaching practices. They supplement it with another framework which proposes a system of structuring features (SF) of classroom practice. This framework originates in an earlier synthesis of ideas and findings from a range of research on classroom processes, teacher thinking and learning, and the integration of new technologies (Ruthven 2009). This SF framework guides Ruthven et al.'s analysis of the basic architecture of lessons. In particular, they highlight how, in the course of appropriating mathematical graphing software, teachers adapt their classroom practice and develop their craft knowledge to establish a coherent *resource system* in which graphware-mediated lesson tasks are aligned with teaching goals and supported by a shared repertoire of graphing techniques; to adapt *activity formats* in ways which capitalize on the interactivity of the graphware; and to extend *curriculum scripts* to encompass these features and to provide for proactive structuring and responsive shaping of student activity on graphware-mediated lesson tasks.

Ruthven et al. also appeal more briefly to two further frameworks. The first of these is the instrumental approach (IA) which focuses on the social shaping of the intertwined development of technical and mathematical proficiency which it refers to as *instrumental genesis*. Further analysis of the critical incidents and teacher actions reported in the lesson summaries brings out the way in which this developmental process is shaped by teacher actions. This highlights in turn issues of semiotic mediation (SM) which call for teachers to scaffold students' appropriation of the multimodal system created by the coordinated use of equations and graphs to represent algebraic forms.

Thus, in this article, Ruthven et al. deploy four different theoretical 'lenses' (PM, SF, IA, SM) to focus on particular aspects of the teaching practice under study. One criticism that could be made of this type of multitheoretical approach is that it leads to each aspect (and the framework used to analyse it) receiving less detailed exposition, examination and discussion than if the article had focused on one aspect alone. Against that must be set the more nuanced and rounded analysis made possible by the use of four complementary lenses.

Studying integration into teaching of a virtual learning environment as the mediator of whole-class activity

The article by Drijvers et al. (2010) examines how teachers employ a virtual learning environment, the Digital Mathematics Environment (DME), to mediate whole-class teaching episodes. The teachers participating in this study were piloting a teaching sequence designed by the researchers to establish a dynamic, multimodal concept of mathematical function. This teaching sequence was organized around a succession of dynamic worksheets within the DME, all of which made use of an Algebra Arrows applet specifically devised by the researchers to support teaching and learning of this mathematical topic.

The study is informed by the theoretical perspective of instrumental orchestration (IO), a development of the instrumental approach that is concerned specifically with achieving coordinated development of the technical and mathematical knowledge of students across a class (Trouche 2004). As the article discusses, the guiding metaphor of orchestration is open to a range of interpretations. The significant achievement of this study is to achieve a sharper operational definition of IO through building a more precise typology of formats for classroom activity mediated by the DME. In three of the orchestration types, the teacher takes the lead in using the projected display of the DME to, respectively, provide a demonstration of technical procedures, explain the mathematical material shown on the screen and establish links between the 'same' mathematics as handled 'on the screen' (i.e. in the digital environment) compared to 'on the board' (i.e. in more traditional media). The other three orchestration types involving use of the DME give a more active role to students as follows: in discussing the current work of the class as shown on the screen; in examining a teacher-chosen example of a student's earlier work; in taking the lead (as 'Sherpa student') in operating and accounting for the publicly projected tool, either to present their own previous work for discussion or to pursue the current collective work of the class.

Although Drijvers et al. note that distinguishing between these orchestration types can be problematic in practice, this system provides relatively concrete characterizations of different templates for classroom interaction mediated by the DME. A more extended analysis of one episode concretizes one type of IO, helping to bring out its characteristic pattern of interaction. As operationalized here, each of the six types of IO identified by Drijvers et al. corresponds to what in SF terms would be the combination of a particular activity format (pattern of classroom interaction between participants) with a specific resource subsystem (deployment and coordination of tools and resources). Equally, Drijvers et al.'s more detailed analysis of one episode brings out how one such combination serves to mediate a particular line of mathematical development within (in SF terms) the teacher's curriculum script (detailed mental map for teaching the topic), so supporting the crucial instrumental genesis in student thinking (development of mathematically proficient tool use) with which the original idea of IO is centrally concerned (Trouche 2004).

By using this typology, Drijvers et al. are better able to describe overall patterns in this aspect of classroom activity, and to pinpoint differences between the profiles of teachers and of teaching cycles. The most common of the IO types, and the only one found in every teaching cycle, was technical demonstration by the teacher. To the surprise of the researchers, a more innovative IO type that their guidance had explicitly highlighted, that of the 'Sherpa' student operating the projected DME, was only taken up by one teacher, and by her only substantially in one teaching cycle. Teachers also employed IO types that had not been anticipated in the guidance: for example, the IO type in which the teacher establishes links between the handling of the 'same' mathematics in different media addresses the important issue of how to achieve a coordinated treatment between accepted approaches to a mathematical topic as mediated by established tools and resources and the more tentative and potentially idiosyncratic approaches emerging with the use of new technologies.

Comparing the profiles of teachers in these terms, Drijvers et al. note some very clear differences. To understand why these might come about, the researchers followed up their observations through discussion with the teachers concerned so as to explore the hypothesis that different profiles of activity may be related to contrasting views on mathematics and technology. Like the researchers in the studies discussed earlier, Drijvers et al. found it necessary to supplement direct observation of classroom activity by accessing the associated mathematical and pedagogical thinking of the participating teachers. The differences that they note between teachers show how a DME can be used to support a variety of patterns of whole-class interaction, and that the degree of teacher- or student-centredness of these patterns relates both to the IOs in the teacher's repertoire and to the underlying models of teaching and learning embraced by the teacher.

Studying integration of dynamic geometry into personal and cultural frameworks for teaching

The study by Zevenbergen and Lerman suggests that the strong uptake of IWBs reflects their compatibility with established instructional pedagogies: indeed, their capacity in the eyes of teachers to enhance such pedagogies. Equally, however, the differences that Zevenbergen and Lerman found between 'IWB lessons' and 'ICT lessons' show that some resource systems better support the use of more reconstructive pedagogies. This has been further illustrated by the cases of mathematical graphing software use studied by Ruthven et al. Nevertheless, the variation between teachers and cycles observed by Drijvers et al. indicates that patterns of use of any technology are conditioned both by contextual factors and teacher characteristics. Drijvers et al. note parallels between the teacher profiles in their study and those identified in a article in which Ruthven et al. (2008) examine the 'interpretative flexibility' of dynamic geometry systems, a type of mathematical tool that, again, has been tailored for classroom use. As in Ruthven et al.'s other study, the focus is on a selected sample of teaching episodes identified through a staged process of professional recommendation.

In analysing interpretations of dynamic geometry systems across their four teaching cases, Ruthven et al. draw out how contrasting ideas of 'employing dynamic geometry to support guided discovery' reflect the differing conclusions that teachers have drawn from 'evaluating the costs and benefits of student software use' and the differing solutions they have devised to 'handling apparent mathematical anomalies of software operation', which have their origins in more fundamental mathematico-pedagogical orientations. In particular, orientations that emphasized 'supporting learning through analysis of mathematical discrepancies' and 'promoting mathematically disciplined interaction' were associated with classroom practices in which students were given much greater opportunity to themselves work with dynamic geometry software.

What is also significant about this study is that it looks beyond individual classrooms and teachers to wider sources of potential influence on teachers' thinking and practice. While echoes of the neoprogressive rhetoric of the missionaries for dynamic geometry can be found in teachers' espousal of ideas of 'guiding students to discover properties for themselves', their enacted practices are more tightly staged and managed than these missionaries envisaged. Other significant factors also emerge. The first is simply the underdeveloped state of detailed knowledge about how dynamic geometry can be used innovatively to support the development of geometrical thinking (Laborde 2001). The second is the failure of curricular guidance to recognize that, just as students need to be supported in learning to make proficient use of classical tools for geometrical construction by hand, a similarly supported development is required in respect of new digital tools. These are better thought of as limitations of the current state of wider mathematico-pedagogical culture than as the failings of individual teachers or curriculum designers or even dynamic geometry advocates: what in the instrumental approach would be thought of as the institutional framing of the process of instrumental genesis (Trouche 2004).

Likewise, Ruthven et al. show how established biases towards experimentation and arithmetization within the culture of English school mathematics have produced preconceptions about how dynamic geometry systems should be used. Accordingly, they note how, in the majority of their cases, the way in which geometrical relations were expressed and reasoned about was primarily in terms of number patterns, and how this influenced the way in which the dragging of dynamic figures was conceived and employed. The sole exception was a case where the teacher was able to draw on personal experience of a classical approach to geometry teaching (now near-extinct in English schools) to produce a very different style of dynamic geometry use.

Again, in this article, Ruthven et al. are theoretically eclectic, drawing explicitly on socio-cultural models from social studies of technological innovation and educational studies of textbook use as well as on the instrumental approach. Notably, they use these simply as orienting theories rather than to provide a more detailed and specialized operational apparatus. Behind this decision lies a judgement that such an apparatus would add little of substance to the analysis and could stand in the way of expressing its findings in a way accessible to educational policy makers and practitioners.

Conclusion

One way of summarizing these articles is to return to activity theory (as shown in Figure 4.1). The integration of digital (and other) technologies into the teaching of mathematics (and other subjects) can be studied simply at the individual level represented by the upper triad of the activity system diagram: in terms of the teacher Subject acting towards their teaching Object(ive) by means of some digital Artefact. Whereas this triad is often read as drawing attention to the way in which the digital Artefact mediates relations between the teacher Subject and the teaching Object(ive), these studies suggest that each element of this triad mediates relations between the other two: first, the already present capacities and beliefs (not to mention habits and attitudes) of the Subject shape the relations that develop between Artefact and Object(ive); likewise, taken-for-granted Object(ive)s (and already established means of achieving them) shape the relations that emerge between Subject and Artefact.

However, to gain a deeper understanding of the social shaping of such relations at the individual level, integration must be studied at the socio-cultural or institutional level represented by the system diagram as a whole. This acknowledges the nesting of the individual triad within an overarching Community and its culture; and it specifically recognizes the way in which the social Rules and norms of Division of Labour of such a Community frame – indeed, typically, condition – interactions within the triad (embedded as these rules and norms are in accumulated cultural and human capital). This is not to discount the contribution made by a myriad of micro-genetic adaptations at the individual Subject level to eventually producing socio-genetic change in the rules and norms of a Community; but it is to recognize that the institutionalization of ideas and practices at the socio-cultural level plays a key part in sustaining them at the individual level. Returning to the example of *Mindstorms* cited in the Introduction to this chapter: the educational rise and fall of *Logo* during the last 20 years of the twentieth century provides a powerful illustration of the waxing and waning of different institutional influences (Agalianos et al. 2001; Ruthven 2008).

Further reading

Artigue, M., 2002. Learning mathematics in a CAS environment: the genesis of a reflection about instrumentation and the dialectics between technical and conceptual work. *International Journal of Computers for Mathematical Learning*, 7 (3), 245–74.

Gueudet, G., Pepin, B. and Trouche, L., eds, 2011. *From text to 'lived' resources: mathematics curriculum materials and teacher development*. New York: Springer.

Laborde, C., 2001. Integration of technology in the design of geometry tasks with Cabri-Geometry. *International Journal of Computers for Mathematical Learning*, 6 (3), 283–317.

Ruthven, K., 2009. Towards a naturalistic conceptualisation of technology integration in classroom practice: the example of school mathematics. *Education & Didactique*, 3 (1), 131–49.

Trouche, L., 2004. Managing the complexity of human/machine interactions in computerized learning environments: guiding students' command process through instrumental orchestrations. *International Journal of Computers for Mathematical Learning*, 9 (3), 281–307.

Villarreal, M. and Borba, M., 2010. Collectives of humans-with-media in mathematics education: notebooks, blackboards, calculators, computers and . . . notebooks throughout 100 years of ICMI. *ZDM – The International Journal on Mathematics Education*, 42 (1), 49–62.

Additional references

Agalianos, A., Noss, R. and Whitty, G., 2001. *Logo* in mainstream schools: the struggle over the soul of an educational innovation. *British Journal of Sociology of Education*, 22 (4), 479–500.

Brock, W. and Price, M., 1980. Squared paper in the nineteenth century: instrument of science and engineering, and symbol of reform in mathematical education. *Educational Studies in Mathematics*, 11 (4), 365–81.

Kidwell, P., Ackerberg-Hastings, A. and Roberts, D., 2008. *Tools of American Mathematics Teaching, 1800–2000*. Baltimore: Johns Hopkins University Press.

Monaghan, J., 2004. Teachers' activities in technology-based mathematics lessons. *International Journal of Computers for Mathematical Learning*, 9 (3), 327–57.

Papert, S., 1980. *Mindstorms: children, computers, and powerful ideas*. London: Harvester Press.

Pea, R., 1985. Beyond amplification: using the computer to reorganize mental functioning. *Educational Psychologist*, 20 (4), 167–82.

Ruthven, K., 1993. Technology and the rationalisation of teaching. In C. Keitel and K. Ruthven, eds, *Learning from computers: mathematics education and technology*. Berlin: Springer, 187–202.

—, 2008. Mathematical technologies as a vehicle for intuition and experiment: a foundational theme of the International Commission on Mathematical Instruction, and a continuing preoccupation. *International Journal for the History of Mathematics Education*, 3 (2), 91–102.

Mathematics Textbooks and How They Are Used

5

Sebastian Rezat and Rudolf Straesser

Core readings

The Core readings addressed in this chapter are as follows:

Pepin, B. and Haggarty, L., 2001. Mathematics textbooks and their use in English, French and German classrooms: a way to understand teaching and learning cultures. *ZDM – The International Journal on Mathematics Education*, 33 (5), 158–75.

Remillard, J. T., 2005. Examining key concepts in research on teachers' use of mathematics curricula. *Review of Educational Research*, 75 (2), 211–46.

Rezat, S., 2008a. Learning mathematics with textbooks. In O. Figueras, J. L. Cortina, S. Alatorre, T. Rojano and A. Sepúlveda, eds, *Proceedings of the 32nd Conference of the International Group for the Psychology of Mathematics Education and PME-NA XXX*, Vol. 4. Morelia, Mexico: PME, 177–84.

Valverde, G. A., Bianchi, L. J., Wolfe, R. G., Schmidt, W. H. and Houang, R. T., 2002. *According to the book: using TIMSS to investigate the translation of policy into practice through the world of textbooks.* Dordrecht, Netherlands: Kluwer, 139–52.

Introduction

We start from a simplistic understanding of a textbook: a textbook in mathematics education is a book about mathematics presented in a way which is considered to support its teaching and learning. The book is normally written for classroom use, involving the most important users of the textbook, the teacher and the learner (or 'student'). If we compare this triad, textbook–teacher–student, with the 'didactical triangle' of teacher–student–content (see, for example, Schoenfeld 2012, for an overview), it becomes clear that a textbook should have something to say about mathematics. The book may be the description, if not the definition of mathematics to be taught (by the teacher) or to be learned (by the student). Usually, the author of the textbook is neither the teacher nor the student. With the textbook author, a third agent comes in, who influences not only the didactical situation, but also other major agents near the didactical triangle. Principals of schools, the parents of the students, (political) decision makers of what is to be taught and learned in schools, mathematicians interested in education and the like, also read textbooks and try to influence their contents. Nowadays, some people think that modern information technology may take over the role of textbooks, but judging from the fact that – at least in industrialized countries – the use of textbooks is taken for granted, while the use of computers is discussed and disputed, a comment from Howson still seems to be valid: 'But despite the obvious powers of the new technology it must be accepted that its role in the vast majority of the world's classrooms pales into insignificance when compared with that of textbooks and other written materials' (1995, p. 21).

The core readings in this chapter are chosen to provide some selective insights into different perspectives within the field of research on mathematics textbooks. In the first part of their article, Pepin and Haggarty (2001) provide a comprehensive overview of research on mathematics textbooks. The second part of the article compares mathematics textbooks and their use by teachers in three European countries. Remillard (2005) looks more closely at what is meant when researchers speak of 'curriculum use' which includes use of textbooks, and identifies four different conceptualizations of the notion of the term. Furthermore, she discusses different core aspects related to curriculum use by teachers. Whereas Pepin and Haggarty, as well as Remillard, investigate textbook use by the teacher, Rezat (2008a) approaches the use of textbooks from the perspective of the student. Finally, Valverde et al. (2002) focus on the textbook itself, as opposed to how it is used, and carry out a cross-cultural comparison of mathematics and science textbooks, which is a seminal work for the whole field of textbook analysis.

Our goal in this chapter is to embed these four core readings in the broader context of research on mathematics textbooks, and to relate different aspects of the articles and chapters to two major issues in the field. These issues are the relationship of textbooks to the *curriculum* (addressed in the next section), and the *book* itself and how it is *used*. Throughout the chapter we shall refer to methodological aspects of textbook research.

The mathematics textbook – curriculum material and artifact

In this section we comment first on the relationship of textbooks to other written materials for classroom use, and then we proceed to clarify the relationship between textbooks and the curriculum.

Mathematics textbooks as curriculum materials

In some countries, and at some levels of education, textbooks are accompanied by other material, offering supplementary ideas for teaching. These can include additional exercises and tests to assess learning. These materials are especially useful in contexts where significant amounts of mathematics teaching are undertaken by non-specialists, including those with no professional training in mathematics didactics. For research purposes, it may be important not to restrict the focus of a study to the textbook as such. Taking into account this supplementary material, accompanying the textbook, this can be an absolute necessity to understanding the role of a textbook in the teaching and/or learning of mathematics. As with the textbook, the accompanying material may be targeted at the student – for example, books containing additional exercises cross-referenced to the textbook chapter it complements. Alternatively, such material can be targeted at the teacher – for example, commentaries offering some didactical background theory and concepts for a specific teaching approach, or additional activities to introduce or scaffold the teaching of a specific mathematical concept or activity.

This supplementary material often indicates an attempt by the textbook author(s) to narrow down the teaching alternatives, in order to secure the 'fidelity' of the teaching to the book in question (for the idea of 'fidelity' to a textbook, see the discussion of different theoretical types of textbook use in Remillard 2005, pp. 215–16).

The discussion in Remillard (2005) implicitly makes another assumption, which should be made explicit: discussing the fit of a textbook to a curriculum (as some major research projects did in the United States in previous decades) assumes that there is a curriculum to be distinguished from the textbook, so that it is meaningful to look into similarities and differences between curriculum and textbook. By contrast, in England, Wales and Northern Ireland before 1988, there was no 'curriculum' to be distinguished from the variety of textbooks in use – although in secondary schools the examination syllabuses effectively defined the curriculum, and arguably the contents of textbooks. The situation in the United States is more complicated insofar as in some states of the United States, the National Council of Teachers of Mathematics (NCTM) 'Standards' serve as a description of what is to be taught, so that one could speak of an 'informally approved' curriculum. In some countries, an official curriculum is in place: in Germany this is regional, with a national document showing common features. Sweden has had a national curriculum for more than 20 years. In Australia, the making of a national curriculum is currently a 'work in progress'. When there is a curriculum defined by the educational authorities (normally some sort of ministry of education), different constraints may work on the textbook. This can vary from official prescription (as in China) at one extreme to a free market (as in the United Kingdom) at the other. For some places and grades (especially in primary and lower secondary) in Germany, textbooks may only be used if they are approved by regional authorities, whereas for upper secondary grades, in most parts of Germany, teachers have freedom to decide on the textbook to be used in their school. Consequently, a research study on textbooks has to take into account the legal constraints of use of different textbooks.

The TIMSS study (Schmidt et al. 2001) identifies three curriculum levels: the *intended* or official curriculum, the *implemented* curriculum, which refers to how the intended curriculum is carried out in the classroom, and the *attained* curriculum, which represents what students actually learn (see also Valverde et al. 2002, p. 14). Within this classification, the textbook and related written material can be conceptualized as the 'potentially implemented curriculum', while the intended curriculum (the 'intentions, aims and goals' (Valverde et al. 2002, p. 5) of the curriculum may not be explicitly stated or obligatory) somehow and in some places controls the textbooks. The textbooks, in turn, by their very existence have potential to influence or even define the 'implemented curriculum' (the 'strategies, practices and activities' of teaching); and these, in turn, influence the 'attained curriculum' (the 'knowledge, ideas, constructs, schemes' of the students). One basic message of the text by Remillard is that all these relations and links are not unidirectional or decisive, but curricula (at different levels) and textbooks must be conceived of as important influencing agents in the teaching and learning of mathematics.

Mathematics textbooks as artifacts

Apart from the relation of textbooks to other written curriculum materials, and to curricula as such, another perspective on textbooks should be considered. If, for the moment, we forget about the *use* of textbooks, it is helpful to think about textbooks in relation to a more general concept, namely that of 'artifacts'. The philosopher Marx Wartofsky defined an 'artifact' as 'anything which human beings create by the transformation of nature and of themselves: thus also language, forms of social organization and interaction, techniques of production, skills' (1979, p. xiii; for details see pp. 200–9). Wartofsky detailed this concept by distinguishing three levels of artifacts: primary artifacts are those 'directly used in the production', while secondary artifacts are 'used in the preservation and transmission of the acquired skills or modes of action or praxis by which this production is carried out'. Tertiary artifacts 'constitute a domain in which there is a free construction in the imagination of rules and operations different from those adopted for ordinary "this-wordly" praxis' (Wartofsky 1979, pp. 202/209). Using this classification of artifacts, textbooks are positioned as secondary artifacts, and share this description with other tools used in the classroom for teaching and learning. This implies that methodological approaches to textbook analysis can act as a prototype for research into other secondary artifacts, such as software to be used for pedagogical purposes.

Mathematics textbooks and their use: artifacts and instruments

In 1955, Cronbach drew attention to the fact that focusing on the text alone provides an incomplete picture:

> No evaluation of texts as they are, or texts as they might be, is possible until we consider how they perform in the classroom. One cannot really judge the functional contribution of the text alone, for the text-in-use is a complex social process wherein a book, an institution, and a number of human beings are interlaced beyond the possibility of separation. (p. 188)

The importance of the use of texts is also underlined by Otte (1986), to whom Remillard refers in the core reading. Otte (1986) distinguishes between the text as an objectively given structure and a subjective scheme. On the one hand, a text is an objectively given structure in the sense that it can be conceived of as structured information or a structured piece of knowledge. On the other hand, reading the text does not simply internalize the objectively given structure: reading is an activity which is guided by subjective schemes encompassing the goals of reading, previous knowledge of mathematics, and previous knowledge about texts. Based on these subjective schemes, the reader selects information from the text, which in turn reorganizes the subjective schemes.

Otte's distinction between an objectively given structure and a subjective scheme as two inseparable aspects of a text is consistent with the more general perspective on textbooks that we are proposing here, and which is also the theoretical foundation for the study presented in the third core reading (Rezat 2008a): the notion of the textbook as an artifact and the textbook as an instrument. This distinction between artifact and instrument goes back to Rabardel (2002/1995) and offers a viable conceptualization of the human use of artifacts (see Wartofsky 1979, pp. 202–9), including texts, textbooks and other curriculum materials. Rabardel defines an instrument as 'a composite entity made up of an artifact component (an artifact, a fraction of an artifact or a set of artifacts) and a scheme component' (2002, p. 86). This distinction between artifact and instrument takes into account the fact that an artifact might be used differently according to the goal it is used for, and that every user of an artifact develops their own ways of using it. Therefore, 'the constitution of the instrumental entity is the product of the subject's activity' (Rabardel 2002, p. 86; see also the chapter by Ruthven, this volume) and *intentional* use of an artifact, that is, the use of an artifact in order to achieve goals, creates the instrument. An important aspect of this perspective is that artifacts shape the user–artifact interaction actively by affording or constraining certain ways of using the artifact. Thus, they are capable of transforming the user's schemes. On the other hand, the user may develop 'utilization schemes', which the developer of the artifact had never thought of, thus extending the range of situations and aims an artifact can be used for.

We believe that the advantage of considering texts and textbooks from an instrumental perspective rather than from the perspective taken by Otte is that it enables us to relate and connect textbook use to the use of other artifacts, including language, computers and software, whereas Otte's perspective only seems to apply to the activity of reading texts.

Mathematics textbooks as artifacts

Following the distinction between artifact and instrument, in this section we will consider textbooks as artifacts – as distinct from their use by teachers, students or other agents in the teaching and learning of mathematics.

Foci of textbook analyses

In the first core reading, Pepin and Haggarty (2001) suggest 'four major areas according to which textbooks have been analysed in terms of their content and structure: the mathematical intentions of textbooks; pedagogical intentions of textbooks; sociological contexts of textbooks; and the cultural traditions represented in textbooks' (p. 160). Explanations of these four areas are given in the core text, but we add here some considerations from Remillard (2005), which specify some foci of interest. In a framework presented on page 235, she lists 'representation of concepts, . . . representation of tasks, structures, voice and look' and in doing so identifies some perspectives on 'objectively given structures' in textbooks. An analysis of the inner structure of textbooks, which we consider in the following subsection, must detail these global perspectives of textbook analysis.

The structure of textbooks

When analysing textbooks as artifacts, it is helpful to have a structure of this type of book, which can be useful to identify the unit of analysis (i.e. the major entity that is analysed in the study). For this purpose, Valverde et al. distinguish the 'macrostructure' and the 'microstructure' of a textbook. According to their definition, macrostructures refer to 'structural features that cut across the entire book', whereas microstructures are 'associated with specific lessons intended for use in a small number of classroom instructional sessions' (Valverde et al. 2002, p. 21). For the macrostructure, Valverde et al. (2002, pp. 63–73) distinguish three categories of textbooks: textbooks with one dominant content theme, textbooks reflecting a progression of sequential themes and textbooks with fragmented content coverage. The vast majority of textbooks analysed by Valverde et al. (2002, p. 77) were in the category with a progression of sequential themes. Specific text elements like the index, table of contents and other lists are also characteristics of the macrostructure of a textbook. Rezat (2008b, p. 48) added a 'meso structure' between the macro- and microstructure to meet the typical organization of textbooks into chapters which contain more material than is necessary or usable in one (or even two) lessons, but are smaller than the whole book. They often contain teaching–learning material for a broader mathematical topic, can be easily detected from the table of contents of the textbook (if there is one) and often have the same inner structure in a given book or book series.

Unfortunately, there is no accepted classification of elements of the microstructure of textbooks, but Valverde et al. (2002) and Rezat (2008a) followed a similar procedure by first identifying units of analysis (called 'blocks' in Valverde et al. 2002, also in Rezat 2008a, p. 180). They offer different descriptions of these 'blocks'. Valverde et al. distinguishes 'narrative' and 'activity elements', and also 'graphical elements; exercise or question sets; worked examples' (2002, p. 141). Rezat only distinguishes 'introductory tasks, exposition, worked examples, kernels, exercises' (2008a, p. 180). The more interesting results in both cases arise when the distributions of these types of blocks in the textbooks together with their respective functions for teaching and/or learning come into play.

Mathematics textbooks as instruments

The preceding section focused on the textbook as an artifact regardless of how it is used. Analyses of textbooks as artifacts only reveal *opportunities* to teach and to learn. They do not allow conclusions to be drawn about actual teaching practices. By contrast, approaching mathematics textbooks as instruments has to take into account the actual use of textbooks. Textbooks are always used by someone for something. Therefore, in considering textbooks as instruments, one always has to specify for whom it is an instrument, and to what end. A common view, expressed in the texts by Remillard and Valverde et al., is that textbooks are used by policy makers and curriculum designers as instruments to promote change in the classroom. Reform efforts like the 'new math' movement that heavily relied on the power of textbooks and other curriculum materials to change instruction were deemed a failure. Two often-cited explanations for this failure are that, on the one hand, the role of teachers and students in shaping the implemented curriculum has been underestimated and, on the other hand, textbook use is not a straightforward process, in the sense that what is written in the book shapes teaching and learning in a deterministic manner. Since the failure of the 'new math' curriculum reforms in the 1960s and 1970s, increasing interest has been paid to the actual use of textbooks by teachers. However, students, as users of textbooks, still remain in the shadows from the perspective of mathematics education research.

Teachers and mathematics textbooks

Remillard's article offers many interesting perspectives on the use of textbooks by teachers, and on some related issues. First of all, the main aim of the article is to draw attention to theoretical issues related to the use of textbooks by teachers. We already referred to one of these, namely the conceptualization of 'curriculum materials'.

A second important theoretical issue is the conceptualization of 'textbook use'. Remillard (2005) draws attention to the fact that this notion can be conceptualized in different ways. On the basis of a literature review, she identifies four different conceptualizations of 'textbook use': that is, curriculum as following or subverting the text; curriculum use as drawing on the text; curriculum use as interpretation of the text; and curriculum use as participation with the text. She argues that these different conceptualizations 'are grounded in different assumptions about curriculum, teaching and reader-text interactions' (Remillard 2005, p. 217). She explains that these conceptualizations are also related to different foci of analysis. Is the focus on the 'agency of the text as an influencing factor', on the 'agency of teachers', on the 'nature of interpretations and resulting classroom practices' or on 'participatory relationship' between text and teacher? In the end, the choice of focus depends on the research questions. The focus of analysis is closely related to methodological issues of the research in terms of the unit of analysis, which might be the text and how it is understood, the teacher and how he or she understands and uses texts and textbooks, or the implemented curriculum and how it is influenced by textbooks.

Remillard's article demonstrates that textbook use – no matter how it is conceptualized – varies tremendously among teachers. No two teachers use textbooks in the same way. Yet, we find a very homogeneous picture of the role of textbooks and how textbooks are used by teachers in the relevant literature: teachers predominantly use tasks from the textbooks, and textbooks influence the implemented curriculum heavily. These results seem contradictory at first sight, so how can they be explained? The answer lies in the attention to detail and related methodological issues, which are hardly considered in Remillard's article. Looking at the big picture, drawn from large-scale, mostly quantitative studies (e.g. Hopf 1980), we find that teachers rely heavily on their textbook, and the mathematical content of the classroom is heavily influenced by the book. Furthermore, teachers use their mathematics textbooks in two dominant ways, namely as a source for tasks and problems and as a guide for instruction. However, as soon as we look in more detail at which tasks are chosen, how teachers choose the tasks, how they understand their pedagogic potential and how they implement them in the classroom, we observe wide variety. Qualitative studies mainly aim at understanding and explaining this variation.

The study reported in the article by Pepin and Haggarty adds an important perspective on teachers' use of textbooks: the cross-cultural dimension. While Remillard's article is merely concerned with studies on the use of textbooks by American teachers, Pepin and Haggarty compare English, French and German teachers' use of textbooks, with a particular interest in cultural influences (see the chapter by Andrews, this volume). This is an important aspect because it draws attention to the problem of comparing the use of textbooks in different cultures. Students' access to textbooks, different learning and teaching cultures and different school systems are only some of the factors influencing textbook use that vary between different cultures. Therefore, it seems almost impossible to speak of 'textbook use by teachers' without at least specifying in which country. Furthermore, Pepin and Haggarty's article also shows that cultural differences are hard to communicate. This is because, first, it is difficult to find a language that describes each culture in a neutral way. Second, every reader interprets the findings of such studies from their own cultural stance.

Research on the use of textbooks by teachers has shown that there seems to be a broad agreement on the role of textbooks in mathematics classrooms among teachers from different countries, but the ways that teachers actually use mathematics textbooks vary greatly. Attention has been paid to many different factors influencing this variation, but it must be acknowledged that a comprehensive framework for a reliable and valid evaluation of the text-in-use-by-teachers has not yet been proposed.

Students and mathematics textbooks

We pointed out earlier that students' use of textbook has not received much attention in mathematics education research. This might be due to the popular (mis)conception that teachers are the (only) designers of the implemented curriculum, and therefore are the audience for educational reforms to be mediated through textbooks. On the other hand, this gap in the research literature might be traced back to methodological problems of obtaining valid data on students' use of textbooks (Love and Pimm 1996). Because of this second reason, a large part of the core reading by Rezat is dedicated to methodological issues of obtaining 'ecologically valid' data on textbook use by students, that is, data on textbook use that is gathered within the natural situation or context, and not in an experimental setting.

Rezat elucidates the activities that the textbook is typically involved in, and describes typical textbook utilization schemes – which he calls Cultural–Historical Utilization Schemes (CHUS) – within these activities. The reason for introducing this (CHUS) terminology is related to the instrumental approach. Since every user of an artifact develops their own, individual utilization scheme, it is not possible at a first glance to identify 'typical' ways of using the textbook. But according to Rabardel (2002, p. 84), utilization schemes have both a private and a social dimension. This takes into account the fact that individuals do not develop utilization schemes in isolation, and that the development is affected by other users and by the artifact itself. Therefore, these schemes can be regarded as historically evolved within a certain culture. Rezat calls them 'cultural–historical' schemes in order to emphasize this aspect.

Rezat's analysis of the use of mathematics textbooks relates to the structural level. The utilization schemes describe how students choose blocks of the textbook within a particular activity. His analysis does not provide insights into how students actually deal with the content of the book. In subsequent work (Rezat 2009), he provides a student typology which describes types of textbooks use depending on favoured utilization schemes. This can be seen as a first step towards the problem of evaluating the text-in-use-by-students, which might also be adaptable to teachers' use of textbooks.

Textbooks and other resources

The primary focus of this chapter is on textbooks and their use in the teaching and learning of mathematics. But the textbook is not the only instrument used by teachers and students to support the teaching and learning of mathematics. Therefore, the sole focus on textbooks in the studies that we have cited can be questioned. This draws attention to the great variety of other material artifacts, including information technologies, that are used in mathematics education. Adler even goes a step further, extending 'common-sense notions of resources beyond material objects and include human and cultural resources such as language and time as pivotal in school mathematical practice' (2000, p. 207).

Connected to this awareness of the variety of resources that influence the implemented curriculum, and likely to be crucial in promoting change in school mathematics practice, a shift from focusing on one resource to studying the interplay of a set of resources can be perceived in mathematics education research. This includes the effects of this resource interplay on teachers' planning and the implemented curriculum. The overall aim is to provide holistic research approaches to teachers' practices. The 'documentation' approach, which again is theoretically based on the instrumental approach, is one example of these efforts. 'Documentation' refers to the complex and interactive ways that teachers work with resources; in-class and out-of-class, individually, but also collectively' (Gueudet et al. 2011, pp. ix–x).

Conclusion

In order to structure the field and relate the core readings to it, we conclude with specific reference to a 'tetrahedron model of textbook use' from Rezat (2008a, p. 177). Four constituents – textbook, student, teacher and mathematical knowledge – form the vertices of a tetrahedron, with the traditional didactical triangle at the bottom and the textbook as an additional vertex creating the three-dimensional tetrahedron (see Figure 5.1).

Valverde et al. elaborate on the vertex 'Mathematics' by presenting the comparison of 418 mathematics and science textbooks from 48 different educational systems, but this article

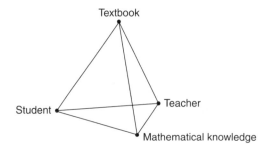

Figure 5.1 Tetrahedron model of textbook use

is basically an artifact analysis, and so does not address the use of this major artifact, or the development of utilization schemes with textbooks. Remillard's article (and especially the framework she proposes towards the end) uses the concept of curriculum to initiate an analysis of the full tetrahedron. Taking the teacher as the main agent of the didactical situation, Remillard's article could also be construed as analysing the teacher–mathematics–textbook triangle, which is also the focus of the article by Pepin and Haggarty. In addition to the introduction of the tetrahedron, Rezat's article describes in detail the student–mathematics–textbook triangle, thus complementing the other three texts. An examination of the whole didactical tetrahedron is yet to be undertaken. In addition to this, one should not forget that the tetrahedron is only a model of the didactical situation, a model which deliberately neglects the influence of its 'environment', including parents, peers, principals and colleagues in a school, the educational administration and the textbook production industry. Therefore, the didactical tetrahedron remains a model which presents only the major constituents of the didactical situation, that is, the teaching and learning of mathematics. Taking into account the complexity of relations within the tetrahedron model will render a more appropriate approach to the field, but can be expected to add further complexity to methodological issues within mathematics education research.

Further reading

Dowling, P., 1996. A sociological analysis of school mathematics texts. *Educational Studies in Mathematics*, 31 (4), 389–415.

Gueudet, G., Pepin, B. and Trouche, L., eds, 2011. *From text to 'lived' resources*. Heidelberg: Springer.

Howson, G., 1995. *Mathematics textbooks: a comparative study of grade 8 texts*. Vancouver: Pacific Educational Press.

Rezat, S., 2009. *Das Mathematikbuch als Instrument des Schülers: Eine Studie zur Schulbuchnutzung in den Sekundarstufen*. Wiesbaden: Vieweg + Teubner.

Additional references

Adler, J., 2000. Conceptualising resources as a theme for teacher education. *Journal of Mathematics Teacher Education*, 3 (3), 205–24.

Cronbach, L. J., 1955. *Text materials in modern education*. Urbana, IL: University of Illinois Press.

Hopf, D., 1980. *Mathematikunterricht: Eine empirische Untersuchung zur Didaktik und Unterrichtsmethode in der 7. Klasse des Gymnasiums*. Stuttgart: Klett-Cotta.

Love, E. and Pimm, D., 1996. 'This is so': a text on texts. In A. J. Bishop, K. Clements, C. Keitel, J. Kilpatrick and C. Laborde, eds, *International handbook of mathematics education*, Vol. 1. Boston: Kluwer, 371–409.

Otte, M., 1986. What is a text? In B. Christiansen, G. Howson and M. Otte, eds, *Perspectives on mathematics education*. Dordrecht, Netherlands: Reidel, 173–203.

Rabardel, P., 2002. *People and technology – a cognitive approach to contemporary instruments*. Available at http://ergoserv.psy.univ-paris8.fr/Site/default.asp?Act_group=1 [accessed on 15 May 2013]. [English version of Rabardel, P., 1995. *Les hommes et les technologies. Approche cognitive des instruments contemporains*. Paris: Armand Colin.]

Rezat, S., 2008b. Die Struktur von Mathematikschulbüchern. *Journal für Mathematik-Didaktik*, 29 (1), 46–67.

Schmidt, W. H., McKnight, C. C., Houang, R. T., Wang, H., Wiley, D. E., Cogan, L. S., et al., 2001. *Why schools matter: a cross-national comparison of curriculum and learning.* San Francisco: Jossey-Bass.

Schoenfeld, A., 2012. Problematizing the didactical triangle. *ZDM – The International Journal on Mathematics Education*, 44 (5), 587–99.

Wartofsky, M. W., 1979. *Models. Representation and the scientific understanding.* Dordrecht, Netherlands: Reidel.

The Affective Domain

Günter Törner

6

Core readings

The Core readings addressed in this chapter are:

Aiken, L. R., 1970. Attitudes toward mathematics. *Review of Educational Research*, 40 (4), 551–96.

Leder, G. C. and Forgasz, H. J., 2006. Affect and mathematics education. In A. Gutiérrez and P. Boero, eds, *Handbook of research on the Psychology of Mathematics Education: past, present and future*. Rotterdam, Netherlands: Sense, 403–27.

McLeod, D. B., 1992. Research on affect in mathematics education: a reconceptualization. In D. A. Grouws, ed., *Handbook of research on mathematics learning and teaching*. New York: Macmillan, 575–96.

Zan, R., Brown, L., Evans, J. and Hannula, M. S., 2006. Affect in mathematics education: an introduction. *Educational Studies in Mathematics*, 63 (2), 113–21.

Foreword

Throughout the literature on teachers' professional knowledge can be found reference to two basic components. Without disregarding their interdependence, these are *cognitive components* and *affective–motivational components* (Bromme 1993, 2005). The same is true with respect to the knowledge of pupils or students. In this chapter, while clearly conscious of cognitive features, we take a closer look at the affective domain.

This chapter should be seen as an introduction that is not intended for experts. However, the chapters in various handbooks (Leder and Forgasz 2006; McLeod 1992; Philipp 2007), articles reviewing the scene (Aiken 1976; Leder 1993) and the relatively recent (2006, volume 63 issue 2) special edition of *Educational Studies in Mathematics* elaborate on aspects of the field and have informed this chapter considerably. That being said, the extent to which this chapter can cover the field is limited, so it has been with great care that the articles and chapters included have been selected. Aiken (1970), more than 40 years ago, introduced the field and his article provides a compact summary of the research on attitudes in the learning of mathematics and on the phenomenon of mathematics anxiety. Most of the categories identified prevail today, although we now know more about some of them. In their chapter, Leder and Forgasz (2006) update Aiken's article and look beyond. In the period to 1990 research typically drew on statistical analyses, but McLeod (1992) introduced a new theory, which, despite developments, has been at the heart of research to the present day. He identified three affect-related concepts: beliefs, attitudes and emotions, to which, interestingly, DeBellis and Goldin (2002) added *values*. Finally, Zan et al. (2006) complete McLeod's contribution and discuss the bridge between cognition and affect – a dialogue that has only just begun.

Introduction

Following McLeod (1992), the affective domain refers here to the wide range of feelings and moods that are generally regarded as something different from pure cognition. We are not interested in the rapidly changing states of feeling typically described as *emotions*; we propose to examine *longer lasting and moderately stable predispositions*, which somehow affect the teaching and learning of mathematics. One component of this, long since established by psychologists, is the construct of attitudes, which is one of the central elements of this chapter. Such matters have been the concern of researchers for more than 50 years (Feierabend 1960).

Since problem solving is working mathematically *in statu nascendi*, it is not surprising that in the area of problem solving the components of affect are often observed, broadly discussed and analysed, especially from the 1990s when problem solving was in the core of curriculum reform in the United States. One should note that although this reform failed, the context of problem solving continues to serve as a promising site for fruitful research on the affective domain (see the chapter by Verschaffel et al., this volume.)

However, by way of introduction to the field, we consider both the origins and consequences of mathematics affect as a general construct before examining in detail the particularities of attitude. In this latter respect, and acknowledging the significance of related constructs like *beliefs*, *ethics*, *values* and *morals*, one is limited by space to examine a single affective component. That being said, Op 't Eynde and De Corte (2002) provide an interesting summary of such matters, confirming that, when dealing with matters psychological, there is seldom a canonical approach, a *royal road* or single construct.

Indeed, as evidence now shows, it is a folklore hypothesis that attitudes might be causally connected to achievement, an idea that has promoted research. Although certain connections cannot be denied, they are not straightforward and, according to Di Martino and Zan

(2010), research has only just begun to understand them. In actual fact, a meta-analysis of existing literature (Ma and Kishor 1997) showed not only that the correlation between attitude and achievement is statistically not significant but also that results emerging from different studies are often beyond comparison or even contradictory. We now know that in general, not only in the context of mathematics, the linkage between attitude and behaviour is more complicated than originally believed (Triandis 1971). This does not free us from asking how attitudes develop and how less favourable attitudes towards teaching and learning might be prevented and how positive attitudes might facilitate students doing mathematics. Research in this area is still at the beginning. In the following, therefore, we attempt to summarize what research has shown with respect to mathematics-related attitudes.

A first phenomenological encounter with the affective domain – an attempt at an inventory

Mathematics is commonly construed, at least from the outside, as a rational activity; everything is determined by logical deduction with no place for emotion. This perception is reinforced by the well-known dialogue between Socrates and the slave, Menon (fourth century BC). Socrates' intention was to send the message that it is possible, even with a slave, to tease out a mathematical result logically. Today we justifiably doubt if this represents a correct recording of a process of mathematical perception; we know, from experience, that learning mathematics is anything but a rational, convincing and exclusively argumentative process. In other words, doing mathematics is not the rational activity of popular conception. It is a highly affective activity in which success and happiness can alternate quickly with failure and disappointment. Indeed, Van der Waerden (1973) discusses letters written, in the middle of the nineteenth century, by Hamilton to his son, highlighting the emotions experienced over both his failures and successes when inventing quaternions. Such letters indicate, also, that mentioning affect when doing mathematics may have been a novelty at the time. Significantly, as I show in the following, we all live with affect and its consequences. It can motivate and challenge and help us experience success. It can also lead us to failure. Dealing with affect is a part of our emancipation, part of our identity (Evans et al. 2006).

Mathematics affect and learning in complex social systems

Most of the time mathematics, whether of the classroom or the professional mathematician, is experienced inside a social network (Ernest 1992). Classes are typically heterogeneous with both high- and low-achieving students working together, which might motivate or frustrate individual learners. Students will inevitably develop attitudes and beliefs and assess themselves in relationship to both the subject and each other. Thus affective relationships are created. In such circumstances students will often reduce their responses to the system to stereotype basic attitudes. That is, affective reactions are often transferred to objects: you love the teacher and thus mathematics; you loathe the teacher and thus dislike mathematics. Even though reality is more complicated than this, it is often observed (for good reasons) that affective attitudes tend to be stereotyped and reduced.

Mathematics affect and the level of mathematical study

The above statements are valid for many areas of life. For students they are true for the subjects they learn at school, and especially for mathematics, for which there is growing evidence. Even at the start of the twentieth century, researchers were concerned with overcoming students' blockages in the learning of mathematics (cf. Billig 1944 and Aiken 1970). Topics like commercial arithmetic and statistics provoked negative reactions (Bendig and Hughes 1954), but affect is not limited to them. Even though some mathematicians might hesitate to talk about it – or because they see it as self-evident – there are prominent *mathematical researchers* who describe mathematics as a highly emotional activity, which they have to experience and to endure (see Singh's 1997 book on Wiles' proof of Fermat's Last Theorem). They all know that there are many ups and downs (see, for example, Hardy 1967; Hersh and John-Steiner 2010), and that this is true of all levels of learning. For example, for first-grade students 7×8 is a difficult and emotionally taxing problem.

Mathematics affect and learner age

According to Evans (2000), all learners, even at university, experience negative affect to the extent that it is not uncommon for undergraduates' failures to be consequences of emotional rather than cognitive reasons.

Mathematics affect and learning difficulties

Much research has identified difficulties for learners, especially in the affective domain, that present obstacles to successful work in mathematics, and that this research permeates the whole of the past century (Billig 1944; Fedon 1958; Leder and Forgasz 2006; McLeod 1992; Philipp 2007). A key focus of much of this research has been *mathematical anxiety* (Ashcraft and Moore 2009; Cates and Rhymer 2003; Krinzinger et al. 2009) in general and *mathematics test anxiety* (Kazelskis et al. 2000) in particular, which has been a consequence of repeated experiences of poor performance. The former, introduced by Dreger and Aiken (1957, p. 344), was described as 'the presence of a syndrome of emotional reactions to arithmetic and mathematics'. Much of the substantial body of research undertaken since then has exploited one or other of the Mathematics Anxiety Rating Scale (MARS) developed by Richardson and Suinn (1972), the Fennema-Sherman Mathematics Attitudes Scales

(Fennema and Sherman 1976) and the Mathematics Anxiety Questionnaire (Wigfield and Meece 1988). Moreover, Szetela's (1973) study linking mathematics test anxiety to student performance was an important early article in the field.

Mathematics affect and achievement

For many years the hypothesis was that mathematics-related attitudes impacted *achievement*. Often asserted by prominent educational psychologists, the evidence for this claim is far from conclusive, although recent studies (see, for example, Pekrun et al. 2004) have indicated that performance is influenced by both cognitive and affective variables.

Mathematics affect and culture

There is evidence that transnationally affective responses towards mathematics are almost bipolar. That is, and irrespective of cultural affinity, wherever a number of mathematics enthusiasts (of any age) is found, a similarly sized group of people who hate mathematics will also be found. For example, a German *Spiegel* survey undertaken in 1995 found 24 per cent of students describing mathematics as a horror subject, while 48 per cent viewed it as their favourite subject. In an American study, Philipp (2007) found similar results although his proportion of students claiming to hate mathematics was higher at 40 per cent. No other subject evokes such polarized reactions between those who like and those who dislike.

As I have shown, research on mathematics affect has grown from lowly beginnings in the first half of the past century to a point whereby a number of research directions have been identified. Significantly, much research on the affective domain in mathematics was stimulated by students' negative experiences of problem solving – a core element of the reform curriculum introduced in the United States in the 1980s. This well-intentioned attempt failed, not least because of the negative affect it induced in both teachers and students (Silver 1985). However, as I have also shown, mathematical affect does not have to be a handicap to effective learning, although we now know that *success in problem solving – and mathematics in general – requires survival in the affective domain.*

An attitude-related theory

When McLeod (1992) mapped out the affective domain for mathematics in the 1990s, the concepts and vocabulary had not yet been well defined by psychologists. Many studies, particularly in mathematics education, failed to define their terms, a problem discussed in Di Martino and Zan (2010). Even today, 20 years after McLeod (1992), these matters remain unresolved (Leder and Forgasz 2006), with still no internationally accepted definitions. That being said, our view is that continuing failures to define subtle distinctions between affective factors such as attitudes and neighbouring constructs allows for flexibility in research.

Interestingly, however, Schoenfeld's new construct of orientation (2010) may offer a means by which various approaches to construct definition may be integrated.

Still, we do not recommend uncritical acceptance of research papers without clear definitions of terminology; it is important to determine what authors mean by the terms they use. Importantly, as we move to the next section, readers should understand that attitudes, the particular affective focus of this chapter, are not construed one-dimensionally along a positive–negative axis, but as multidimensional constructs. Also, all psychological constructs, including attitude, typically refer to a state internal to the person and are not, therefore, directly observable. They are assumed to exist and it is the researcher's responsibility to find evidence of them. However, it is easy to assume that actions reflect attitudes and although this may be true in isolated cases, it is not generally the case. The relationship between attitudes and actions is complicated and, in this sense we must constantly pose the question if and to what extent attitudes can be inferred from actions.

In the following sections we attempt a working definition of mathematical attitude. Eagly and Chaiken (1993, p. 1) write, in general terms, that attitude 'is a psychological tendency that is expressed by evaluating a particular entity with some degree of favor or disfavor'. In one of the earliest studies in the field, Aiken (1970, p. 551) writes that it is 'a learned predisposition or tendency on the part of an individual to respond positively or negatively to some object, situation, concept, or another person'. Thus, it is clear that attitude has an affective element involving positive or negative feelings of moderate intensity and reasonable stability. Examples of attitudes towards mathematics include liking geometry, disliking story problems, being curious about topology and being bored by algebra (McLeod 1992).

Although Eagly and Chaiken's (1993) description is relatively open, we would like to present a more precise point of view recently developed by DeBellis and Goldin (1991 and 2006), which acknowledges the now common understanding that affective and cognitive systems are interrelated. In other words, attitudes must be seen as representational systems, which can additionally be accessed by cognitive systems. This description is both functional and a metaphor for the construct around which we are building a theory. Later we will model the postulated representation as an evaluation component ε, but first we are introducing further terminology; the attitude object O.

Attitude objects

In order to describe attitudes as adequately as possible it is important to acknowledge that they are always associated with an attitude object O (Eagly and Chaiken 1993). Attitude objects can be abstract, concrete, large or small. Basically, every entity might be regarded as an attitude object. The attitude object of interest to us is mathematics. In this context the well-known work by Aiken (1970) remains well worth reading today. But what is mathematics in this context? Is it school mathematics and, if so, on what experiences is it based and in what kinds of school? Is it those mathematical applications that society sees as important in a world beyond school or cherished cultural artefact? Is it the mathematics presented in the recreational textbooks that comprise puzzles that require the mental acrobatics that only experts seem to possess? Such questions highlight the need to describe an attitude object carefully. What is more, one can have two, apparently dissonant, attitudes towards mathematics: one being a respect for an awe-inspiring and unattainable genius and the other a disapproval of the school mathematics which one can never quite master. In other words, it is quite possible for mathematical attitudes not to be entirely consistent with respect to their object although they are, typically, stable over time. Moreover, such matters present us with our first indication that attitudes in general and mathematics-related attitudes must not be viewed as unidimensional. Of course, mathematics comprises subdomains (like geometry, statistics or algebra) and even smaller entities like theorems, formulae and even specific tasks (like 7×8), all of which can be regarded as attitude objects to which long-lasting affect is adherent. Even readers of this book, whom we might regard as people familiar and comfortable with mathematics, may have different attitudinal responses to different theorems according to their experiences of those theorems, typically as learners of mathematics.

Measuring attitudes

As we have discussed, attitudes towards an attitude object are not unidimensional. Therefore, in considering how we might measure attitudes towards an object it is important that we are aware of the various manifestations that attitude may take. For example, one attitude-related factor that historically has received more attention than most has been mathematics anxiety (Ma 1999; McLeod 1992), alongside other interesting attitude 'variables' like *confidence*, *frustration* and *satisfaction*. In fixing an attitude object we can then develop scales for measuring each of the possible attitude dimensions variables (DeBellis and Goldin 1991).

Having identified our variables it is now necessary to find suitable measurement scales. The easiest case is a dichotomous scale with only two values, 0 or 1, black or white, hot or cold. Here, a person's attitude towards an attitude object is – in the mathematical sense – a function with the values 0 and 1, which models Eagly and Chaiken's (1993) definition. A similar evaluation would be the spontaneous assessment of a test item as easy or hard, when a mathematics problem is regarded as an attitude object O. In addition to such dichotomized sets of values, attitudes to object could be assigned values between 0 and 1 on a continuous scale (e.g. 0.7). On other occasions, a Likert type scale – with five (sometimes more, sometimes fewer) options, for example, very easy, easy, normal, hard, and very hard – is used. The five point scale allows a neutral or 'don't know' option. Such approaches have been widely used with both primary (Chapman 2003; Georgiou et al. 2007; Meelissen and Luyten 2008) and secondary aged children (Gruehn and Roeder 1995; Hargreaves et al. 2008; Papanastasiou 2000; Randhawa and Gupta 2000).

Associated with all such measures is the assumption that the different components or dimensions of attitude can be represented in linguistically simple and unambiguous ways.

Moreover, it is not sufficient to evaluate attitude by means of a single item that presents, for example, mathematics as easy or hard, one should also consider alternative phrases such as interesting, familiar, challenging, as each of these would refer, essentially, to a different component of mathematics-related attitude. In this sense the collection of measures equates, in mathematical terms, to a vector, and a questionnaire with 20 related questions or items would yield a bundle of responses for a single attitude object. Of course, in many situations a complete measure of attitude would draw on several scales, each comprising several items, with each scale evaluating a different component of attitude. Thus, if one were measuring, for example, students' attitudes towards their mathematics lessons then several scales relating to, for example, pleasure taken from learning, pride in performing well, hope, irritation, shame or boredom, each of which may comprise several items, could be incorporated into the whole measure.

Of course, while survey approaches exploiting the sorts of scales described earlier have been widely adopted, others have exploited case-study approaches to examine the individual nature of these deep-seated responses to mathematics, particularly with secondary students (Hannula 2002; Op 't Eynde and Hannula 2006).

The formation of attitudes

Attitudes are perceived as widely constituted by the dynamic interplay of cognitive, physiological and motivational processes in a specific context where it is often difficult to describe the details of such interplay. Moreover, recent research has indicated that attitudes tend to take one of two forms, explicit and implicit. The former refer to a person's 'deliberate, carefully considered evaluative judgments of beliefs' and are typically examined by means 'of direct procedures such as questionnaires or interviews' (Hughes and Barnes-Holmes 2011, p. 391). The latter, also known as automatic attitudes, form over time as a consequence of people's membership of particular social or cultural groups. As such, they are constantly exposed to information that 'links different social groups to positive and negative attributes. Because these links are repeatedly and chronically activated, their activation eventually becomes automatic for all members of that culture' (Gregg et al. 2006, p.2). In other words, attitudes are part of a system; they tend, particularly implicit attitudes, to develop over long period of time and despite evidence of their stability (McLeod 1992), they are prone to change. The nature of their formation confirms that it would be foolish to separate them from cognition. Indeed, one of the most important problems for research on mathematics-related affect lies in understanding the interrelationship between affect and cognition (Zan et al. 2006) because attitudes are often rooted in experiences that may be so subtle in their impact as to be beyond articulation. However, with respect to the dominant theme of this chapter, an aversion to mathematics cannot be altered in just one lesson!

Conclusion

I conclude this chapter with a few summarizing remarks and suggestions for future research. It has become clear that behind individuals' decisions and behaviours are very often attitudes towards mathematics, which on the one hand have an affective and emotional character, while, on the other, are of cognitive origin. These apply to all classroom participants, whether student or teacher and it is important for future research to acknowledge this.

Very often we create and characterize our image of mathematics prototypically. But everyone who observes lessons, learning processes and behaviour in the context of mathematical learning must be aware of the existence of this background and the need to avoid judging it prototypically; we should focus our attention on understanding the interrelations of affective and cognitive contexts.

Attitudes, whether explicit or implicit, are social constructs. In this respect, individual experiences are important constituents of attitude development; our concerns as researchers should be to go beyond what questionnaire surveys can tell us to discover and describe the stories that emerge from those experiences. By way of example, I have, on many occasions, invited students and teachers with whom I have worked to write one page on *Me and Mathematics* in order to initiate a discussion on the affective domain and its relationship to mathematics. Such an approach can be extremely enlightening, as highlighted by the study of Di Martino and Zan (2010). Adopting a similar approach they found that students' mathematics-related attitude draws on three interconnected components. These are their emotional dispositions towards mathematics, which can be construed as reflecting a traditional perspective on attitudes, their visions of mathematics and their perceived competence in mathematics.

This latter component of Di Martino and Zan's (2010) model of attitudes is a learner's perception of mathematical competence. Such a construct has significant links to other concepts well known in the literature: concepts like self-regulation, self-concept, self-esteem, self-confidence and self-control. It would seem sensible for future research to examine more closely the relationship between attitude and these important constructs. This leads to my next point.

As was indicated early in this chapter, the relationship between attitude and achievement is poorly understood with, frequently, poor correlations being identified. Such problems are exacerbated when one reads the results of large-scale international assessments of mathematics achievement like TIMSS and its various repeats. These have found that in some cultural groups, poor attitudes are associated with high achievement, while in others the opposite is true. In other words, we need to explore such matters more fully than has currently been the case, which leads me to my closing comment.

If attitude is a correlate with achievement, then the role of the teacher in the development of positive attitudes is crucial; teachers as mediators of both mathematics and the affective processes are key.

Further reading

Eagly, A. H. and Chaiken, S., 1993. *The psychology of attitudes*. San Diego, CA: Harcourt, Brace and Janovich.

Op 't Eynde, P., De Corte, E. and Verschaffel, L., 2006. Accepting emotional complexity: a socioconstructivist perspective on the role of emotions in the mathematics classroom. *Educational Studies in Mathematics*, 63, 193–207.

Di Martino, P. D. and Zan, R., 2010. 'Me and maths': towards a definition of attitude grounded on students' narratives. *Journal of Mathematics Teacher Education*, 13, 27–48.

Philipp, R. A., 2007. Mathematics teachers' beliefs and affect. In F. K. Lester, ed., *The handbook of research on mathematics education* (2nd edn). Charlotte, NC: Information Age Publishing, 257–314.

Törner, G., 2002. Mathematical beliefs – a search for a common ground. In G. C. Leder, E. Pehkonen and G. Törner, eds, *Beliefs: a hidden variable in mathematics education?* Dordrecht, Netherlands: Kluwer, 73–94.

Triandis, H. C., 1971. *Attitude and attitude change*. New York: Wiley.

Additional references

Aiken, L. R., 1976. Update on attitudes and other affective variables in learning mathematics. *Review of Educational Research*, 46 (2), 293–311.

Ashcraft, M. H. and Moore, A. M., 2009. Mathematics anxiety and the affective drop in performance. *Journal of Psychoeducational Assessment*, 27 (3), 197–205.

Bendig, A. W. and Hughes, J. B., 1954. Student attitude and achievement in introductory statistics. *Journal of Educational Psychology*, 45, 268–76.

Billig, A. L., 1944. Student attitude as a factor in the mastery of commercial arithmetic. *Mathematics Teacher*, 37, 170–72.

Bromme, R., 1993. Beyond subject matter: a psychological topology of teachers' professional knowledge. In R. Biehler, R. W. Scholz, R. Strasser and B. Winkelmann, eds, *Didactics of mathematics as a scientific discipline*. Dordrecht, Netherlands: Kluwer, 73–88.

—, 2005. Thinking and knowing about knowledge: a plea for and critical remarks on psychological research on programs on epistemological beliefs. In H. G. Hoffmann, J. Lenhard and F. Seeger, eds, *Activity and sign – grounding mathematics education*. New York: Springer, 191–202.

Cates, G. L. and Rhymer, K. N., 2003. Examining the relationship between mathematics anxiety and mathematics performance: an instructional hierarchy perspective. *Journal of Behavioral Education*, 12 (1), 23–34.

Chapman, E., 2003. Development and validation of a brief mathematics attitude scale for primary-aged students. *Journal of Educational Enquiry*, 4 (2), 63–73.

DeBellis, V. A. and Goldin, G. A., 1991. Interactions between cognition and affect in eight high school students' individual problem solving. In R. Underhill, ed., *Proceedings of the 13th Annual Meeting of the North American Chapter of the International Group for the Psychology of Mathematics Education* (PME), Vol. 1. Blacksburg VI: Virginia Tech, 29–35.

—, 2006. Affect and meta-affect in mathematical problem solving: a representational perspective. *Educational Studies in Mathematics*, 63 (2), 131–47.

Dreger, R. M. and Aiken, L. R., 1957. The identification of number anxiety in a college population. *Journal of Educational Psychology*, 48 (6), 344–51.

Ernest, P., 1992. The nature of mathematics: towards a social constructivist account. *Science and Education* 1 (1), 89–100.

Evans, J., Morgan, C. and Tsatsaroni, A., 2006. Discursive positioning and emotion in school mathematics practices. *Educational Studies in Mathematics*, 63 (2), 209–26.

Evans, J. T., 2000. *Adults' mathematical thinking and emotions: a study of numerate practices*. London. Routledge.

Fedon, J. P., 1958. The role of attitude in learning arithmetic. *Arithmetic Teacher*, 5, 304–10.

Feierabend, R. L., 1960. Review of research on psychological problems in mathematics education. In *Research problems in mathematics education. US Office of Education, Cooperative Research Monograph No. 3 (3–46)*.

Fennema, E. and Sherman, J. A., 1976. Fennema-Sherman Mathematics Attitudes Scales: instruments designed to measure attitudes toward the learning of mathematics by males and females. *Catalog of Selected Documents in Psychology*, 6 (1), MS No. 1225.

Georgiou, S. N., Stavrinides, P. and Kalavana, T., 2007. Is Victor better than Victoria at maths? *Educational Psychology in Practice*, 23 (4), 329–42.

Goldin, G., 2002. Affect, meta-affect, and mathematical belief structures. In G. Leder, E. Pehkonen and G. Törner, eds, *Mathematical beliefs – a hidden variable in mathematics education?* Dordrecht, Netherlands: Kluwer, 59–72.

Gregg, A. P., Seibt, B. and Banaji, M. R., 2006. Easier done than undone: asymmetry in the malleability of implicit preferences. *Journal of Personality and Social Psychology*, 90 (1), 1–20.

Gruehn, S. and Roeder, P. M., 1995. Concomitants of achievement in mathematics: a comparative analysis. In W. Bos and R. H. Lehmann, eds, *Reflections on educational achievements: papers in honour of T. Neville Postlethwaite*. Münster: Waxmann, 88–106.

Hannula, M. S., 2002. Attitude towards mathematics: emotions, expectations and values. *Educational Studies in Mathematics*, 49 (1), 25–46.

Hardy, G. H., 1967. *A mathematician's apology*. Cambridge: Cambridge University Press.

Hargreaves, M., Homer, M. and Swinnerton, B., 2008. A comparison of performance and attitudes in mathematics amongst the 'gifted'. Are boys better at mathematics or do they just think they are? *Assessment in Education: Principles, Policy & Practice*, 15 (1), 19–38.

Hersh, R. and John-Steiner, V., 2010. *Loving and hating mathematics: challenging the myths of mathematical life*. Princeton, NJ: Princeton University Press.

Hughes, S. and Barnes-Holmes, D., 2011. On the formation and persistence of implicit attitudes: new evidence from the implicit relational assessment procedure (IRAP). *Psychological Record*, 61 (3), 391–410.

Kazelskis, R., Reeves, C., Kersh, M. E., Bailey, G., Cole, K., Larmon, M., et al., 2000. Mathematics anxiety and test anxiety: separate constructs? *The Journal of Experimental Education*, 68 (2), 137–46.

Krinzinger, H., Kaufmann, L. and Willmes, K., 2009. Math anxiety and math ability in early primary school years. *Journal of Psychoeducational Assessment*, 27 (3), 206–25.

Leder, G. C., 1993. Reconciling affective and cognitive aspects of mathematics learning: reality or a pious hope? In I. Hirabayashi, N. Nohda, K. Shigematsu and F.-L. Lin, eds, *Proceedings of the 17th International Conference of the International Group for Psychology of Mathematics Education* (PME), Vol. 1. Hawthorn, Victoria: ACER, 46–65.

Ma, X., 1999. A meta-analysis of the relationship between anxiety and achievement in mathematics. *Journal for Research in Mathematics Education*, 30 (5), 520–40.

Ma, X. and Kishor, N., 1997. Assessing the relationship between attitude toward mathematics and achievement in mathematics: a meta-analysis. *Journal for Research in Mathematics Education*, 28 (1), 26–47.

Meelissen, M. and Luyten, H., 2008. The Dutch gender gap in mathematics: small for achievement, substantial for beliefs and attitudes. *Studies in Educational Evaluation*, 34 (1), 82–93.

Op 't Eynde, P. and De Corte, E., 2002. Accepting emotional complexity: a socio-constructivist perspective on the role of emotions in the mathematics classroom. *Educational Studies in Mathematics*, 63 (2), 193–207.

Op 't Eynde, P. and Hannula, M., 2006. The case study of Frank. *Educational Studies in Mathematics*, 63 (2), 123–9.

Papanastasiou, C., 2000. Effects of attitudes and beliefs on mathematics achievement. *Studies in Educational Evaluation*, 26 (1), 27–42.

Pekrun, R., Götz, T., vom Hofe, R., Blum, W., Jullien, S., Zirngibl, A., et al., 2004. Emotionen und Leistung im Fach Mathematik: Ziele und erste Befunde aus dem Projekt zur Analyse der Leistungsentwicklung in Mathematik (PALMA). In J. Doll and M. Prenzel, eds, *Bildungsqualität von Schule: Lehrerprofessionalisierung, Unterrichtsentwicklung und Schülerförderung als Strategien der Qualitätsverbesserung.* Münster: Waxmann, 345–63.

Randhawa, B. S. and Gupta, A., 2000. Cross-national gender differences in mathematics achievement, attitude and self-efficacy within a common intrinsic structure. *Canadian Journal of School Psychology*, 15 (2), 51–66.

Richardson, F. C. and Suinn, R. M., 1972. The mathematics anxiety rating scale: psychometric data. *Journal of Counseling Psychology*, 19 (6), 551–4.

Schoenfeld, A. H., 2010. *How we think: a theory of goal-oriented decision making and its educational applications.* New York: Routledge.

Silver, E. A., 1985. Research on teaching mathematical problem solving: some underrepresented themes and needed directions. In E. A. Silver, ed., *Teaching and learning mathematical problem solving: multiple research perspectives.* Hillsdale, NJ: Lawrence Erlbaum, 247–66.

Singh, S., 1997. *Fermat's last theorem.* London: Fourth Estate.

Szetela, W., 1973. The effects of test anxiety and success/failure on mathematics performance in grade eight. *Journal for Research in Mathematics Education*, 4 (3), 152–60.

Van der Waerden, B. L., 1973. *Hamilton's entdeckungen der quaternionen.* Göttingen: Vandenhoeck and Ruprecht.

Wigfield, A. and Meece, J. L., 1988. Math anxiety in elementary and secondary school students. *Journal of Educational Psychology*, 80 (2), 210–16.

Mathematics and Language

Richard Barwell

7

Core readings

The Core readings addressed in this chapter are as follows:

Pimm, D. and Sinclair, N., 2009. Audience, style and criticism. *For the Learning of Mathematics*, 29 (2), 23–7.

Sfard, A., 2001. There is more to discourse than meets the ears: looking at thinking as communicating to learn more about mathematical learning. *Educational Studies in Mathematics*, 46 (1–3), 13–57.

Morgan, C., 2006. What does social semiotics have to offer mathematics education research? *Educational Studies in Mathematics*, 61 (1–2), 219–45.

Barwell, R., 2009a. Researchers' descriptions and the construction of mathematical thinking. *Educational Studies in Mathematics*, 79 (2), 255–69.

Introduction

Language is a significant issue in mathematics education and has been a focus of research since the 1970s. In this chapter, I will sketch some of the broad contours of that research, in order to introduce and situate the four core readings. As I do so, I will argue that research in this area has matured considerably in recent years. This maturity is suggested by a broader and more developed range of theoretical influences, by a greater scope in terms of the substantive focus of research, and by an increasing willingness to engage with the complexities of language, learning and mathematics. The chapter will be organized around four themes: linguistic perspectives, discursive perspectives on mathematical cognition, socio-political perspectives and the discourse of mathematics education research. Each core reading is used to illustrate one of these areas of development. Of course, this way of organizing the material is a simplification. In reality, there is much overlap and shared interest across the different themes, some of which I will point out along the way. The concluding section will discuss some of these commonalities and a little of what has been left out, as well as considering what the future might hold.

Linguistic perspectives

The most salient feature of mathematical language is probably its vocabulary. Words like 'dimension', 'cylinder' and 'matrix' are prominent. Without them, students cannot develop their thinking. Mathematical language, however, needs to be seen more broadly. Linguistically, mathematical language also involves, for example, specific syntax (e.g. how to form an expression like 'one-dimensional'), or the use of as innocuous a word as 'a' to express generality (in the statement 'a square is a kind of rectangle,' 'a' is a determinant, though the statement is about squares in general, rather than one particular square).

Simply focusing on the formal linguistic features of mathematical language is of limited value; language is brought to life by people. The linguist Michael Halliday (1978) captured this idea in his definition of the 'mathematics register' as:

> the meanings that belong to the language of mathematics (the mathematical use of natural language, that is: not mathematics itself), and that a language must express if it is being used for mathematical purposes. (p. 195)

This definition is about how language is used to create mathematics, and it suggests the relevance of investigating how this happens: how language is used to make meaning in mathematics.

This task was taken up by Pimm (1987), in the book that has become a standard reference point for research in this area. In particular, Pimm examined how mathematics is used to make meaning in mathematics classrooms (in English). For if students are to learn mathematics, they must learn 'how to mean' like a mathematician. Pimm's exploration includes some attention to the formal features of spoken and written language in mathematics. He points out, for example, how much mathematical vocabulary arises through metaphorically extending everyday words (think of 'product' or 'function'). Students must learn to distinguish between mathematical and everyday uses of such words. Pimm also looks at more diffuse aspects of the mathematics register. He discusses, for example, the nature of authority, as produced through things like choice of pronouns (see also Rowland 1999). Teachers and mathematicians often use 'we', implying a wider community of mathematicians. This 'we' also constructs a mathematical authority in classrooms that can be problematic.

More recently Morgan (1998), Burton and Morgan (2000) and O'Halloran (2005) have examined the formal features of written mathematics. These features include the use of passive voice, imperatives ('let', 'define') and nominalization (i.e. turning a process, 'to integrate', into an object, 'integration'). The general effect of these kinds of features is to render formal mathematical writing impersonal; the authors depersonalize the mathematics. This kind of writing is consistent with the idea that mathematics is a kind of truth that exists beyond human thought. Different ways of writing mathematics may construct differently the relationship between mathematicians and mathematics (see the chapter by Ernest, this volume).

In the first of the core readings, Pimm and Sinclair (2009) add a new dimension to the way in which mathematical writing may be understood: they discuss 'mathematical style', including the rhetorical and aesthetic features of mathematical writing. Style has not previously been discussed in mathematics education, perhaps being seen as the preserve of literary theorists. Nevertheless, style can be significant. In Morgan's (1998) study of secondary school students' extended mathematical writing, the style adopted by a student had an effect on how the teacher evaluated the work. Writing that was closer to the canonical form was likely to be seen as (mathematically) better. Pimm and Sinclair (2009) refer to historical examples of written mathematics, including writing by the nineteenth-century mathematician, Hamilton, known for, among many accomplishments, his work on quaternions, a higher dimensional complex number system. Hamilton wrote many kinds of mathematical texts, including academic papers, but also letters, diary entries and even a graffito carved into a bridge in Dublin. Some of this writing includes narrative accounts of his discoveries as well as more formal mathematical presentations.

Pimm and Sinclair go on to develop three related points. First, they ask what a narrative style of written mathematics might look like. Narratives are temporally organized and include protagonists and, usually, some kind of 'trouble' that must be overcome. Most of us, I suspect, experience mathematics in this way. And yet it is not (or is no longer) written like this: published mathematics is often in the form of carefully refined, atemporal, dehumanized accounts of logical relations. The tricky words are not so much the vocabulary, as what linguists call the cohesion markers: 'hence', 'thus' and even 'then'.

Second, Pimm and Sinclair discuss how the style of a mathematical text is related to the intended audience. Indeed, any text or utterance is shaped by the looming presence of the intended audience. We speak differently to different people (our boss, our students, our mother) and we also write differently for them.

Third, Pimm and Sinclair discuss the connection between style and aesthetics. Style is not simply a technical matter of choosing the right words and formulations. It is implicated in the values associated with different kinds of writing. Mathematicians are fond of words like 'elegant' to describe their proofs. But elegance is an aesthetic quality, some of which derives from the style used to present the proof. And the idea of aesthetics raises the question of how such things should be evaluated. Is it possible to imagine a literary theory of mathematics? What value would such a theory have?

Linguistic perspectives on mathematics have moved on, then, from a fairly narrow concern with such formal features as vocabulary, to a much broader and richer account. Pimm and Sinclair move this work in new directions, linking language, style and aesthetics. Underlying their article, moreover, there is an important rationale. Halliday's definition of the mathematical register constructs a separation between language and mathematics. For Pimm and Sinclair, however, doing mathematics is inseparable from writing (or, I would add, speaking) mathematics. The two are intertwined. Mathematical style, then, is more than a frivolous curiosity: it tells us something of the nature of mathematics.

Discursive perspectives on mathematical cognition

If, as suggested in the previous section, doing mathematics and speaking or writing mathematics cannot easily be separated, what is the relationship between language and mathematical thinking? Much research in mathematics education has been concerned with different aspects of mathematical thinking, or learning or understanding (see other chapters in this volume). In the past 20 years or so, research on language and mathematics has become more integrated with research on different aspects of mathematical cognition. This trend has particularly been prompted by the growing influence of (Western interpretations of) Vygotsky's work in mathematics education research. Vygotsky's theoretical work was taken up for its more satisfying account of children's learning, including its emphasis on the role of society in individual learning and mechanisms like the Zone of Proximal Development and internalization (see the chapter by Lerman, this volume). In Vygotsky's theory, however, language plays a central role. Language mediates between individuals and society, acting as a 'cultural tool' through which shared ways of thinking can be taken up by individuals and used to make meaning and solve problems. From this perspective, the nature of mathematical language is no longer a question of the formal features of the means of expressing mathematical ideas; mathematical language is central to mathematics learning (see, for example, Cobb et al. 1993). Students are not simply acquiring new words; they are learning to use words like 'dimension' in culturally (i.e. mathematically) appropriate ways. In so doing, the students internalize the meaning of the words and construct mathematical concepts. This deep role for language as the means by which cultural traditions, ideologies and practices are propagated is reflected in the preference for the term 'discourse'. Where 'language' can indicate a narrow concern with the system of language itself, 'discourse' connotes both language-in-use and language as cultural, historical and ideological.

The second of the core readings appeared in a collection of articles largely inspired by this Vygotskian approach (Kieran et al. 2002). Sfard's contribution is particularly interesting, since it captures a shift in perspective from a more cognitivist approach to a more discursive one. As such, the article is symbolic of the wider shift in mathematics education more generally. Sfard evokes this shift through direct comparison. She summarizes two approaches to mathematical cognition. The more cognitivist approach she refers to is in terms of a learning-as-acquisition metaphor. That is, learning is the process of acquiring concepts and methods that are stored in the brain and retrieved when needed. Sfard refers to the more discursive approach as learning-as-participation. In this approach, learning is a process of entering a community and taking on the practices of that community. Learning mathematics is, therefore, the process of entering a mathematical community and, in so doing, developing the practices of doing mathematics. The influence of Vygotskian theory is evident in this latter approach.

Having set up these two contrasting approaches, Sfard takes another step, which can be traced back to the role of language in Vygotsky's theory. A key part of this theory is the idea that in taking on practices of a wider community, individuals internalize the meanings associated with these practices. Sfard argues that mathematical thinking has its origins in the communication that happens at the social level. Learners do not simply internalize meanings, however; they internalize the communication practices themselves, which then form the basis for individual thinking. Sfard's position, therefore, is that 'thinking may be conceptualized as a case of communication' (p. 26). From this point, Sfard is able to refine the idea of learning from simply 'participation' to 'initiation to a discourse' (p. 28).

Sfard illustrates these ideas by discussing two examples of mathematical thinking, first from a learning-as-acquisition perspective and then from a thinking-as-communicating perspective. (She also discusses some of the methodological tools that make such analyses possible, although I will not discuss them here.) The comparison highlights some of the limitations of the former approach and the explanatory power of the latter. In one of Sfard's examples, two high school students work together on tasks relating to functions. One of the boys' contributions to their discussion suggests that, from a learning-as-acquisition perspective, he does not understand the concepts involved and the discussion with his peer is not helpful in developing such an understanding. But this perspective is limited in its ability to explain why he does not understand. Taking a learning-as-participation perspective, one starts to notice that one of the boys works on the task with little concern for the understanding of the other. Although there is interaction between them, it is not productive, with one pursuing his own agenda and the other trying, but not succeeding, to join in. Sfard concludes that the lack of understanding of one of the boys is a result of the poor quality of their interaction. And this interaction is, of course, jointly produced.

In the second example, a girl and a teacher discuss numbers. At one point, the girl appears to think that there is a 'biggest number', but after some questioning by the teacher concludes that there is no such number. Sfard uses the learning-as-participation approach to argue that the girl's transition from misconception to understanding the infinitude of numbers can be attributed to the resolution of a discursive (and not a cognitive) conflict: the teacher and the student are using the same words in different ways and the student must rework her way of using the word 'number' in particular, so that it is more consistent with mathematical discourse.

In more recent work, Sfard has continued to develop these ideas, moving more squarely to a position of seeing communicating and thinking as the same thing. Her book *Thinking as Communicating* (2008) sets out this position and considerably extends her account of the discursive nature of mathematical thinking. In particular, she identifies some key features of mathematical discourse that, by definition, are also features of mathematical thinking. These features include visual mediators, routines and, in an interesting connection with Pimm and Sinclair's (2009) article, narratives. Sfard's sense of narrative, however, is in the narrower sense of a descriptive account, in contrast to Pimm and Sinclair's more literary approach.

Socio-political perspectives

The two perspectives discussed so far in this chapter have a couple of limitations. First, they do not take sufficient account of the social organization of language. As both Halliday and Vygotsky noted in different ways, language is a social phenomenon. This means, however, that the way language is used in mathematics is not simply shaped by the structure of language, nor by the structure of cognition. Language use is shaped, at least in part, by the social organization of human relations. In many mathematics classrooms, for example, the teacher is able to offer evaluative remarks about what students say – things like 'well done'. Students cannot typically evaluate the teacher's utterances. As Pimm (1987) noted, mathematical discourse includes aspects of authority.

The social organization of mathematics classroom interaction has been the subject of much research (e.g. Cobb and Bauersfeld 1995). Much of this work has been accompanied by a theoretical approach that extends the perspectives discussed so far in this chapter, by drawing on ideas largely drawn from sociology, including symbolic interactionism and ethnomethodology (see the chapter by Jablonka, this volume). This work has focused in some detail on how language is used to teach and learn mathematics, highlighting, for example, the implicit norms that guide both interaction and mathematics. Yackel and Cobb (1996) make a distinction between social and sociomathematical norms. A social norm concerns the conventions of general classroom life, such as who can make evaluative comments. An example of a sociomathematical norm is the sense of what counts as an acceptable mathematical explanation – something that, for students, must develop over time.

In the third core reading, Morgan (2006) proposes a more rigorous, linguistics-based approach to examining the social organization of mathematical discourse, including, unlike the research mentioned in the previous paragraph, written texts. This approach is based on Halliday's work – the same Halliday whose definition of the mathematical register is mentioned earlier. His conceptualization of language is multilayered and I will not summarize it all here, since Morgan gives a clear account of it in her article. A key idea of his work, however, is that using language involves making choices. Using one word or expression instead of another realizes a particular meaning from the space of potential meanings. A second important idea is that language is multifunctional – it simultaneously conveys meanings related to conceptual content, interpersonal matters and the organization of the text itself. The mathematical register includes all of these functions. This approach brings together various different insights about mathematical discourse; for example, that it includes social organization as well as conceptual content, and that cohesion markers, which concern the organization of mathematical text, are also important.

Morgan uses Halliday's ideas to develop some new insights. She points out, for example, that the way in which mathematical language is used depends on the context in which it is used. At the same time, this context is encoded in the language choices made. A classroom discussion, for example, is recognizably taking place in a classroom setting. In her article, Morgan includes examples of mathematical discourse from a Portuguese classroom and from students' written work. The classroom exchange involves three boys and has a similar asymmetry to that observable in Sfard's (2001) first example. Morgan discusses the participation of two of the boys. As in Sfard's example, one appears to be doing more mathematical work; the other is tagging along and seems not to really understand. The social semiotic approach presented by Morgan in her article, however, gives her finer tools with which to tease out what is going on. She is able, for example, to look at the interpersonal function to understand how one student comes to be positioned more dominantly than another. For Morgan, this kind of analysis of the interpersonal allows an understanding of 'where power lies and what form it takes' (p. 238). Similarly, in her examination of contrasting examples of students' written mathematics, she shows how different identities are constructed through the language choices made by the students. One student writes more authoritatively about the mathematics, while the other is more explicitly writing for a test. In the former, it is frequently mathematical objects that act ('the slant increases'), while in the latter, it is the student ('I found the formula for hexagons quite quickly'). The former might be considered more mathematically appropriate and, for Morgan, what is appropriate is once again a matter of power. There is a link here to Pimm and Sinclair's (2009) point about audience. We might infer that the student who wrote the more authoritative text has a sense of a mathematical audience, while the other student is writing more for the person who will mark his work.

In subsequent work, Morgan (e.g. 2012) has been increasingly concerned with this issue of power, and the related problem of the apparently unequal access to 'appropriate' mathematical discourse. These kinds of problems involve a more large-scale, political dimension, for which Morgan has turned to sociological theory. We know that children from some backgrounds (e.g. middle class) generally do better in school mathematics than children from some other backgrounds (e.g. working class). Explaining why this is so can include a focus on language, since part of school 'success' is about learning to speak and write 'appropriately'. Furthermore, as noted, discursive perspectives see language as a vehicle for ideology. By extension, language is implicated in oppression and disequity. Similar issues have been discussed in different contexts of mathematics education by Zevenbergen (2000) and Setati (2005).

The discourse of mathematics education research

The last theme I will address involves a slight shift in emphasis. The work discussed so far examines different aspects of the language of mathematics, of mathematical thinking and of mathematics classrooms. Doing research in mathematics education is also, however, a language-dependent activity. Most, if not all, of the research discussed in this book is based on language data of some kind, such as interview data, classroom transcripts or students' written work. And the way mathematics education research is reported also depends on language, whether the formal prose of academic journal articles or the spoken language of a conference presentation. Mathematics education research is, then, a discursive activity and, as such, language constructs its concepts and ideas as much as it constructs mathematics in classrooms. A transcript, for example, is a text, carefully prepared. As Morgan points out in her article, language involves choices, and the construction of a transcript also involves choices. The use of punctuation, standard spelling and brief descriptive details all create a particular portrayal of the discussion. The point is not that such choices can be avoided, but that different choices highlight or construct different interpretations (see Staats 2008).

How mathematics education research is constructed is the subject of my own article (Barwell 2009a), the fourth of the core readings. Some version of this general argument has been around for some time. In the article, I refer to Walkerdine (1988), who wrote (at about the same time as Pimm's book):

> The central concepts in . . . mathematics education may themselves be regarded as signifiers, that is, aspects of discourse. . . . What is crucial about this analysis is that *language* and *cognition* become similarly amenable to the analysis. (p. 202, original emphasis)

Walkerdine is first saying that key concepts in mathematics education research, including such basic ideas as 'cognition', are themselves discursive constructions. Second, she is saying that having recognized the first point, the way is clear to examine how exactly things like 'cognition' are produced through discourse. While others have taken up this idea to critique the structure of mathematics teaching or examine how teachers' identities are formed (e.g. Brown 2001), the purpose of my article is to look in detail at the discursive practices and mechanisms that are used to produce mathematical thinking.

Theoretically and methodologically, my analysis is based on discursive psychology, rather than Walkerdine's broadly Foucauldian approach. Discursive psychology is more focused on the details of discursive practice, usually in spoken interaction, but also in written text.

Furthermore, discursive psychology emphasizes some ideas in common with the work discussed in this chapter. For example, it emphasizes the socially situated nature of language use, and the idea that all spoken or written language is shaped or 'designed' for its audience or 'recipient'.

In other work, I have used this approach to examine students' mathematical interaction in different settings (e.g. Barwell 2013) but in the core reading, I turn the lens on the production of research. In particular, I focus on the role of description in mathematics education research discourse. From the perspective of discursive psychology, description is never neutral. In particular, descriptions account for things like the motives or intentions of the participants and observers. The sense that an observer is neutral or impartial is a construction achieved by presenting the observations in a particular way. Research discourse, of course, involves a good deal of description, including accounts of students' mathematical thinking.

In the article, I analyse two research articles, one of which is the second core reading, by Sfard (2001). I discuss two different discursive practices. One prevalent practice is known as a contrast structure. In Sfard's article, for example, she includes some description of the actions of the student who discussed 'the biggest number' with a teacher. This description is the basis for the claim that the student has learned that the set of (positive whole) numbers is infinite. Sfard describes how the student starts off 'convinced' that there is a number called 'the biggest' and ends with an account of her 'emphatically' stating the opposite. The choice of words like 'convinced' and 'emphatically' contribute to our sense of what happened, but these words also construct what happened in particular ways. The key point is that by building such words into her descriptions, Sfard makes possible her subsequent claims about the student's mathematical thinking. As I have already mentioned, it is not possible to avoid the constructed nature of descriptions of mathematical thinking; my analysis highlights some of the ways in which such descriptions are implicated in researchers' analyses, however, and opens the door to more critical readings of research in mathematics education.

Conclusion

Research on language and mathematics education has developed considerably over the past 30 years, as the work discussed in this chapter shows. First, and most straightforwardly, there is now much more research conducted on this topic. Second, research in this area now draws on a wider range of more thoroughly worked-out theoretical perspectives. Theorists who have inspired research on language and mathematics education include Bernstein, Halliday, Fairclough, Bourdieu, Gee, Edwards, Harré, Bakhtin, Foucault and Lacan and range from the strongly structuralist, to the post-structuralist to the psychoanalytic. Third, there has been a degree of methodological development. While all the work discussed in this chapter is based on analysis of naturally occurring discourse data, whether spoken or written, they vary in the nature and form of their analyses. Morgan's work, for example, draws on some of the tools provided by Halliday's systemic functional linguistics. This approach entails analysing discourse data using a complex coding structure to look at the different functions of language. In her work, Sfard (2008) has developed concepts of her own (e.g. endorsed narratives) and then shows how these concepts are apparent in her data. My own work involves looking at specific discursive practices (e.g. use of contrast structures) to understand what these practices achieve. Pimm and Sinclair's approach, by contrast, is more akin to literary criticism; it involves a careful, informed reading of texts selected to illuminate significant overlooked features of mathematical discourse.

Finally, research on language in mathematics education has moved on from being a somewhat peripheral interest that, while undoubtedly fascinating, perhaps did not concern the 'big' problems of why children struggle to learn mathematics and how best to teach them. In common with the broader linguistic turn in the social sciences in general, there is now recognition that language and cognition are inseparable and may even be the same thing. To understand why children struggle to learn mathematics, we need to look at how they talk and write about mathematics. As a result, the breadth of research topics in mathematics education that are examined from a linguistic or discursive perspective has also increased considerably. This chapter does not have the space for me to discuss, for example, important research on teaching and learning mathematics in second language, bilingual, multilingual classrooms or other settings of language diversity (see Barwell 2009b; Setati 2005). Nor is there room to discuss research on the relationship between linguistic and cultural aspects of learning mathematics, including valuable work on language and ethnomathematics (e.g. Barton 2008). And I have not made reference to research on how mathematics teachers may most effectively focus on their use of language in their teaching or professional development (e.g. Lampert and Blunk 1998).

Given this great richness and increasing diversity, it is not easy to see what trends might emerge in future research on language and mathematics. I foresee an increasing interest in the more technical tools of applied linguistics. Until now, most mathematics education researchers have made use of theoretical ideas derived from linguistics, Morgan's article being a good example. But they have made less use of the more technical methods of analysis, including those supported by technology. This may change in future. There will certainly also be more research relating to language and diversity, reflecting the increasingly mobile and diverse student populations of most mathematics classrooms around the world. And, as a third prediction, I anticipate a more widespread use of post-modern approaches to research in mathematics education. Since such approaches are inherently linguistic, there may well be an increasing feeling that learning mathematics is, in some sense, all about language.

Further reading

Barwell, R., ed., 2009b. *Mathematics in multilingual classrooms: global perspectives*. Bristol, UK: Multilingual Matters.

Morgan, C., 1998. *Writing mathematically: the discourse of investigation*. London: Falmer.

Pimm, D., 1987. *Speaking mathematically: communication in mathematics classrooms*. London: Routledge.

Sfard, A., 2008. *Thinking as communicating: human development, the growth of discourses, and mathematizing*. Cambridge: Cambridge University Press.

Additional references

Barton, B., 2008. *Language and mathematics: telling mathematical tales*. London: Springer.

Barwell, R., 2003. Patterns of attention in the interaction of a primary school mathematics student with English as an additional language. *Educational Studies in Mathematics*, 53 (1), 35–59.

—, 2013. The academic and the everyday in mathematicians' talk: the case of the hyper-bagel. *Language and Education*, 27 (3), 207–22.

Brown, T., 2001. *Mathematics education and language: interpreting hermeneutics and post-structuralism* (2nd edn). Dordrecht, Netherlands: Kluwer.

Burton, L. and Morgan, C., 2000. Mathematicians writing. *Journal for Research in Mathematics Education*, 31 (4), 429–53.

Cobb, P. and Bauersfeld, H., eds, 1995. *The emergence of mathematical meaning: interaction in classroom cultures*. Hillsdale, NJ: Lawrence Erlbaum, 229–69.

Cobb, P., Wood, T. and Yackel, E., 1993. Discourse, mathematical thinking, and classroom practice. In E. Forman, N. Minick and C. A. Stone, eds, *Contexts for learning: sociocultural dynamics in children's development*. New York: Oxford University Press, 91–119.

Halliday, M. A. K., 1978. *Language as social semiotic: the social interpretation of language and meaning*. London: Edward Arnold.

Kieran, C., Forman, E. and Sfard, A., eds, 2002. *Learning discourse: discursive approaches to research in mathematics education*. Dordrecht, Netherlands: Kluwer.

Lampert, M. and Blunk, M. L., eds, 1998. *Talking mathematics in school: studies of teaching and learning*. Cambridge: Cambridge University Press.

Morgan, C., 2012. Studying discourse implies studying equity. In B. Herbel-Eisenmann, J. Choppin, D. Wagner and D. Pimm, eds, *Equity in discourse for mathematics education: theories, practices and policies*. Dordrecht, Netherlands: Springer, 181–92.

O'Halloran, K. L., 2005. *Mathematical discourse: language, symbolism and visual images*. Continuum: London.

Rowland, T., 1999. Pronouns in mathematics talk: power, vagueness and generalisation. *For the Learning of Mathematics*, 19 (2), 19–26.

Setati, M., 2005. Teaching mathematics in a primary multilingual classroom. *Journal for Research in Mathematics Education*, 36 (5), 447–66.

Staats, S., 2008. Poetic lines in mathematics discourse: a method from linguistic anthropology. *For the Learning of Mathematics*, 28 (2), 26–32.

Walkerdine, V., 1988. *The mastery of reason*. London: Routledge.

Yackel E. and Cobb, P., 1996. Sociomathematical norms, argumentation, and autonomy in mathematics. *Journal for Research in Mathematics Education*, 27 (4), 458–77.

Zevenbergen, R., 2000. 'Cracking the code' of mathematics classrooms: school success as a function of linguistic, social, and cultural background. In J. Boaler, ed., *Multiple perspectives on mathematics teaching and learning*. Westport, CT: Ablex, 201–24.

Mathematics Teacher Knowledge

Tim Rowland

Core readings

The Core readings addressed in this chapter are as follows:

Shulman, L. S., 1986. Those who understand: knowledge growth in teaching. *Educational Researcher*, 15 (2), 4–14.

Ball, D. L., 1990a. The mathematical understandings that prospective teachers bring to education. *Elementary School Journal*, 90, 449–66.

Ball, D. L., Thames, M. H., and Phelps, G., 2008. Content knowledge for teaching: what makes it special? *Journal of Teacher Education*, 59 (5), 389–407.

Rowland, T., Huckstep, P. and Thwaites, A., 2005. Elementary teachers' mathematics subject knowledge: the Knowledge Quartet and the case of Naomi. *Journal of Mathematics Teacher Education*, 8 (3), 255–81.

Introduction

The four articles selected as the core readings for this chapter offer complementary and, in some respects, cumulative perspectives on the complex relationship between what a teacher knows and how this knowledge relates to their professional role. This relationship is not well understood in general, and it can be oversimplified to the point of caricature. However, there is increasing recognition that effective teaching calls for distinctive forms of subject-related knowledge and thinking. Before homing in on the core readings, and to set the scene, it will make sense to consider the nature of teacher knowledge in general and mathematics teacher knowledge in particular.

Every profession – every 'job', for that matter – has its own knowledge base: physicians, lawyers, priests, plumbers, motor mechanics, and so on. A moment's thought about what it would be like to *do* these jobs exposes the fact that most of us could not do what lawyers, plumbers, and the rest, do, because we lack the necessary knowledge – although we could aspire to acquire it, of course. Discussion of the relation between knowledge and the profession of teaching is particularly convoluted because knowledge is itself the commodity at the heart of education, and the very goal of teaching. Kelly (1995, p. 103) writes that:

> knowledge is the very stuff of education; it is impossible to conceive of, or to plan, any educational activity without recognising the central role that some knowledge-based transaction must play in it.

Teacher knowledge is the prerequisite of the education enterprise, and student knowledge its objective. The question arises, then, as to whether these two kinds of knowledge are the same; and if not, how they are related.

For some sort of starting point in theory about knowledge and teaching, it is usual to turn to Aristotle's (384–322 BC) aphorism 'it is a sign of the man who knows, that he can teach' (*Metaphysics*, Book 1). The Oxford philosopher John Wilson (1975) has endorsed and extended Aristotle's position on teacher knowledge with the argument that comprehension of the logic of concepts offered guidance on how to teach them. In other words, not only do we need to know what we teach in the sense of understanding it, but such a profound quality of knowing actually acts as a guide to the pedagogy, that is, the 'how to teach' of subjects such as mathematics. This position has recently been developed by Watson and Barton (2011) in terms of pedagogical application of 'mathematical modes of enquiry'.

But research has shown that the relationship between knowledge of mathematics and effective teaching is complicated and counterintuitive. Begle (1979), and later Ball (1990b), challenged the common-sense assumption that more subject knowledge (as measured by quantity of mathematics instruction received) results in more 'effective' teaching. Indeed, they questioned whether some aspects of higher-level education in mathematics might actually be counterproductive in preparation for teaching. Askew et al. (1997) also found that 'more' was not necessarily 'better' when they correlated primary teachers' mathematical knowledge, measured in terms of qualifications, against pupil learning over one academic year. The study cohort of ninety teachers included ten who had taken post-compulsory 'advanced level' mathematics at school. The median pupil gain was slightly lower for the classes taught by these ten teachers. Given the complexity of the knowledge-teaching relationship, the work of Lee Shulman and his colleagues is a helpful starting point in an attempt to understand what mathematics teachers know, and how they use it in teaching.

Lee Shulman

The importance of Shulman's thinking, and this article in particular, in the field of teacher knowledge, can hardly be exaggerated. As I write, a Google Scholar check suggests that his original work (Shulman 1986, 1987) has been cited in nearly 8,000 papers in the 25 years since its publication. The core reading article is the text of Shulman's 1985 presidential address to the American Educational Research Association, in which he argued that too much emphasis had been placed in recent (American) research on general pedagogical processes and not enough on the subject-matter under consideration: he called this omission 'the missing paradigm'. Its measured and rather poetic prose could be mistaken for musings of a theoretical kind, and the fruits of distillation of diverse experiences. In fact Shulman's multifaceted perspective on teacher knowledge arose from empirical research, the *Knowledge Growth in a Profession* project, conducted by Shulman and his colleagues at Stanford University in the mid-1980s. This study examined how beginning secondary school teachers learned to transform their own knowledge of academic subjects in order to teach them. Shulman's conception of teachers' knowledge of the *content* that they teach includes not only knowledge of 'subject-matter', but also *pedagogical* content knowledge, as well as knowledge of curriculum. The concept of pedagogical content knowledge is now embedded in the discourse of mathematics teacher education, expressing that mathematical 'something extra' that mathematics teachers know and bring to their work with students.

The Stanford project also recognized aspects of teacher knowledge that are not (so) subject-specific. These are set out in a kind of sequel or companion paper to the core 1986 reading, in which Shulman delineated seven categories of teacher knowledge including, for example, generic principles of classroom management, and knowledge of educational purposes and values (Shulman 1987, p. 8; see also Wilson et al. 1987, p. 113). A valuable elaboration of the content-related aspects is provided in Grossman et al. (1989), who draw out the distinction, due to Schwab (1978), between *substantive* and *syntactic* content knowledge. Broadly speaking, substantive knowledge can be characterized as knowledge of the facts and concepts of a discipline, and the ways that they are organized. Syntactic knowledge is about the nature of *enquiry* in the field, and the mechanisms through which new knowledge is introduced and accepted in that community; in the case of mathematics it includes knowledge about inductive and deductive reasoning, the affordances and limitations of exemplification, about problem-solving heuristics and proof.

Grossman et al. (1989) also enhance Shulman (1986) with a discussion of the role of teachers' *beliefs* about teaching, learning and the subject-matter itself. In particular, they refer to 'orientation' towards the subject-matter as a type of belief. The same word was picked up by a team at King's College, London (Askew et al. 1997) in the afore-mentioned study of the qualities of effective teachers of primary mathematics. Teachers found to be highly effective tended to have an orientation described by the researchers as 'connectionist', characterized by the belief that children's learning is best supported by teaching that explicitly makes links between different aspects of mathematics.

The overwhelming interest in Shulman's taxonomy of *kinds* of teacher knowledge, and in pedagogical content knowledge as a new way of giving recognition to teachers' distinctive expertise, has perhaps diverted attention from the equally inspired, and overtly poetic, passages about the *forms* of teacher knowledge. Shulman draws out three such forms: first, propositional knowledge, consisting of statements about what is 'known' about teaching and learning; second, case knowledge, being salient instances of theoretical constructs which serve to illuminate them; and third, strategic knowledge, where propositional and case knowledge are applied in the exercise of judgement and wise action. Shulman separates each of the first two forms of knowledge into three subcategories – it is useful to draw a tree to help organize the presentation. In particular, *principles* are types of propositions deriving from empirical knowledge, typically outcomes of systematic research. In turn, *prototypes* are cases which exemplify such principles. In fact, Shulman and his colleagues make significant use of such prototypes in their subsequent exposition (Wilson et al. 1987; Grossman et al. 1989).

The following scenario from a lesson that took place in 2002 (Rowland 2010) is offered here to demonstrate the power of the prototype, and the value of Shulman's conceptualization of teacher knowledge. Jason was reviewing elementary fraction concepts with a Year 3 class (student age 7–8). The pupils each had a small oblong whiteboard and a dry-wipe pen. Jason asked them to 'split' their individual whiteboards into two. Most of the children predictably drew a line through the centre of the oblong, parallel to one of the sides, but one boy, Elliot, drew a diagonal line. Jason praised him for his originality, and then asked the class to split their boards 'into four'. Again, most children drew two lines parallel to the sides, but Elliot drew the two diagonals. Jason's response was to bring Elliot's solution to the attention of the class, but to leave them to decide whether it is correct.

This scenario is interesting mathematically, and not so 'elementary' in the context of the Year 3 curriculum. Responding to Elliot's solution, either by teacher exposition, or in interaction with the class, makes demands on Jason's content knowledge in each of the ways described by Shulman. Jason has to decide not only whether the non-congruent parts of Elliot's board are equal, but also what notions of 'equal' will be meaningful to his 7–8 year-old students, and what kinds of legitimate mathematical arguments about area will be accessible to them.

Shulman's conceptualization of teacher knowledge has not been without its critics. Meredith (1995), for example, argued that Shulman perpetuates an expository, transmissionist view of teaching; McNamara (1991) questioned the distinction between subject-matter knowledge and pedagogic knowledge, on the grounds that all mathematics subject-matter is itself a form of representation; Hodgen (2011) sees teacher knowledge as being 'held' in a collective way, distributed within professional communities, in contrast to Shulman's more individualist conception. These critiques must be evaluated against Shulman's (1987) own clear admission that his framework was provisional, tentative and most probably incomplete. There is, we would suggest, an undeniable sharpness of insight in Shulman's analysis – a blend of philosophy and empirical reasoning – and for that reason it remains the agreed and accepted starting point for subsequent analyses of, and further investigation into, teachers' professional knowledge base.

Deborah Ball

Deborah Ball's contribution to research in the field of mathematics teacher knowledge has been extensive and far-reaching. Before taking up her doctoral studies in the 1980s, Ball worked as an elementary (primary) school teacher in publicly funded schools in Michigan State. Videotapes and other records of her own classroom teaching have been an important source of data in the investigations of her now world-famous research group at the University of Michigan. Ball entered the research field on the cusp of Shulman's work at Stanford: this 1990 core reading reports selected findings from a project (Teacher Education and Learning to Teach – TELT) which built on her Ph.D. study (see Ball 1990b). This research is characteristic of many studies that set out to probe what mathematics teachers (more often, prospective teachers) know and – significantly – what they appear not to know. Such identification of 'gaps' in teacher knowledge has been criticized for adding to the 'deficit discourse' about teaching; at the same time, it highlights priorities for teacher education in potentially useful ways (Goulding et al. 2002). A Ph.D. study by Liping Ma, using Ball's methods and TELT items, compared serving US elementary teachers with their counterparts in Shanghai, China. The very readable book that reports her findings (Ma 1999) has been embraced by proponents on both sides of the reform/traditional divide in debates about mathematics teaching ('math wars') in the United States.

Ball's TELT project investigated the participants' content knowledge through questionnaires administered to 252 student teachers, both elementary and secondary, at the beginning of their teacher education program. More in-depth, task-based interviews were conducted with 35 of the participants. In these interviews, participants were presented with a 'classroom scenario' and a related problem, or a teaching-related issue of some kind. The topic at the heart of the item under scrutiny in this article – division, and division by a fraction in particular – is rich with potential, for a number of reasons. First, because justifying the 'invert-and-multiply' rule is not easy; in any case, most educated citizens do not have reason to think about it. Second, because natural, meaningful representations of division by $\frac{1}{2}$ appeal to the 'measurement' (or quotative) interpretation, rather than the more familiar 'partitive' alternative (see the chapter by Julia Anghileri, this volume). Again, awareness of these *two* division structures is important in the professional knowledge repertoire of mathematics teachers, elementary teachers especially, but outside the 'common content knowledge' of educated citizens – so much so that Ball devotes a whole page (p. 452) of this article to an exposition of the partitive and quotitive division structures. The difficulty experienced by one novice teacher – and a mathematically well-qualified one at that – in explaining 'invert-and-multiply' in the classroom is powerfully documented in the celebrated case of Ms Daniels (Borko et al. 1992). The full account in the Borko article is well worth reading.

As Ball remarks, the questionnaire task was in some sense 'easier' than the interview task, because it involved choosing rather than proposing a representation of division by $\frac{1}{2}$. We are told that only around 30 per cent of the 252 prospective teachers chose the story problem for which $1\frac{3}{4} \div \frac{1}{2}$ would yield a solution. This might disguise the extent of the 'problem' in that the participants were instructed to 'circle all that apply', so the 30 per cent could include those that selected the correct option (c) 'just in case', along with others. (In fact, given that Ball herself says that some respondents selected both correct and incorrect answers, it is not clear why the columns in Table 1 sum to 100, and not more.) Although this statistic is the stuff of tabloid newspaper panic headlines, it is hard to know what to make of it, whether the 'only 30 per cent' is a cause for concern, or not a great surprise before these participants have not even begun their professional training. One message we can confidently draw from it, however, is that these trainee teachers do have something to learn in their professional education. The interview situation, in which the participants had to *actively* devise a representation that might 'explain' the meaning of division by a half, constituted a much more exacting 'test' of teaching-specific knowledge, and the success rate is even lower, with just over 10 per cent of the 35 intending teachers able to propose an appropriate model. An abundance of pizzas ('round models') was in evidence, but only rarely did the respondents know what to do with them. The 'story' generated by Abby (p. 455) in which the pizzas are shared ('split') by two people reflects a well-documented preference for partition as default division structure, but it results in division by 2, rather than $\frac{1}{2}$. I referred earlier to Ma's (1999) comparison of serving US and Chinese teachers: Ma reports that 90 per cent of her 72 Chinese elementary teacher participants offered a suitable representation of the same division problem, whereas only one of the 23 US teachers were able to do so. However, comparison between the 2 sample populations is complicated in a number of respects.

An enduring contribution of Ball's early work, underpinned by her findings about 'gaps' in what prospective teachers know about mathematics, is her prophetic questioning of three 'common-sense' assumptions about elementary mathematics and preparing teachers to teach it. Essentially, Ball cautions that teaching elementary mathematics is not 'easy', because it requires a way of knowing mathematics that is not acquired at school, or even by those who specialize in mathematics in higher education. This is something that needs to be understood by policy makers, and also by prospective teachers themselves.

Mathematical knowledge for teaching

In the past 15–20 years, Deborah Ball's research team at the University of Michigan has worked towards better understanding of the demands that the work of teachers places on their mathematical knowledge and understanding. This stream of research developed from Ball's collaboration, since 1996, with the mathematician Hyman Bass (www.msri.org/attachments/teachcollabcombined.pdf [accessed on 16 May 2013]), directed towards a 'practice-based theory of knowledge for teaching' (Ball and Bass 2003). This work was grounded in the analysis of a database documenting a year of mathematics teaching (the teacher being Ball herself) in a 'third grade public school classroom' in 1989–90. These multimodal data include records of teaching and student work, as well as of teacher planning and reflection (Ball and Bass 2003). The theory that emerges from the Michigan studies, expounded in our third core reading, unpicks and reconfigures the three kinds of content knowledge – subject-matter, pedagogical and curricular – identified by Shulman (1986). The elements of this new theory are summarized in the 'egg' model of 'Mathematical Knowledge for Teaching' (MKfT) shown in figure 5 (p. 403) of the core reading. This model has been widely acclaimed and adopted by several researchers as a theoretical framework for interpreting their own classroom data, as well as a language for articulating their findings.

In this deconstruction of Shulman, Subject Matter Knowledge (SMK) is separated into 'common content knowledge' (CCK), 'specialized content knowledge' (SCK) and 'horizon content knowledge' (HCK). CCK is essentially 'school mathematics', applicable in a range of everyday and professional contexts demanding the ability to calculate and solve problems. SCK, on the other hand, is that 'something extra' that mathematics teachers need in their work, but others do not, which Ball herself had highlighted in our second reading, in her challenge to the three commonly held assumptions about preparation for mathematics teaching. But surely this second kind of mathematical knowledge, peculiar to teachers and teaching, was precisely what Shulman intended by PCK? Why then, does the MKfT theory include it as a component of SMK? The conception of SCK within MKfT is exemplified by reference to the evaluation of student responses to column subtraction. The authors argue (p. 398) that the kinds of knowledge required to diagnose incorrect strategies, or to understand correct but non-standard ones, are essentially *mathematical*, rather than pedagogical. On the other hand, they suggest that knowing about typical errors (and alternative strategies too, I would suggest) in advance, thereby enabling them to be anticipated, is *pedagogical* content knowledge: specifically, what they call 'knowledge of content and students' (KCS). This is a subtle but reasonably clear distinction, on the basis of which one might conclude that SCK is accessible to the competent mathematician, and can be developed by such a person by reference to their knowledge of mathematics (see also Watson and Barton 2011). KCS, on the other hand, seems to be conceived as a body of knowledge deriving from empirical research in the behavioural and social sciences (including mathematics education, of course). This seems fine, but one can envisage instances or situations that do not fit unequivocally into the SCK or KCS categories as conceived. Take, for example, knowledge of the two division structures (partition and measurement/quotition) discussed in Ball's 1990a core reading (see the previous section, this chapter). Ball et al. (2008, p. 400) locate this particular 'piece' of knowledge within SCK; yet, most of the prospective teacher participants in her TELT study, some of them well-qualified mathematically, were unable to access it in response to the questionnaire or the task-based interview. At a personal level, I can attest that this accords with my own awareness of these structures, and that my explicit knowledge of the corresponding take-away/comparison structures for subtraction (e.g. Carpenter and Moser 1983) came about only through instruction in mathematics education. However, the Michigan team is at pains to emphasize that the categories are not static, and that the boundaries between categories are not always clear: it is for users to decide whether annexing part (SCK) of what Shulman seems to have conceived as PCK to SMK is helpful for their purpose.

It is immediately apparent that the 'egg' model is not a simple elaboration of Shulman's three content categories, since curriculum knowledge is no longer a major category. In effect, it has been partitioned into two: HCK, which becomes the third component of SMK; and knowledge of content and curriculum, which is now one of three components of PCK. In fact, Ball et al. (2008, p. 391) draw out two aspects of curriculum knowledge, as conceived by Shulman, that are often overlooked. The first, lateral curriculum knowledge, relates to cross-curricular mathematical connections, invoking conceptions and applications that enrich students' experience and appreciation. The second, vertical curriculum knowledge, is about knowing what mathematical experiences preceded those in the current grade-level, and what will follow in the next, and subsequent, grades. Ball et al. seem to have relabelled 'vertical knowledge' as 'horizon content knowledge', and included it within SMK. Reference to the horizon evokes places and events that are some way off, but where one can hope to arrive eventually. Whereas Ball et al. seem to emphasize the 'what comes later' direction of HCK (p. 403), Shulman (1986, p. 10) referred to 'preceding and later years in school'. The importance of this Janus-like quality in mathematics teachers is clear. On the one hand, we need to know what knowledge our students can be expected to bring with them as a result of previous instruction, as well as the kinds of 'baggage' they might bring in terms of restricted conceptions and even misconceptions. On the other hand, Dewey (1903, p. 217) cautioned teachers against fostering 'mental habits and preconceptions which have later on to be bodily displaced or rooted up in order to secure a proper comprehension of the subject', and it is helpful in the long run to avoid the kind of narrow, instrumental teaching that loads students with more baggage and half-truths, thereby impeding progress in the later grades.

The Knowledge Quartet

In this chapter, and these core readings, we see something of the range of methodological possibilities available to researchers in the investigation of mathematics teacher knowledge.

The principal data collection methods have used questionnaires, interviews and observations. Observations of classroom practice are at the heart of our fourth and final core reading, but the research reported in it came out of a stream of activity in the United Kingdom involving questionnaires, known as 'audits' – in effect, 'tests'. Reflecting UK government concern about teachers' knowledge of the subjects that they taught, regulations for initial teacher education (ITE) in England, introduced in 1998, required teacher educators to 'audit' trainees' knowledge and understanding of mathematics, and to ensure that 'gaps' identified be 'filled' during the training. Within the teacher education community, few could be found to support the imposition of the 'audit and remediation' culture. And yet the introduction of this 'testing' regime ignited a new strand of UK research on prospective primary teachers' mathematics subject-matter knowledge: the proceedings of a research symposium held in 2003 usefully bring together some of the threads of this audit-provoked research (BSRLM 2003).

One study, with 150 London-based graduate trainee primary teachers (Rowland et al. 2000), found that trainees obtaining high (or even middle) scores on a 16-item audit of content knowledge were more likely to be assessed as strong mathematics teachers on school-based placements than those with low scores; whereas those with low audit scores were more likely than other participants to be assessed as weak mathematics teachers. Although this was interesting in itself, and attracted some media attention, a team at the University of Cambridge wanted to find out more about what was 'going on', and took forward this new line of enquiry. If superior content knowledge really does make a difference when teaching elementary mathematics, it ought somehow to be observable in the practice of the knowledgeable teacher. Conversely, the teacher with weak content knowledge might be expected to misinform their pupils, or somehow to miss opportunities to teach mathematics 'well'. In a nutshell, the Cambridge team wanted to identify, and to understand better, the ways in which elementary teachers' mathematics content knowledge, or the lack of it, is made visible in their teaching.

The core reading (Rowland et al. 2005) describes the process of data collection, and the 'grounded theory' approach to analysing video-recordings of the 24 lessons. In 'theory-driven' (or deductive) approaches to the analysis of data, the researcher brings a ready-made theory, or theories, about the kind of situation being investigated, and applies them to the data. By contrast, grounded theory (inductive) research does not bring existing theory to make sense of the data, but aims to use the data for the purpose of generating or 'discovering' a theory or theories. We were looking for ways in which these teachers' mathematical content knowledge 'played out' in their work in the classroom and, to the best of our knowledge, no existing framework existed to organize the complexity of what we saw in the lessons, with that particular focus on teacher knowledge. We did not come to our analysis of the tapes devoid of influences, however, and this 'insider knowledge' was made explicit in our interpretative 'analytical accounts' of the lessons (see p. 258), in which we made reference to connections of various kinds that came to mind when we viewed the lessons.

In the event, 18 agreed codes emerged from this grounded analysis, subsequently grouped into 4 categories. Briefly: the *foundation* dimension consists of knowledge and understanding of mathematics per se and of mathematics-specific pedagogy, as well as beliefs concerning the nature of mathematics, the purposes of mathematics education and the conditions under which students will best learn mathematics. The second dimension, *transformation*, concerns the presentation of ideas to learners in the form of analogies, illustrations, examples, explanations and demonstrations. The third, *connection*, includes the sequencing of material for instruction, and an awareness of the relative cognitive demands of different topics and tasks. The final dimension, *contingency*, is the ability to make cogent, reasoned and well-informed responses to unanticipated and unplanned events.

The core reading paves over the details of the process whereby we partitioned the 18 codes into 4 categories, but it took almost a year for us to agree on the number of code-sub-sets, and their constituents: a warts-and-all account can be found in Rowland (2008). The outcome, the Knowledge Quartet, is a theoretical tool for observing, analysing and reflecting on actual mathematics teaching. It offers a four-dimensional framework against which mathematics lessons can be discussed, with a focus on their subject-matter content, and the teacher's related knowledge and beliefs. A book aimed at mathematics teachers and teacher educators (Rowland et al. 2009) explains how to analyse and give feedback on mathematics teaching, using the Knowledge Quartet. In the previous section I noted that the Michigan research team refer to MKfT as a 'practice-based theory of knowledge for teaching' (Ball and Bass 2003). The same description could be applied to the Knowledge Quartet, but while parallels can be drawn between the methods and some of the outcomes, the two theories look very different. In particular, the theory that emerges from the Michigan studies aims to unpick and clarify the formerly somewhat elusive and theoretically undeveloped notions of SMK and PCK. In the Knowledge Quartet, however, the distinction between different *kinds* of mathematical knowledge is of lesser significance than the classification of the situations in which mathematical knowledge surfaces in teaching. In this sense, the two theories are complementary, so that each has useful perspectives to offer to the other.

Conclusion

Taken as a whole, these four articles offer an overview of the direction of research into mathematics teacher knowledge in the past 25 years, and where it stands at present. It is fair to observe that the field is skewed towards primary mathematics, and to inexperienced teachers-in-training. It is also important to keep in mind that that these articles give us a glimpse of Anglo-American perspectives on the topic. Views from Europe outside the United Kingdom look a little different (see, for example, Rowland and Ruthven 2011, and the chapter by Andrews, this volume), as do those from the Far East (see the chapter by Wong, this volume). One recent German project (COACTIV: Baumert et al. 2010) is of major significance because it investigates secondary mathematics teacher knowledge and builds bridges between European thinking and the Anglo-American Shulman-inspired tradition. In a sophisticated quantitative study, the COACTIV group succeeded in establishing empirically that PCK and SMK (or 'content knowledge', CK) represent distinct knowledge categories. Furthermore, their findings indicate that weak CK puts limits on the growth of PCK. However, teacher PCK (as measured by the COACTIV instruments) predicts student progress – in the German secondary setting – better than teacher CK. There is continuing, significant interest in research on mathematics teacher knowledge, and more studies of this quality can be anticipated in the future.

Further reading

Baumert, J., Kunter, M., Blum, W., Brunner, M., Voss, T., Jordan, A., et al., 2010. Teachers' mathematical knowledge, cognitive activation in the classroom, and student progress. *American Educational Research Journal*, 47 (1), 133–80.

Ma, L., 1999. *Knowing and teaching elementary mathematics: teachers' understanding of fundamental mathematics in China and the United States.* Mahwah, NJ: Lawrence Erlbaum.

Rowland, T. and Ruthven, K., eds, 2011. *Mathematical knowledge in teaching.* London and New York: Springer.

Shulman, L. S., 1987. Knowledge and teaching: foundations of the new reform. *Harvard Educational Review*, 57, 1–22.

Additional references

Askew, M., Brown, M., Rhodes, V., Johnson, D. and Wiliam, D., 1997. *Effective teachers of numeracy.* London: King's College.

Ball, D. L., 1990b. Prospective elementary and secondary teachers' understanding of division, *Journal for Research in Mathematics Education*, 21 (2), 132–44.

Ball, D. L. and Bass, H., 2003. Toward a practice-based theory of mathematical knowledge for teaching. In B. Davis and E. Simmt, eds, *Proceedings of the 2002 annual meeting of the Canadian Mathematics Education Study Group.* Edmonton, Alberta, Canada: CMESG, 3–14.

Begle, E. G., 1979 *Critical variables in mathematics education: findings from a survey of empirical research.* Washington, DC: Mathematics Association of America and the National Council of Teachers of Mathematics.

Borko, H., Eisenhart, M., Brown, C. A., Underhill R. G., Jones, D. and Agard P. C., 1992. Learning to teach hard mathematics: do novice teachers and their instructors give up too easily? *Journal for Research in Mathematics Education*, 23 (3), 194–222.

BSRLM, 2003. *Proceedings of the British Society for Research into Learning Mathematics*, 23 (2). Available at www. bsrlm.org.uk/informalproceedings.html [accessed on 16 May 2013].

Carpenter, T. P. and Moser, J. M., 1983. The acquisition of addition and subtraction concepts. In R. Lesh and M. Landau, eds, *The acquisition of mathematical concepts and processes.* New York: Academic Press, 7–44.

Dewey, J., 1903. The psychological and the logical in teaching geometry. *Educational Review*, 25, 387–99.

Goulding, M., Rowland, T. and Barber, P., 2002. Does it matter? Primary teacher trainees' subject knowledge in mathematics. *British Educational Research Journal*, 28 (5), 689–704.

Grossman, P., Wilson, S. and Shulman, L., 1989. Teachers of substance: subject matter knowledge for teaching. In M. Reynolds, ed., *Knowledge base for the beginning teacher.* Oxford: Pergamon, 23–36.

Hodgen, J., 2011. Knowing and identity: a situated theory of mathematical knowledge in teaching. In T. Rowland and K. Ruthven, eds, *Mathematical knowledge in teaching*. London and New York: Springer, 27–42.

Kelly, A. V., 1995. *Education and democracy: principles and practices*. London: Paul Chapman.

McNamara, D., 1991. Subject knowledge and its application: problems and possibilities for teacher educators. *British Educational Research Journal*, 28 (5), 113–28.

Meredith, A., 1995. Terry's learning: some limitations of Shulman's pedagogical content knowledge. *Cambridge Journal of Education*, 25 (2), 175–87.

Rowland, T., 2008. Researching teachers' mathematics disciplinary knowledge. In P. Sullivan and T. Wood, eds, *International handbook of mathematics teacher education. Vol. 1: Knowledge and beliefs in mathematics teaching and teaching development*. Rotterdam, Netherlands: Sense, 273–98.

—, 2010. Back to the data: Jason, and Elliot's quarters. In M. M. F. Pinto and T. F. Kawasaki, eds, *Proceedings of the 34th Conference of the International Group for the Psychology of Mathematics Education*, Vol. 4. Belo Horizonte, Brazil: PME, 97–104.

Rowland, T., Martyn, S., Barber, P. and Heal, C., 2000. Primary teacher trainees' mathematics subject knowledge and classroom performance. *Research in Mathematics Education* 2, 3–18.

Rowland, T., Turner, F., Thwaites, A. and Huckstep, P., 2009. *Developing primary mathematics teaching: reflecting on practice with the Knowledge Quartet*. London: Sage.

Schwab, J. J., 1978. Education and the structure of the disciplines. In I. Westbury and N. J. Wilkof, eds, *Science, curriculum and liberal education*. Chicago: University of Chicago Press, 229–72.

Watson, A. and Barton, B., 2011. Teaching mathematics as the contextual application of modes of mathematical enquiry. In T. Rowland and K. Ruthven, eds, *Mathematical knowledge in teaching*. London and New York: Springer, 65–82.

Wilson, J., 1975. *Education theory and the preparation of teachers*. Windsor: NFER.

Wilson, S., Shulman, L. and Richert, A., 1987. '150 different ways' of knowing: representations of knowledge in teaching. In J. Calderhead, ed., *Exploring teacher thinking*. London: Cassell, 104–24.

Part II
Aspects of Mathematics Curriculum

Proof

9

Andreas J. Stylianides

Core readings

The Core readings addressed in this chapter are as follows:

Balacheff, N., 2002. The researcher epistemology: a deadlock for educational research on proof. In F. L. Lin, ed., *Proceedings of the 2002 International Conference on Mathematics: understanding proving and proving to understand*. Taipei, Taiwan: NSC and NTNU, 23–44. Pre-publication version available at www.tpp.umassd.edu/proofcolloquium07/reading/Balachef_Taiwan2002.pdf [accessed on 25 November 2011].

Stylianides, A. J., 2007. Proof and proving in school mathematics. *Journal for Research in Mathematics Education*, 38, 289–321.

Sowder, L. and Harel, G., 1998. Types of students' justifications. *Mathematics Teacher*, 91, 670–5.

Stylianides, G. J. and Stylianides, A. J., 2009. Facilitating the transition from empirical arguments to proof. *Journal for Research in Mathematics Education*, 40, 314–52.

Introduction

The core readings focus on the notion of *proof* in mathematics education research and address a set of related conceptual and instructional issues in this area. I begin with an overview of the role of proof in the field of mathematics and its place (both current and recommended) in students' mathematical education as early as the primary school years. Then I use a classroom episode as a context to introduce the specific issues and I discuss separately each core reading, referring also back to the episode in order to exemplify some ideas.

In the field of mathematics, the notion of proof has a pivotal role, serving at least three major functions. First, it is the principal means by which mathematicians validate mathematical assertions and derive new knowledge (Kitcher 1984). Second, it is central to the process of mathematical discovery. As it is portrayed by Lakatos (1976), this process is not a steady accumulation of indubitably established truths, but rather the incessant improvement of conjectures by attempts to prove them and by criticism of these attempts through refutations expressed mainly in the form of counterexamples (see the chapter by Ernest, this volume). Third, it can promote mathematical understanding by showing why an assertion is true and by illuminating logical connections between different mathematical ideas (Kitcher 1984).

Despite the pivotal role that proof plays in the field of mathematics, proof has traditionally had a marginal place in mathematics teaching and learning in many countries, especially at the primary school level. According to a group of researchers from different countries (the United States, England, Germany and Israel), primary school mathematics teaching tends to focus 'on arithmetic concepts, calculations, and algorithms, and, then, as [pupils] enter secondary school, pupils are suddenly required to understand and write proofs, mostly in geometry' (Ball et al. 2002, pp. 907–8). The limited attention to proof in primary school, students' subsequent abrupt introduction to proof in secondary school, and the insufficient learning opportunities that traditional secondary school mathematics teaching offers to students for meaningful engagement with proof, all help explain (at least in part) the findings of a large body of research (e.g. Chazan 1993; Coe and Ruthven 1994; Healy and Hoyles 2000; Küchemann and Hoyles 2001–3; Senk 1985) that even advanced secondary school students face difficulties with proof.

In recent years, many researchers from different countries have called for more attention to proof in students' mathematical education (e.g. Ball et al. 2002; Hanna and Jahnke 1996; Healy and Hoyles 2000; Mariotti 2000; Zack 1997). In North America, for example, the current research and policy discourse is not simply tilted in favour of a more central presence of proof in school mathematics, but recommends also that proof be incorporated into all students' mathematical experiences and as early as the primary school (e.g. Ball and Bass 2003; National Council of Teachers of Mathematics 2000; Schoenfeld 1994; Yackel and Hanna 2003).

From a philosophical standpoint, the recommendation to engage even young children in activities related to proof is consistent with the thinking of educational scholars such as Bruner (1960) and Schwab (1978). These scholars argued that there should be continuity between what experts do on the forefront of their disciplines and what children do in approaching the disciplines for the first time. Given the central role that proof plays in the field of mathematics, the limited attention to proof in primary school mathematics can be considered to be, then, a serious threat to the integrity of the school mathematics curriculum and students' opportunities to learn mathematics. Schwab (1978, p. 242) wrote:

> *How* we teach will determine what our students learn. If a structure of teaching and learning is alien to the structure of what we propose to teach, the outcome will inevitably be a corruption of that content. And we will know that it is.

From a pedagogical standpoint, the recommendation to engage even young children in activities related to proof is aligned with the goal to promote learning mathematics with understanding (e.g. Hanna 1995), a goal that is prioritized in many school mathematics curricula internationally. It would appear contradictory to talk about an emphasis on mathematical understanding without attending to issues of proof. Indeed, in classes whose teachers took proof seriously, students' engagement with proof was interlinked with mathematical sense making (e.g. Ball and Bass 2003; Lampert 1992; Zack 1997). Furthermore, students' engagement with proof could allow them to become more active participants in knowledge construction, for new knowledge would then be validated by means of the logical structure of the mathematical system rather than by appeal to the authority of the teacher (e.g. Ball and Bass 2000; Reid 2002; Zack 1997).

To conclude, the core readings belong to a body of research that derived from the growing appreciation of the importance of proof in all students' mathematical education and the problems associated with the failure of traditional mathematics teaching to promote student learning of proof. This body of research aimed, among other things, to theorize the notion of proof in mathematics education and to develop knowledge that could inform or support the teaching and learning of proof as early as the primary school years.

A classroom episode as a context to introduce the focal issues

Next I look in on an episode from an American third-grade class where the students (7-year-olds) were working on the conjecture that the sum of any two odd numbers is an even number. The episode is known to many mathematics education researchers, in part because there is scarcity in the literature of episodes where young children engage with proof. This scarcity echoes the concerns I described earlier about the limited emphasis that is currently placed on proof in many primary school classes. Indeed, the few examples of episodes of this kind that are reported in the literature came from classes taught by teacher-researchers, in this case Deborah Ball (whose work is discussed further in the chapter by Rowland, this volume). A lot can be said about the episode, but in this chapter I use it in a very specific way: as a context to introduce some issues that span the four core readings and on which I will focus next in the chapter.

The following description derives from Stylianides and Ball (2008, pp. 323, 328), and begins with a student responding to the teacher's invitation for comments about the conjecture, which the class called 'Betsy's conjecture'.

9. Jeannie: Me and Sheena were working together, but we didn't find one [i.e. an example] that didn't work. We were trying to prove that, um, Betsy's conjecture, um, that you can't prove that Betsy's conjecture always works [murmurs from other children].

10. Ball: Go on, Jeannie. Say more about why you think that.

11. Jeannie: Because um there's um like numbers go on and on forever and that means odd numbers and even numbers, um, go on forever and, um, so you couldn't prove that all of them work.

12. Ball: What are people's reactions to what Jeannie and Sheena thought? [pause] They said they didn't find one that didn't work, but they don't think we can prove it always works because numbers go on forever and ever.

13. Ofala: I think it can always work because I um tried almost, um, [she counted the examples she had in her notebook] eighteen of them, and I also tried a Sean number [i.e. an even number with an odd number of groups of 2] so I think, I think it can always work.

More students expressed objections to Jeannie and Sheena's idea, saying that the conjecture could be proved in ways that were similar with Ofala's argument. In the next lessons, Ball helped the students think how they could construct a general argument for the conjecture. A notable aspect of Ball's intervention was that she directed students' attention to their definitions of even and odd numbers as the numbers which when made in groups of 2 there is, respectively, 'nothing' or '1' left over. Ultimately, Betsy proposed the following argument:

14. Betsy: [A]ll odd numbers if you circle them, what we found out, all odd numbers if you circle them by twos, there's one left over, so if you . . . plus one, um, or if you plus another odd number, then the two ones left over will group together, and it will make an even number.

The episode shows young children debating about what it means to prove a conjecture that involves an infinite number of cases, and raises several related conceptual and instructional issues: What might we mean by 'proof' in school mathematics, especially at such an early stage of students' education? What might a proof look like for the specific conjecture? Would Ofala's or Betsy's arguments in the episode meet the standard of proof? How might teachers help students recognize the limitations of non-proof arguments?

The core readings help address these and other related issues. In my discussion of the four core readings, I will refer back to the episode to exemplify some ideas.

Discussion of the core readings

Balacheff (2002)

Balacheff's (2002) critical review of the literature drew attention to the lack of clarity in the use of the term 'proof' in mathematics education research, and pointed out the adverse consequences of this lack of clarify for communicating, interpreting, synthesizing and further developing relevant research findings. Balacheff discussed seven research strands in the area of proof that he considered to be (1) illustrative of different researcher epistemologies of proof and (2) representative of different perspectives on proof from which research in this area was done in various countries.

Balacheff's thesis in the chapter was presented (and I think rightly so) as being applicable to the overall state of the field at the time. His thesis is summarized in the following quotation:[1]

> I went through a large number of research papers to figure out whether beyond the keywords we [researchers in mathematics education] had some common understanding [for the meaning of proof]. To discover that this is not the case was in fact not surprising. The issue then is to see where the differences are and what the price for them is in our research economy. My main concern is that if [we] do not clarify this point, it will be hardly possible to share results and hence to make any real progress in the field. (p. 1)

Balacheff clarified further his thesis later in the chapter (on p. 2) when he talked about the role of researchers' epistemologies of proof – that is, their acquaintance with truth and validity – in their research work in this area. According to Balacheff, researchers' epistemologies of proof shape their selection of research questions, theoretical frameworks and related methodologies, and so limited awareness of, or attention to, these epistemologies can hinder significant advancements in the field.

Turning back to the episode, we can consider two different (hypothetical) researcher epistemologies of proof according to each of which Ofala's argument (line 13) could be considered, or not, a proof. Ofala's argument could be considered a proof if, for example, proof were loosely defined to denote a justification (or an explanation), without any expectations imposed upon the qualities of this justification. On the other hand, Ofala's argument could not be considered a proof according to a researcher epistemology that viewed proof as a deductive argument offering conclusive evidence for the truth or falsity of a conjecture.[2] This illustrates the point that, unless researcher epistemologies are made explicit, there is little basis on which to explain apparently contradictory research findings such as whether or not the episode exemplifies Ofala's ability to prove.

Other mathematics education researchers such as Reid (2005) expressed similar concerns about the lack of a clear conceptualization of the meaning of proof in the field of mathematics education. The acknowledgement of this problem by different researchers was the first step towards addressing the problem. According to Reid (2005, p. 458), '[p]erhaps it is a sign of the maturity of research into the teaching and learning of proof and proving that we are beginning to reflect on what it is we are researching, and whether, as a community, we are successful in communicating our work to each other.'

Stylianides (2007)

In Stylianides (2007), I offered a proposal of how mathematics education research can take a further step towards addressing the problem described earlier about the lack of a clear conceptualization of the meaning of proof in the field. Specifically, I set out a conceptualization of the meaning of proof in school mathematics that aims to be: (1) developmentally sensitive and thus sufficiently 'elastic' to guide the design of coherent student learning experiences with proof throughout their schooling, and (2) compatible with disciplinary norms about the meaning of proof. The first aim is intended to address the problem I described earlier about the limited place that proof has traditionally had in the primary school and the corresponding 'didactical break' that results in many countries from students' abrupt transition to proof in the secondary school. The second aim is intended to address philosophical views, such as those I described earlier with reference to Bruner (1960) and Schwab (1978), that the treatment of proof in the school curriculum should not be alien to fundamental aspects of the nature of proof in the field of mathematics.

In addition to discussing the theoretical grounding of the proposed conceptualization, I used three classroom episodes to elaborate on and exemplify two related applications of the conceptualization: (1) how it may be used by researchers as an analytic framework for studying teaching practices related to proof as early as the primary school years, and (2) how it may be used by teachers to manage their decision making as they try to help a classroom community develop more mathematically acceptable forms of argument. The three episodes are derived from the same third-grade class as the episode I presented earlier. As explained in the article (pp. 300–2), this class offered an appropriate context within which to examine and illustrate the potential affordances of the proposed conceptualization.

The proposed conceptualization is, of course, not the only possible approach to conceptualizing the meaning of proof in school mathematics. Yet, by presenting my proposal in an explicit way, I hoped to provide a specific context for discussions among researchers about the topic. To use Balacheff's (2002, p. 1) words, 'I do not expect every researcher to come on a same line, but we may benefit from being able to witness our convergences and to turn our differences into research questions.' Reid's (2005, p. 465) words are also relevant here: '[I]f we can acknowledge that there is an issue here, and discuss the characteristics of proof, we may be able to come to, if not agreement, then at least agreement on how we differ.'

Turning back to the episode from Ball's third-grade class, Ofala's argument (line 13) would not meet the standard of proof, for, according to the conceptualization in Stylianides (2007), the argument used invalid modes of argumentation: it offered inconclusive evidence for the truth of the conjecture by verifying its truth only in a proper subset of all the possible cases covered by the conjecture. On the other hand, and again according to the conceptualization, Betsy's argument (line 14) would qualify as a proof for the conjecture in the particular classroom community. This is because Betsy's argument: (1) used true statements that were readily accepted by the specific community, notably, the definitions of odd and even numbers; (2) employed the valid mode of argumentation associated with the use of definitions to logically deduce the statement of the conjecture; and (3) was represented appropriately using verbal language in a way that was understandable to the students in the class.

Sowder and Harel (1998)

Sowder and Harel (1998) discussed a framework for classifying students' justification (or proof) schemes, whereby a student's *justification scheme* signifies what argument convinces the student (ascertaining) and what argument the student offers to convince others (persuading). The authors' aim in the article was 'to give a framework for thinking about students' justifications, with an eye toward shaping their mathematical reasoning' (p. 670).

The framework that is presented in the article is derived from the authors' teaching experiences and from interviews they conducted with secondary and university students. The article was published in a professional journal and omitted discussion of methodology, which can be found in a research paper by the same authors on the same topic (Harel and Sowder 1998). According to the framework, justification schemes can be classified into three broad categories: externally based justification schemes, empirical justification schemes and analytic justification schemes. Each of these categories includes several subcategories as shown in figure 1 of the article (p. 671). The authors noted that their framework provides instructors with 'a way to evaluate the justifications given by [their] students, so that [they] can plan instruction to move them toward more sophisticated ways of reasoning' (p. 674). Yet, issues such as what this planning can involve and how it can actually support students' advancement towards more sophisticated ways of reasoning are not addressed in the article.

Turning back to the episode, Ofala's argument (line 13) is illustrative of an *empirical justification scheme* and, in particular, the example-based justification scheme: Ofala convinced herself and tried to persuade others for the truth of the conjecture on the basis of few examples that covered only a proper subset of all the possible cases. Betsy's argument (line 14) is more sophisticated (from a mathematical standpoint) than Ofala's and illustrative of an *analytic justification scheme*. In particular, Betsy's argument illustrates the transformational justification scheme, for it was concerned with the general aspects of the conjecture and involved reasoning oriented towards settling the conjecture in general.

Sowder and Harel noted that '[s]tudents who place full faith in examples should at least find out that examples can betray them and that patterns found in several examples are not completely trustworthy' (p. 674). This point is illustrated well by the failing patterns in problems 1–5, which are presented on pages 672–3 of the article. Yet, practice and research (e.g. Zazkis and Chernoff 2008) suggested that the mere presentation of failing patterns to students is not enough to challenge their faith in empirical arguments and help them see an 'intellectual need' (Harel 1998) for more general arguments: students tend to consider the counterexamples in such problems as exceptions that have no bearing on their empirical justification scheme. More complex didactical engineering is required to help students recognize the limitations of empirical arguments, and this requirement is reinforced by the findings of research that showed the pervasiveness of the empirical justification scheme among students of all levels of education including prospective primary school teachers (e.g. Chazan 1993; Coe and Ruthven 1994; Goulding et al. 2002; Healy and Holyes 2000; Martin and Harel 1989; Sowder and Harel 2003).

Stylianides and Stylianides (2009)

As noted earlier, much research has documented the deeply rooted misconception, illustrated in Ofala's argument, that empirical arguments are proofs. Yet, little progress has been made thus far in identifying effective ways to help students overcome this misconception. The research reported in Stylianides and Stylianides (2009) took a step in addressing this problem. Specifically, the article presented the theoretical foundation and implementation of an instructional intervention that we designed and found to be effective in helping students begin to recognize the limitations of empirical arguments as methods for validating mathematical generalizations and see an intellectual need to learn about more secure methods for validation. In other words, the instructional intervention supported students to move beyond the empirical justification scheme.

The theoretical framework underpinning the instructional intervention was developed and refined on the basis of data (e.g. classroom videos, field notes of small-group activities, written student work) that we collected and analysed over the five research cycles of a four-year design experiment. As it is typical of design experiment methodology, in which theory and instructional design grow in dialectic (e.g. Cobb et al. 2003), the refinements of the framework were accompanied by parallel refinements of the intervention, both of which reached their final forms in the last research cycle as discussed in the article.

The intervention relied heavily on two deliberately engineered cognitive conflicts that motivated stepwise progressions in students' knowledge about proof, moving away from the empirical justification scheme. It should be noted, though, that it took us five research cycles of implementation, analysis and refinement before we satisfactorily theorized and managed to achieve the intended function of these cognitive conflicts. In the early research cycles of the design experiment, we faced a major problem that is well documented in the literature (e.g. Zazkis and Chernoff 2008), to which I alluded earlier, namely, students dismissing as exceptions apparent contradictions in their empirical justification schemes and thus not experiencing intended cognitive conflicts. The article discussed and exemplified two instructional conditions whose fulfilment increases the likelihood of students experiencing the intended cognitive conflict in the area of proof. The article also elaborated on the key role of the instructor in helping students resolve the emerging cognitive conflicts and develop knowledge about proof that better approximates conventional understandings.

The research participants in the design experiment that was reported on in the article were American undergraduate students who were preparing to join a primary teacher education course. A slightly modified version of the intervention was subsequently implemented, with researcher support and with remarkably similar results, by a secondary mathematics teacher in a Year 10 class in England (A. Stylianides 2009). The successful replication of the results of the intervention in a new cultural setting and with students of a different educational level provides further support to the theoretical framework that underpinned the design and implementation of the intervention. Also, the replication opens up a window of optimism that appropriately modified versions of the intervention may be used successfully in other settings and with younger students.

Conclusion

The four core readings addressed a set of related conceptual and instructional issues, and exemplified an important body of research within mathematics education that focuses on the notion of proof. Specifically, the readings addressed the following issues: the meaning of proof and adverse consequences of the use of unclear terminology for mathematics education research in the area of proof (Balacheff 2002; Stylianides 2007); students' different ways of thinking about proof, some of which derive from deeply rooted misconceptions such as that empirical arguments are proofs (Sowder and Harel 1998); and the role of instruction to support the development of students' ways of thinking about proof and to help them overcome misconceptions they have in this area (Stylianides 2007; Stylianides and Stylianides 2009).

Although not all readings focused on the same level of education, they form in my view a coherent reading package that can inform research and practice across all levels of education. This can be partly attributed to the fact that, unlike many mathematical topics (e.g. fractions) or operations (e.g. addition) whose curricular treatment is typically age specific, the notion of proof is, or can be, relevant throughout students' mathematical education as a vehicle to mathematical sense making.

There are several other important issues within the selected body of research that I have not discussed in this chapter. These include the elements of teacher knowledge about proof that can be important for effective mathematics teaching (e.g. Stylianides and Ball 2008), the role that technology can play in the teaching and learning of proof (e.g. Jones 2000; Mariotti 2000; Marrades and Gutiérrez 2000), practices involved in reading or evaluating proofs (e.g. Inglis and Mejia-Ramos 2009; Stylianides and Stylianides 2009;

Weber and Mejia-Ramos 2011), the place of proof in curriculum or textbook materials (e.g. G. Stylianides 2009), and so on.

Notes

1. The page numbers in this section refer to the online version of Balacheff (2002).
2. Betsy's argument (line 14) would likely meet the stricter standard of proof set by the second researcher epistemology.

Further reading

Hanna, G. and Jahnke, H. N., 1996. Proof and proving. In A. J. Bishop, K. Clements, C. Keitel, J. Kilpatrick and C. Laborde, eds, *International handbook of mathematics education*. Dordrecht, Netherlands: Kluwer, 877–908.

Healy, L. and Hoyles, C., 2000. A study of proof conceptions in algebra. *Journal for Research in Mathematics Education*, 31, 396–428.

Marrades, R. and Gutiérrez, Á., 2000. Proofs produced by secondary school students learning geometry in a dynamic computer environment. *Educational Studies in Mathematics*, 44, 87–125.

Stylianides, G. J., 2009. Reasoning-and-proving in school mathematics textbooks. *Mathematical Thinking and Learning*, 11, 258–88.

Additional references

Ball, D. L. and Bass, H., 2000. Making believe: the collective construction of public mathematical knowledge in the elementary classroom. In D. Philips, ed., *Constructivism in education: Yearbook of the National Society for the Study of Education*. Chicago, IL: University of Chicago Press, 193–224.

—, 2003. Making mathematics reasonable in school. In J. Kilpatrick, W. G. Martin and D. Schifter, eds, *A research companion to principles and standards for school mathematics*. Reston, VA: National Council of Teachers of Mathematics, 27–44.

Ball, D. L., Hoyles, C., Jahnke, H. N. and Movshovitz-Hadar, N., 2002. The teaching of proof. In L. I. Tatsien, ed., *Proceedings of the International Congress of Mathematicians*, Vol. 3. Beijing, China: Higher Education Press, 907–20.

Bruner, J., 1960. *The process of education*. Cambridge, MA: Harvard University Press.

Chazan, D., 1993. High school geometry students' justification for their views of empirical evidence and mathematical proof. *Educational Studies in Mathematics*, 24 (4), 359–87.

Cobb, P., Confrey, J., diSessa, A., Lehrer, R. and Schauble, L., 2003. Design experiments in educational research. *Educational Researcher*, 32 (1), 9–13.

Coe, R. and Ruthven, K., 1994. Proof practices and constructs of advanced mathematics students. *British Educational Research Journal*, 20, 41–53.

Goulding, M., Rowland, T. and Barber, P., 2002. Does it matter? Primary teacher trainees' subject knowledge in mathematics. *British Educational Research Journal*, 28, 689–704.

Hanna, G., 1995. Challenges to the importance of proof. *For the Learning of Mathematics*, 15 (3), 42–9.

Harel, G., 1998. Two dual assertions: the first on learning and the second on teaching (or vice versa). *American Mathematical Monthly*, 105, 497–507.

Harel, G. and Sowder, S. (1998). Students' proof schemes. In A. H. Schoenfeld, J. Kaput and E. Dubinsky, eds, *Research in College Mathematics Education III*. Providence, RI: American Mathematical Society, 234–83.

Inglis, M. and Mejia-Ramos, J. P., 2009. The effect of authority on the persuasiveness of mathematical arguments. *Cognition & Instruction*, 27, 25–50.

Jones, K., 2000. Providing a foundation for deductive reasoning: students' interpretations when using dynamic geometry software and their evolving mathematical explanations. *Educational Studies in Mathematics*, 44, 55–85.

Kitcher, P., 1984. *The nature of mathematical knowledge*. New York: Oxford University Press.

Küchemann, D. and Hoyles, C., 2001–3. *Longitudinal proof project* (Technical reports for Year 8–10 surveys). London, UK: Institute of Education. Available at www.mathsmed.co.uk/ioe-proof/techreps.html [accessed on 3 May 2009].

Lakatos, I., 1976. *Proofs and refutations: the logic of mathematical discovery*. Cambridge, UK: Cambridge University Press.

Lampert, M., 1992. Practice and problems in teaching authentic mathematics. In F. K. Oser, A. Dick and J. Patry, eds, *Effective and responsible teaching: the new synthesis*. San Francisco, CA: Jossey-Bass, 295–314.

Mariotti, M. A., 2000. Introduction to proof: the mediation of a dynamic software environment. *Educational Studies in Mathematics*, 44, 25–53.

Martin, W. G. and Harel, G., 1989. Proof frames of preservice elementary teachers. *Journal for Research in Mathematics Education*, 20, 41–51.

National Council of Teachers of Mathematics, 2000. *Principles and standards for school mathematics*. Reston, VA: National Council of Teachers of Mathematics.

Reid, D. A., 2002. Conjectures and refutations in Grade 5 mathematics. *Journal for Research in Mathematics Education*, 33, 5–29.

—, 2005. The meaning of proof in mathematics education. In M. Bosch, ed., *Proceedings of the 4th Conference of the European Society for Research in Mathematics Education*. Sant Feliu de Guixols, Spain, 458–68. Available at http://ermeweb.free.fr/CERME4/CERME4_WG4.pdf [accessed on 11 December 2011].

Schoenfeld, A. H., 1994. What do we know about mathematics curricula? *Journal of Mathematical Behavior*, 13, 55–80.

Schwab, J. J., 1978. Education and the structure of the disciplines. In I. Westbury and N. J. Wilkof, eds, *Science, curriculum, and liberal education: selected essays*. Chicago & London: University of Chicago Press, 229–72.

Senk, S. L., 1985. How well do students write geometry proofs? *Mathematics Teacher*, 78 (6), 448–56.

Sowder, L. and Harel, G., 2003. Case studies of mathematics majors' proof understanding, production, and appreciation. *Canadian Journal of Science, Mathematics and Technology Education*, 3, 251–67.

Stylianides, A. J., 2009. Breaking the equation 'empirical argument = proof'. *Mathematics Teaching*, 213, 9–14. Available at http://nrich.maths.org/6664 [accessed on 16 December 2011].

Stylianides, A. J. and Ball, D. L., 2008. Understanding and describing mathematical knowledge for teaching: knowledge about proof for engaging students in the activity of proving. *Journal of Mathematics Teacher Education*, 11, 307–32.

Stylianides, G. J. and Stylianides, A. J., 2009. Proof constructions and evaluations. *Educational Studies in Mathematics*, 72, 237–53.

Weber, K. and Mejia-Ramos, J. P., 2011. Why and how mathematicians read proofs: an exploratory study. *Educational Studies in Mathematics*, 76, 329–44.

Yackel, E. and Hanna, G., 2003. Reasoning and proof. In J. Kilpatrick, W. G. Martin and D. Schifter, eds, *A research companion to principles and standards for school mathematics*. Reston, VA: National Council of Teachers of Mathematics, 227–36.

Zack, V., 1997. 'You have to prove us wrong': proof at the elementary school level. In E. Pehkonen, ed., *Proceedings of the 21st Conference of the International Group for the Psychology of Mathematics Education*, Vol. 4. Lahti, Finland: University of Helsinki, 291–8.

Zazkis, R. and Chernoff, E. J., 2008. What makes a counterexample exemplary? *Educational Studies in Mathematics*, 68, 195–208.

Mathematical Problem Solving

Lieven Verschaffel, Fien Depaepe and Wim Van Dooren

10

Core readings

The Core readings addressed in this chapter are as follows:

Schoenfeld, A., 1983. Beyond the purely cognitive: belief systems, social cognitions, and metacognitions as driving forces in intellectual performance. *Cognitive Science*, 7, 329–63.

Hiebert, J., Carpenter, T. P., Fennema, E., Fuson, K., Human, P., Murray, H., et al., 1996. Problem solving as a basis for reform in curriculum and instruction: the case of mathematics. *Educational Researcher*, 25 (4), 12–21.

Verschaffel, L., De Corte, E., Lasure, S., Van Vaerenbergh, G., Bogaerts, H. and Ratinckx, E., 1999. Design and evaluation of a learning environment for mathematical modeling and problem solving in upper elementary school children. *Mathematical Thinking and Learning*, 1, 195–230.

Dewolf, T., Van Dooren, W. and Verschaffel, L., 2011. Upper elementary school children's understanding and solution of a quantitative problem inside and outside the mathematics class. *Learning and Instruction*, 21, 770–80.

Introduction

Consideration of the role of problem solving in (mathematics) education goes to the heart of radical reappraisals of the purposes of schooling. For much of the past century schools focused on teaching low-literacy skills of reading, writing and calculating. Developments during the latter part of the century – the explosion of knowledge and its accessibility, globalization, political instability, resource management and climate change – have accelerated the need for high literacy, including gathering and interpreting new information, evaluating complex arguments, identifying and solving problems (Kuhn 2005; National Research

Council 2000). Thus, we see a major shift from the accumulation of factual knowledge and facility in routine operations to cognitive tools for making sense of and evaluating complex information, and the ability to deal with novel situations.

Mathematics (education) is a domain wherein this shift in orientation towards high literacy has manifested itself most clearly. For instance, when asked what mathematics is, many now give problem solving a central, integrated, place in their definition (De Corte et al. 1996), a centrality that extends to most countries' current mathematics curricula (Törner et al. 2007). As an illustration, the National Council of Teachers of Mathematics (2000) acknowledges that an evolving societal context requires from its citizens increased mathematical thinking and higher-order problem-solving skills. In its standards, students' acquisition of a new set of mathematics basics, including metacognitive and heuristic skills, is privileged above the teaching and practising of procedures and algorithms.

What is a mathematical problem?

In general, a mathematical problem[1] is a task for which no routine method of solution is available. Relatedly, problem solving may be defined as 'cognitive processing directed at transforming a given situation into a goal situation when no solution method is obvious to the problem solver' (Mayer and Wittrock 2006, p. 2007). Thus, whether a task is a problem or not depends on the existing routine expertise of the solver(s) and the nature of the tools available. For example, the task 'divide 120 marbles equally among 8 children' may be a problem (though solvable) for a young child, but not for one who has learnt the long division algorithm or who has (and knows how to use) a calculator. The problematic character of a task also depends on the classroom culture and practice: 'Tasks are inherently neither problematic nor routine, whether they become problematic depends on how teachers and students treat them' (Hiebert et al. 1996, p. 16). Thus, virtually any mathematics can, at any level, be taught by presenting it as a problem to be solved given the resources available to the learners and guidance from the teacher. As Hiebert et al. (1996) argue convincingly, even topics usually treated as routine skills, such as the development of arithmetic facts, knowledge or computational algorithms, can be made 'problematic'.

Types of problems

In the literature on (mathematical) problem solving, distinction is made between various types of problems. A first distinction is between well-defined and ill-defined problems (Newell and Simon 1972). In the former, the given state, the goal state and the allowable operators are clearly specified – chess problems offer a prototypical example. An example in the domain of mathematics is to find the value of the unknown x in the expression $5x - 12 = 2x + 8$. In an ill-defined problem, by contrast, one or more of the given state, goal state and allowable operators are less clearly specified. An example here could be choosing between different subscription formulas offered by mobile phone companies in relation to one's personal phone habits.

Second, researchers have developed problem typologies, each associated with the particular cognitive operation or skill necessary to solve them (Greeno 1991). There are inductive problems, in which several instances are given and the problem solver must discover the rule or pattern involved (as in the well-known Fibonacci sequence mathematical series such as 1, 1, 2, 3, 5, 8, 13, . . .). There are transformation problems, where an initial state is given and the problem solver must find a sequence of operation that will produce the goal state (as in a mathematical word problem or a mathematical proof). Lastly, there are arrangement problems, in which all of the elements are given and the problem solver must arrange them in such a way that the problem is solved (as in a magic square puzzle). Greeno points out that not all problems will neatly fall into one of these three classifications and that some consist of a combination of classifications.

Third, focusing on the importance of subject-matter knowledge, is the distinction between 'knowledge-lean' and 'knowledge-rich' problems (Glaser 1984). Puzzle-like tasks (such as the well-known 'Tower of Hanoi' puzzle) are examples of the former category. Constructing a mathematical model for a complex social phenomenon is an example of the latter.

Finally, a distinction is frequently made between pure problems and application or modelling problems (De Corte et al. 1996). Although some authors consider application and modelling problems as synonyms, others use the term 'modelling problems' for a specific subset of (application) problems wherein the main difficulty relates to the relationship between real-world situation wherein the problem is embedded and the abstract formal mathematical structure that can be used to model and solve that problem. These problems, in which real-world considerations play a critical role during the various phases of the solution process, may serve as appropriate vehicles for teaching and learning mathematical modelling (Greer 1997).

Scientific views on problem solving

Historically, problem-solving research has been undertaken within psychology. Greeno et al. (1996) distinguished three broad psychological approaches, that is, the behaviourist, cognitive/rationalist and situative perspective. The first, and earliest, draws on behaviourism and has been largely discredited in relation to higher-level cognitive processes, including problem solving. The second had its roots in Gestalt Psychology and Piaget's theory. In the 1970s and 1980s, in parallel with work in Artificial Intelligence, the information-processing view of problem solving became dominant. In this tradition, a central concept is the 'problem space', which is assumed to contain (1) the initial state of the problem, (2) a set of operators transforming given states into new states, (3) a set of possible states of the problem, (4) the desired goal states, as well as (5) additional knowledge available to the problem solver (see Newell and Simon 1972). Problem solving is then defined as searching the problem space in order to transform the initial state into a goal state. According to this theory, success in problem solving and transfer is assumed to depend on the quality of activated knowledge schemata and of general cognitive strategies (heuristics). A well-known example is the general heuristic 'means–end analysis', the key idea of which is to analyse differences between the goal state and the current state of a problem and to strategically apply operators to reduce the difference.

As the richness and complexity of mathematical and other tasks, and the accompanying methodologies used by cognitive psychologists, increased, researchers became increasingly aware that their conceptualization of problem solving was too narrow and that a more comprehensive theory was needed encompassing aspects that are not rational in a narrow sense, such as intuition (Fischbein 1987), metacognition (Schoenfeld 1992), affect (beliefs, attitudes and emotions) (McLeod 1992) and visually and bodily mediated thinking (Lakoff and Núñez 2000). These developments, which are sometimes referred to as the 'second wave of the cognitive revolution' (Greer and Verschaffel 1990), as opposed to the first wave characterized by Newell and Simon (mentioned earlier) gave rise to the third perspective, the situative perspective, wherein knowing and problem solving are viewed in terms of practices of communities and the abilities of individuals to function and participate in these practices: whether one is able to solve a problem and the nature of that solution depend on the culture and the practices of the group in which one has been initiated, and how well one is able to participate in these practices. Illustrating this broadening of the scope 'beyond the purely cognitive' is Schoenfeld's (1983) multidimensional analysis and interpretation of mathematical problem-solving behaviour, wherein he raised a series of theoretical and methodological issues that represented a clear break away from the dominant cognitive paradigm and made a plea for considering a much wider variety of knowledge and behaviour – including the problem solver's knowledge base, heuristics, control strategies, belief systems and their mutual interplay. Later he would, in line with the situative perspective, also include another element, namely the classroom practices in which the problem solver is participating.

Another important line of research has contrasted learning and problem solving in the context of school mathematics with other contexts, such as informal mathematical practices out of school, as in Nunes et al.'s (1993) study that compared the solution processes of Brazilian street-vendors in the formal context of the mathematics lesson with an informal selling context at a street corner or on an open market. Their study showed that children performed better and applied qualitatively different strategies on problems in the out-of-school contexts compared to their performance on and strategies for isomorphic school mathematical tasks.

More recently, Dewolf et al. (2011) investigated two representative groups of students solving the same problem about fair sharing in either mathematics or religion classes. Also, students were asked to evaluate different fictional students' responses to that problem. Their results revealed that students in the mathematics class preferred precise numerical answers motivated by calculations, whereas students in the religion class had a preference for a verbal description of the solution based on non-numerical arguments. Moreover, 'fairness' was interpreted and used differently in both class contexts, leading to different preferential situational and mathematical models and solutions. Such studies provide a clear illustration for the general phenomenon that people's ways of thinking and problem solving are context-sensitive, and that even such seemingly context-immune tasks as mathematical problems may be represented and solved differently in different situations.

Whereas mathematics has always been a major source of examples and applications for psychological theories of problem solving, mathematicians have also contributed to theory and research about mathematical problem solving through reflections on their own experiences as (mathematical) problem solvers. In particular, the mathematician Polya (1945) proposed a four-phase model of problem solving involving understanding the problem, devising a plan, carrying out the plan and, finally, looking back. Each phase was accompanied by a set of heuristics, or guidelines, to support the process. For example, as part of devising a plan, one might ask, have I seen this problem before (possibly in a different format), do I know a related problem, could I reformulate the problem? Polya's framework has acted as a starting point for much analytic and intervention research. Being influenced by Gestalt theory, Polya can be considered the most important source of ideas about mathematical problem solving in recent decades.

Phases and components of problem solving

Drawing on Polya, it seems clear that solving a problem can be summarized as representing, planning, executing and evaluating – frequently with an overarching monitoring or self-regulatory process (De Corte et al. 1996; Mayer and Wittrock 2006; Polya 1945; Schoenfeld 1992). In actual problem-solving behaviour, it may be that some phases are bypassed. In competent problem solving, it is frequently difficult to distinguish between the different stages and the process is typically cyclic rather than linear.

There is now a rather broad consensus that success in mathematical problem solving (and modelling) requires the integrated mastery of the following five categories of cognitive, affective and cognative components (De Corte et al. 1996; Schoenfeld 1992):

- Well-organized and flexibly accessible domain-specific knowledge base involving the facts, symbols, concepts, rules, algorithms and other procedures that constitute the content of a subject-matter field (e.g. knowing that a rectangle is a special case of quadrilateral or knowing how to calculate the area of a rectangle).
- Heuristic methods, or search strategies for problem analysis and transformation which significantly increase the probability of finding a satisfactory solution because they induce a systematic approach to the problem at hand.

- Positive mathematics-related affect, involving positive emotions and attitudes towards mathematics and mathematics learning and teaching (see the chapter by Törner, this volume), as well as mathematics-related beliefs that comprise, in turn, the implicitly and explicitly held subjective conceptions about mathematics and mathematics education, about the self as a learner of mathematics, and about the social context of the mathematics classroom.
- Meta-knowledge involving knowledge about one's cognitive functioning – knowing that one's cognitive potential can be developed through learning and effort – as well as knowledge about one's motivation and emotions.
- Self-regulation embracing skills for the regulation of one's cognitive processes. These include metacognitive skills, for example, planning and monitoring one's problem-solving processes and meta-volitional skills, for example, keeping up one's attention and motivation to solve a given problem.

Instructional methods that promote problem solving

As a consequence of perceived societal needs for general problem-solving skills, and developments within (the first wave of) cognitive science, the 1970s and 1980s witnessed a strong trend among scientists and practitioners to develop general, domain-independent courses in problem solving. While some evaluation studies showed gains on various intelligence and/or problem-solving measures for children involved in such programmes, the overall results were disappointing, especially against the considerable investment of extra student time required (Mayer and Wittrock 2006; Schoenfeld 1992).

Several related reasons explain this disappointing finding (for a more detailed discussion see Schoenfeld 1985). First, descriptions of heuristics, such as those of Polya, were not sufficiently detailed for students, not yet familiar with them, to implement the strategies. For example, 'finding an easier related or analogous problem' can take very different forms for distinct kinds of problems. Second, teaching isolated heuristics does not substantially improve performance on new problems because learners are often unable to discover and decide which strategy is appropriate for the problem at hand. Besides heuristics, also meta-cognitive skills should be developed, with a view to enable students to self-regulate their problem-solving process and select the most appropriate heuristics dependent on the nature of the task and personal characteristics. Accordingly, they need to learn what a heuristic entails and how, when and why to apply it. Third, the fact that domain-independent problem-solving skills do not automatically transfer to specific knowledge domains (e.g. mathematics, writing) shows the importance of domain-specific training of problem-solving expertise. Fourth, complementary attention should be paid to the promotion of appropriate mathematics-related beliefs about mathematics education in general, and problem solving in particular.

Although such general courses retain some popularity, a newer generation of instructional programmes emerged focused on teaching relevant cognitive skills within the context of specific subjects (Mayer and Wittrock 2006). This shift from domain-independence to domain-specificity was accompanied by a change in instructional goals as well as in instructional approaches, as characterized by the inclusion of principles and ideas from the situative view, and, in particular, the notion of 'cognitive apprenticeship' (Collins et al. 1989).

A pioneering example is Schoenfeld's (1985) instructional program in which specific heuristics were taught to college students alongside metacognitive skills and beliefs. The core of the program comprised a five-stage metacognitive strategy that helps the learner to select the right heuristic(s) to solve a given problem. Besides modelling and whole-class discussion, Schoenfeld frequently used small-group problem solving whereby students are given ample opportunities to apply the learned heuristic and metacognitive skills. By asking three questions – (1) What are you doing? (2) Why are you doing this? and (3) If what you are doing now is successful, how will it help to find the solution? – students were encouraged to articulate and reflect on their problem-solving strategies and their accompanying beliefs. Schoenfeld's instructional program for mathematical problem solving served as one of the three exemplarily cases for Collins et al.'s (1989) cognitive apprenticeship model.

As a second example, we review a study by Verschaffel and his co-workers (Verschaffel et al. 1999). Unlike Schoenfeld's (1985) instructional program, which was designed to teach pure mathematical problem solving to college students, Verschaffel et al.'s (1999) study addressed upper primary school children solving mathematical application problems. They developed a learning environment in which eight heuristic strategies (e.g. make a drawing, make a scheme) were taught embedded in a five-stage self-regulatory strategy for solving complex, unfamiliar word problems. By creating an innovative classroom culture the learning environment aimed to foster in children positive beliefs about mathematical problem solving. The cornerstones of the learning environment were: (1) a set of functional, exciting and realistic application, and modelling problems; (2) a number of varying and powerful instructional techniques and classroom organization forms; and (3) an appropriate classroom culture, which aims at developing positive beliefs and attitudes towards problem solving. Overall, when compared with students working in traditional mathematics classrooms, the powerful learning environment had a positive effect on students' beliefs about and attitudes towards problem solving, their problem-solving behaviour, their use of heuristic strategies and their development of metacognitive skills. And, this was not only the case for the mathematically most able children, children of medium and low ability also benefited from the positive effects of the learning environment. As such, Verschaffel et al.'s study, reflective of other design experiments (see Cobb et al. (2003) for a summary of this research tradition[2]), shows that it is possible to substantially enhance elementary and secondary school students' problem-solving skills, strategies, attitudes and beliefs by putting them in an innovative classroom practice and culture that is intentionally and systematically aimed at these various problem-solving goals. Based on a review of this research evidence, Niss (2001, p. 8) concludes that students' capability in solving application and modelling problems 'can be learnt, and, according to the above-mentioned findings, has to be learnt, but at a cost, in terms of effort, complexity of task, time consumption and reduction of syllabus in the traditional sense'. A more general and more recent meta-analysis of intervention studies at the primary and secondary school level in the domains of mathematics as well as in the domain of reading and writing confirms the positive outcomes of such initial investigations (Dignath and Büttner 2008).

Problem solving as a vehicle for learning mathematics

Problem solving is important not only as a goal of instruction in itself, but also as a vehicle for learning mathematics. A number of related research projects in the United States and South Africa addressed children's well-known arithmetical deficiencies through a 'problem-solving approach' which Hiebert et al. (1996, p. 12) described and explained as follows:

> students should be allowed to make the subject problematic. We argue that this single principle captures what is essential for instructional practice. . . . Allowing the subject to be problematic means allowing students to wonder why things are, to inquire, to search for solutions, and to resolve incongruities. It means that both curriculum and instruction should begin with problems, dilemmas, and questions for students.

Hiebert et al.'s article is illustrative of a view among many mathematics educators that the activity of 'problematizing' leads to the construction of mathematical understanding. It reviews several examples of design experiments, realized by the authors, wherein this basic instructional design principle has been systematically applied as a basis for learning multidigit calculation, that have been successfully implemented and tested in different educational settings (including predominantly low socio-economic status classrooms). Hiebert et al. (1996) conclude that there are several advantages of a problem-based curriculum compared to a more traditional skills-based approach. First, students confronted with problems develop a deeper understanding of mathematical concepts and stronger links between their conceptual and procedural knowledge. Second, students immersed in problem-based approaches outperform those in traditional approaches on general metacognitive skills, enabling them to develop strategies, adapt them and apply them successfully in new problem situations, without performing weaker on traditional measures of mathematical performance. Third, such students develop more appropriate beliefs and more positive attitudes towards (learning) mathematics, influencing, in turn, their orientation towards future learning and problem-solving activities.

The notion that problem solving can be used as a vehicle for learning mathematics is also prominent in realistic mathematics education (Freudenthal 1983; see also the chapter by Anghileri, this volume) and related approaches that take a so-called modelling approach to mathematics education (Lesh and Doerr 2003), whereby learners are confronted with 'model eliciting activities', through which they can invent, extend, revise and refine many of the important mathematical ideas (such as the idea of multiplication, fractions or proportionality) throughout the mathematics curriculum. Through such activities students actively and constructively develop the intended mathematical ideas, by going through a series of increasingly abstract and formal modelling cycles in which the givens, goals and relevant solutions of a certain problem situation are continuously reinterpreted, rethought and renegotiated.

Conclusion

In this chapter, we have argued that problem solving has become both a central goal and an import feature of (mathematics) education. It is generally agreed that teaching mathematical problem solving and teaching mathematics through problem solving can increase interest, motivation and a sense of ownership of problem solving and learning in the individual student, and that these skills are essential in educating creative and critical citizens to collectively address the real problems that face humankind. However, many questions remain.

First, although we have used the term 'mathematical problem' to refer to non-routine tasks that solvers experience as 'problematic', it should be clear that there are no canonical definitions of the terms 'mathematical problem' and 'mathematical problem solving' (Törner et al. 2007). For instance, the term 'mathematical problem' often refers to traditional, routine (arithmetic or word) problems that can be solved by simple and straightforward application of standard procedures. But, partly as a consequence of the growing complexity of the personal and professional problems with which many people are confronted, some authors have introduced the notion of *complex* problem solving, referring to problems that comprise many highly interrelated variables that have to be considered in order to transfer a current state of a problem into a desirable goal state. Solving complex problems usually implies the acquisition and application of knowledge in opaque, complex, dynamic systems (Funke and Frensch 1995). However, it remains unclear whether this new category is theoretically needed and educationally helpful.

Second, although research on mathematical problem solving has yielded many insights into the nature and role of the components of the problem-solving model described, many questions remain, especially about the relative importance of and the interaction between these various components in general and the role of the various affective elements in particular. Probably, the rapidly developing fields of cognitive and affective neuroscience, which now also starts to explore the neuropsychological basis of the processes involved in the solution of more complex mathematical tasks, may yield research methods and findings to deepen our understanding of how these various components contribute in an integrated way to the solution of a mathematical problem (De Smedt et al. 2010).

Third, research has shown that learners frequently fail to solve mathematical problems they should be able to solve correctly given their domain-specific knowledge and skills.

Fischbein (1987) emphasized that some errors may be the consequence of pervasive intuitions that interfere with correct reasoning. The assumption is that students' problem-solving related reasoning is often led by external task features that are not intrinsically relevant to the task but draw students' attention away from those features that are pertinent to the problem situation. Of course, students' lack of metacognitive knowledge and skills plays a crucial role in this phenomenon.

Fourth, even though recent design experiments have yielded positive outcomes in terms of performance, underlying processes, and motivational and affective aspects of mathematics learning and problem solving, the results of these studies are not unanimously positive. In their review of the research literature on problem-based learning environments, Kirschner et al. (2006) argue that, although such instructional approaches are increasingly popular and intuitively appealing, they ignore the structures that constitute human cognitive architecture and evidence from many empirical studies consistently indicating that minimally guided instruction is less effective and less efficient than instructional approaches that emphasize strong guidance of the learning process. In their view, the advantage of guidance recedes only when learners have sufficiently high prior knowledge and skills to provide 'internal' guidance (Kirschner et al. 2006). More research is needed to further reveal for what purposes and under what conditions problem-based instruction is effective in mathematics education.

Finally, although problem solving and modelling are gradually being implemented in mathematical frameworks in many countries, it is still the case internationally that genuine and extensive problem-solving and modelling activities continue to be scarce in everyday school practice. There are several important barriers that may jeopardize a fluent and efficient implementation: (1) the difficulty of getting problem solving and modelling into (high-stakes) tests (partly because such higher-order skills are not viewed by many people as part of mathematics and partly because it is difficult to assess such complex skills in such tests), and (2) the high demands this problem-based and/or modelling approach puts on teachers' knowledge of the subject-matter domain, their pedagogical content knowledge, and their subjective beliefs about and attitudes towards mathematics, mathematical problem solving and its teaching and learning, as well as their more general didactical skills (e.g. classroom management). Therefore, pre-service as well as in-service teacher training should provide teachers with ample curricular material and support them in establishing a problem-based and modelling approach in their classroom.

Notes

1. Although the term 'problem' is often used in case of traditional, routine (arithmetic or word) problems that can be solved by a simple and straightforward application of standard procedures, we use the term 'problem' in this chapter in the strictly psychological meaning of the concept, that is, to refer to the 'problematic' (i.e. non-routine) nature of a task.

2. According to Cobb et al. (2003, p. 9) 'design experiments entail both "engineering" particular forms of learning and systematically studying those forms of learning within the context defined by the means of supporting them. This designed context is subject to test and revision, and the successive iterations that result play a role similar to that of systematic variation in experiment.'

Further reading

Lesh, R. and Doerr, H. M., eds, 2003. *Beyond constructivism. Models and modeling perspectives on mathematical problem solving, learning and teaching.* Mahwah, NJ: Lawrence Erlbaum.

Mayer, R. E. and Wittrock, M. C., 2006. Problem solving. In P. A. Alexander and P. H. Winne, eds, *Handbook of educational psychology.* New York: Macmillan, 287–303.

Schoenfeld, A. H., 1992. Learning to think mathematically. Problem solving, metacognition and sense-making in mathematics. In D. A. Grouws, ed., *Handbook of research on mathematics teaching and learning.* New York: Macmillan, 334–70.

Törner, G., Schoenfeld, A. H. and Reiss, K. M., eds, 2007. Problem solving around the world: summing up the state of the art. *ZDM – The International Journal on Mathematics Education,* 39 (5–6).

Additional references

Cobb, P., Confrey, J., diSessa, A., Lehrer, R. and Schauble, L., 2003. Design experiments in educational research. *Educational Researcher,* 32 (1), 9–13.

Collins, A., Brown, J. S. and Newman, S. E., 1989. Cognitive apprenticeship: teaching the crafts of reading, writing, and mathematics. In L. Resnick, ed., *Knowing, learning, and instruction: essays in honor of Robert Glaser.* Hillsdale, NJ: Erlbaum, 453–94.

De Corte, E., Greer, B. and Verschaffel, L., 1996. Mathematics teaching and learning. In D. C. Berliner and R. C. Calfee, eds, *Handbook of educational psychology.* New York: Macmillan, 491–549.

De Smedt, B., Ansari, D. Grabner, R. H., Hannula, M. M., Schneider, M. and Verschaffel, L., 2010. Cognitive neuroscience meets mathematics education. *Educational Research Review,* 5, 97–105.

Dewolf, T., Van Dooren, W. and Verschaffel, L., 2011. Upper elementary school children's understanding and solution of a quantitative problem inside and outside the mathematics class. *Learning and Instruction,* 21, 770–80.

Dignath, C. and Büttner, G., 2008. Components of fostering self-regulated learning among students. A meta-analysis on intervention studies at primary and secondary school level. *Metacognition and Learning,* 3, 231–64.

Fischbein, E., 1987. *Intuition in science and mathematics: an educational approach.* Dordrecht, Netherlands: Reidel.

Freudenthal, H., 1983. *Didactical phenomenology of mathematical structures.* Dordrecht, Netherlands: Kluwer.

Funke, J. and Frensch, P., eds, 1995. *Complex problem solving – the European perspective.* Hillsdale, NJ: Erlbaum.

Glaser, R., 1984. Education and thinking. The role of knowledge. *American Psychologist,* 39, 93–104.

Greeno, J., 1991. A view of mathematical problem solving in school. In M. U. Smith, ed., *Toward a unified theory of problem solving.* Hillsdale, NJ: Erlbaum, 69–98.

Greeno, J. G. Collins, A. M. and Resnick, L., 1996. Cognition and learning. In D. C. Berliner and R. C. Calfee, eds, *Handbook of educational psychology.* New York: Macmillan, 15–46.

Greer, B., 1997. Modelling reality in mathematics classrooms. *Learning and Instruction,* 7, 293–307.

Greer, B. and Verschaffel, L., 1990. Introduction to the special issue on mathematics as a proving ground for information-processing theories. *International Journal of Educational Research*, 14, 3–12.

Hiebert, J., Carpenter, T. P., Fennema, E., Fuson, K., Human, P., Murray, H., et al., 1996. Problem solving as a basis for reform in curriculum and instruction: the case of mathematics. *Educational Researcher*, 25 (4), 12–21.

Kirschner, P. A., Sweller, J. and Clark, R. E., 2006. Why minimal guidance during instruction does not work: an analysis of the failure of constructivist, discovery, problem-based, experiential, and inquiry-based teaching. *Educational Psychologist*, 41 (2), 75–86.

Kuhn, D., 2005. *Education for thinking*. Cambridge, MA: Harvard University Press.

Lakoff, G. and Núñez, R. E., 2000. *Where mathematics comes from*. New York: Basic Books.

McLeod, D., 1992. Research on affect in mathematics education: a reconceptualization. In D. A. Grows, ed., *Handbook of Research on Mathematics Teaching and Learning*. New York: Macmillan, 575–96.

National Council of Teachers of Mathematics, 2000. *Principles and standards for school mathematics*. Reston, VA: National Council of Teachers of Mathematics.

National Research Council, 2000. *How people learn: brain, mind, experience, and school*. Committee on Developments in the Science of Learning and Committee on Learning Research and Educational Practice. Washington, DC: National Academy Press.

Newell, A. and Simon, H. A., 1972. *Human problem solving*. Englewood Cliffs, NJ: Prentice-Hall.

Niss, M., 2001. Issues and problems of research on the teaching and learning of applications and modelling. In J. F. Matos, W. Blum, S. K. Houston and S. P. Carreira, eds, *Modelling and mathematics education. ICTMA 9: applications in science and technology*. Chichester, UK: Horwood, 72–89.

Nunes, T., Schliemann, A. D. and Carraher, D. W., 1993. *Street mathematics and school mathematics*. Cambridge: Cambridge University Press.

Polya, G., 1945. *How to solve it*. Princeton, NJ: Princeton University Press.

Schoenfeld, A. H., 1983. Beyond the purely cognitive: belief systems, social cognitions, and metacognitions as driving forces in intellectual performance. *Cognitive Science*, 7, 329–63.

—, 1985. *Mathematical problem solving*. New York: Academic Press.

Verschaffel, L., De Corte, E., Lasure, S., van Vaerenbergh, G., Bogaerts, H. and Ratinckx, E., 1999. Design and evaluation of a learning environment for mathematical modeling and problem solving in upper elementary school children. *Mathematical Thinking and Learning*, 1, 195–230.

Verschaffel, L., Greer, B. and De Corte, E., 2007. Whole number concepts and operations. In F. Lester, ed., *Second handbook of research on mathematics teaching and learning*. Charlotte, NC: Information Age Publishing, 557–628.

Algebra 11

Daniel Chazan

Core readings

The Core readings addressed in this chapter are as follows:

Herbst, P. and Chazan, D., 2012. On the instructional triangle and the sources of justification for the actions of the mathematics teacher. *ZDM – The International Journal on Mathematics Education*, 44 (5), 601–12.[1]

Schwartz, J. and Yerushalmy, M., 1992/2003. Getting students to function in algebra. In I. Wirszup and R. Streit, eds, *Developments in school mathematics education around the world, Volume 3: Proceedings of the 3rd UCSMP International Conference on Mathematics Education*. Reston, VA: National Council of Teachers of Education, 303–18.[2]

Mesa, V., 2004. Characterizing practices associated with functions in middle school textbooks: an empirical approach. *Educational Studies in Mathematics*, 56 (2), 255–86.

Yerushalmy, M. and Chazan, D., 2002. Flux in school algebra: curricular change, graphing technology, and research on student learning and teacher knowledge. In L. English, ed., *Handbook of international research in mathematics education*. Hillsdale, NJ: Erlbaum, 725–55.

Introduction

This chapter is primarily situated in the content of school algebra, but its focus is on exploring two related ways of conceptualizing what mathematics educators might mean by a 'curricular approach' to an area of mathematics to be taught. It draws on four core readings. Framed against a discussion of the changing nature of school algebra as summarized in the chapter by Yerushalmy and Chazan (2002), the chapter explores first Schwartz and Yerushalmy's (1992/2003) notion of fundamental objects of study and a 'processes on objects' approach to curriculum. Second, it examines the notion of instructional situations (Herbst and Chazan 2012) and curriculum as a collection of instructional situations – or practices from Mesa's (2004) textbook analysis – aimed at developing particular student conceptions. In this way, the chapter suggests that our field should continue to push forward to develop a more carefully defined and theoretical register for communicating its questions, results and understandings.

Exploring the meaning of approach: Approaches to school algebra

Labaree (2003) suggests that a lack of a theoretical 'register' (see the chapter by Barwell, this volume) in educational research causes a set of challenges when educators steeped in practice and its registers seek to become educational researchers. He suggests that when doing social science, scholars often use everyday terms in a theoretical sense or continue to use everyday terms with meanings that are not yet connected to theoretical frameworks. One instance of this challenge can be found in the ways in which scholars working in mathematics education use the term 'approach', a challenge that is particularly acute when it comes to discussions of the school algebra curriculum and how it is changing. As scholars seek to understand how what is taught to students in school under the label of algebra is shifting (Kilpatrick and Izsak 2008), many have attempted to characterize these shifts by describing competing approaches to, or perspectives on, school algebra; the word 'approach' has been tasked with capturing a wide range of dimensions of classroom interaction. Descriptors have included a focus on processes like generalization, problem-solving and modelling perspectives on introducing school algebra (Bednarz et al. 1996); ones that focus on tools like a spreadsheet approach to algebra (e.g. Sutherland and Rojano 1993); or content-focused descriptions like structural algebra (in Sutherland et al. 2001) or functions-based approaches to school algebra (Schwartz and Yerushalmy 1992/2003); in addition to terms that tag either pedagogical or epistemological perspectives (The APPA Group and Sutherland 2004).

Substantive structures in mathematics and the curriculum

To begin to work towards a narrower view of what an approach to curricular content might mean, I'll begin with science educator Joseph Schwab's (1978) way of conceptualizing one narrow aspect of what one might mean by an approach to school algebra. In particular, his work suggests a way to examine and describe a curricular approach to a content area. Schwab proposes that in considering education and the disciplines (like science and mathematics), it can be useful to consider the disciplines from perspectives that examine their substantive structures, as well as perspectives that examine what he calls the syntactic perspective on the structure of disciplines (which we will not examine here, but might lead towards processes like generalizing, modelling, etc. Schwab's distinction is also discussed in the chapter by Rowland, this volume). An example Schwab gives for the substantive structure of the disciplines involves 'ways in which biologists can conceive the organism for purposes of investigation' (p. 247). Furthermore, he suggests that most disciplines have more than one substantive structure. Based on this notion of Schwab's, elsewhere (Chazan 2000, pp. 59–75), I have tried to articulate how mathematics curricula in general, and algebra curricula in particular, include a perspective on the fundamental objects of study of an area of study. In the remainder of this chapter, I would like to explore this narrower sense of what one might mean by an approach to a mathematical field of study; that is, identifying how a curriculum might want teachers and students to conceptualize the fundamental objects of study in the mathematical arena they are engaged in teaching and learning. But, before continuing, there is one more observation to make.

On page 244 of his 1978 chapter, Schwab comes close to suggesting that mathematics may have only one substantive structure. If this view were correct, there would be little utility to describing a curricular perspective on the fundamental objects of study in a mathematical arena. However, this way of thinking does not seem to fit how mathematicians view their subject. For example, in *How Mathematicians Think*, mathematician William Byers suggests that 'ambiguity involves a single situation or idea that is perceived in two self-consistent but mutually incompatible frames of reference' (2007, p. 28) and that conceptualized in this way 'ambiguity is a crucial mechanism in mathematics' (p. 77). Byers is well aware that his formulation might sound strange to many, especially to non-mathematicians, but he then shows that others have appreciated the power of ambiguity in mathematics. For example, he quotes approvingly from a piece by William Thurston, a noted mathematician, about the variety of 'different ways of thinking about or conceiving of the derivative' (Table 11.1).

Table 11.1 Different ways of conceiving the derivative listed in Thurston (1994, p. 163)

1. Infinitesimal: The ratio of the infinitesimal change in the value of a function to the infinitesimal change in a function.

2. Symbolic: The derivative of x^n is nx^{n-1}, the derivative of $\sin(x)$ is $\cos(x)$ etc.

3. Logical: $f'(x) = d$ if and only if for every ε there is a δ such that when $0 < |\Delta x| < \delta$

$$\left| \frac{f(x + \Delta x) - f(x)}{\Delta x} - d \right| < \varepsilon$$

4. Geometric: The derivative is the slope of a line to the graph of the function, if the graph has a tangent.

5. Rate: The instantaneous speed of $f(t)$, when t is the time.

6. Approximation: The derivative of a function is the best linear approximation to the function near a point.

7. Microscopic: The derivative of a function is the limit of what you get by looking at it under a microscope of higher and higher power.

Consonant with Byers' perspective, I suggest that when it comes to representing mathematics to students, there are, to paraphrase Thurston, different ways of thinking about or conceptualizing the mathematics itself. Furthermore, I suggest that the importance of understanding this aspect of the choices made in the development of curriculum suggests developing the term 'curricular approach' to capture this understanding.

Different ways of thinking about equations in two variables: The curricular challenge of multiple substantive structures

Thurston's point is not only true for advanced mathematical subjects, but also for the mathematics that is at the heart of the school curriculum. Related to Thurston's argument, Zalman Usiskin (1988) famously points out that different equations have different 'feels' to them. He uses five equations to make his point, which can be seen in Table 11.2.

Typically equation (1) is called a formula, (2) an equation (or open sentence) to solve, (3) an identity, (4) a property, and (5) an equation of a function of direct variation (not to be solved) (Usiskin 1988, p. 9). Differences in the names mathematicians use 'reflect different uses to which the idea of variable is put'. For example, in (1) A, L and W stand for quantities and have the 'feel' of knowns, while it is only with (5) that the 'feel' of variability emerges.

In an effort to underline Usiskin's point, Yerushalmy and Chazan (2002, p. 728) add a sixth equation to Usiskin's list, $5x + y = 5$. Their argument being that such equations present, essentially, a range of perspectives on the nature of variables, each with a different 'feel'. They write that, 'when focusing on solutions to equations . . . the xs and ys in an equation in two "variables" seem less fixed than the xs in an equation in one "variable"', even though when 'one is given a value for x in $5x + y = 5$, one then has an equation in one variable that can be solved.' Also, an equation like $5x + y = 5$, even though it is equivalent to the function $f(x) = 5 - 5x$, 'feels' different. In the former 'the focus is solely on the values of the letters for which the equation is true', that is unknown numbers, 'rather than quantities that vary'.

In so doing they outline how different perspectives on what an equation represents (different substantive structures) bring with them particular understandings of the question that is being asked when one solves an equation, as well as differences in the roles which graphical and tabular representations might play in answering such questions.

Table 11.2 Five example equations provided in Usiskin (1988)

(1) A = LW	(2) 40 = 5x	(3) sin$x$ = cos$x$ • tan$x$
(4) $1 = n \cdot \dfrac{1}{n}$	(5) y = kx	

Table 11.3 Ways of thinking about equations adapted from Yerushalmy and Chazan (2002)

What does an equation in two variables represent?	Questions asked when solving an equation in two variables	Linked tabular and graphical representations
A 2D solution set	In a conditional statement of the form 'For this set of replacement values for x and y, the equation generates true statements', what coordinated pairs of numbers can be used to make the conditional statement a true statement?	Two column table of coordinated xs and ys. Graph of an equation in the Cartesian plane (any point can be on or off).
A relation between replacement sets for the two variables	What coordinated pairs of values are related in the way indicated by this equation?	Two column table: x and y, where one is computed from the other. Graph of an equation in the Cartesian plane (any point can be on or off).
A set of arithmetic sentences	Which arithmetic sentences generated from the template provided by this equation are true and which are false?	Two-dimensional table with x values on one dimension, y on another, and T or F in the cells. Graph in the Cartesian plane (any point can be on or off).
A coordinate triple with unknown inputs	What inputs to the expression on one side will produce the output on the other?	Two-dimensional table with x values on one dimension, y on another, and output of the expression in the cells. A point on a graph in 3D space.
A function of one variable	What coordinated pairs of values are generated by replacing x with members of a given set (the domain)?	Tables with x, and f(x) computed from x. Graph of a function in the plane (only one point a particular x value).
A comparison of two functions of two variables	For what inputs to the expressions on either side of the equality, will the outputs of each be the same?	Table with x values on one dimension, y on another, and output of the two expressions in each cell. Graph of two functions in 3D space.

The point in adding this additional equation, and in outlining the varieties of meanings equations can take on, is to show that one's perspective on what the objects of study in algebra are – in this case, equations – shapes the sorts of curricular expectations one might have for how students solve problems (similar to Balacheff and Gaudin's (2010) notion of conception). Thus, to go back to Schwab, the examples in Table 11.3 show how different substantive structures for the discipline have differing curricular ramifications in terms of what students can be expected to do when solving equations.

Processes on Objects: One way to characterize choices made about substantive structures in school curriculum

Continuing with algebra, it is evident that what is meant by algebra in the discipline has changed over time. While historically algebraic techniques developed to solve varieties of equations (captured in a field of study labelled the Theory of Equations), beginning in the early twentieth century, modern ideas of algebra conceive of polynomials and of the solving of equations in dramatically different ways (for one telling of the story of this shift, see van der Waerden 1985). Algebraists now consider groups, rings and fields as the ways to conceive of the mathematical objects that they explore. As the substantive structures of the discipline itself shifted, educators at the time of the New Math (see the chapter by Jablonka, this volume) considered whether the substantive structures of the school algebra curriculum should also shift. Critics of the New Math (e.g. Thom 1986) suggested that if the substantive structures of the school algebra curriculum should change then they should not necessarily change to match the abstractions of the discipline. Instead, as Jim Kaput (1995) has argued, when considering how to conceptualize the school algebra curriculum, in addition to considering the discipline of mathematics, one must also take into account the role that school algebra plays in the process of allocating life opportunities in society. Teachers and schools have other obligations besides an obligation to disciplinary points of view (Herbst and Chazan 2011).

It is against this background that Schwartz and Yerushalmy's core reading can be read as a particular proposal for describing the substantive structures of mathematics that lie behind a mathematics curriculum. In this piece, the authors stress the importance of having a curricular point of view on the fundamental objects of study in a curricular area, as well as a description of the nature of the operations on those objects of study.

Operations on functions: One way to understand school algebra

In addition to making a general point about curriculum, Schwartz and Yerushalmy also suggest that when it comes to much of the secondary school curriculum, from Algebra to Calculus, functions are a viable candidate for a fundamental object of study; they argue that 'the function, and its entailed concept – the variable, can serve as the root construct on which all of the mathematical objects of algebra can be built' (p. 18). Central to their argument is the way in which many of the common tasks carried out in school algebra can be (re)conceived as involving operations on single functions or on pairs of functions (see the chart on p. 6 of their article). Operating on individual functions (e.g. functions on points, linear functions, quadratic functions, absolute value functions, rational functions, exponential and logarithmic functions), students early on learn to:

- represent a given function symbolically (e.g. moving from 'number recipes' given in words to expressions and function notation);
- represent a given function graphically (by learning about key points like intercepts, vertices, points of inflection, slope, concavity, etc.);
- manipulate functions symbolically to create new functions (to learn about the influence of coefficients of different sorts on the behaviour of functions);
- re-represent functions symbolically while maintaining function values (known in school as simplifying or rewriting the function);
- manipulating functions graphically to create new functions (to understand the impact of graphical transformations on the coefficients of functional expressions in different forms).

Later, when learning Calculus and focusing on single functions, they learn to examine how the values of a function

- change, and come to create a new derivative function from an original function;
- accumulate, and come to create new functions with the semi-definite integral and families of functions with the indefinite integral.

And, when operating on pairs of functions, students early on learn to

- identify the solution sets for equations and inequalities depending on the nature of the functions that are involved (linear equations, quadratic equations, absolute value inequalities, etc.);
- demonstrate that pairs of expressions represent the same function (known in school as proving identities);
- construct new functions from binary operations on given functions.

And, in calculus, they learn about ways to

- understand the behaviour of the derivative of a complicated function from the behaviour of its constituent functions;
- re-represent complicated functions as created from simpler functions in order to be able to take particular classes of integrals.

Schwartz and Yerushalmy's proposal for conceptualizing school algebra is one attempt to make the unruly school algebra curriculum more coherent and focused. They propose one particular substantive structure for understanding large swathes of school mathematics that puts many aspects of school algebra in a new light. Perhaps overstating their case for the utility of this perspective, they maintain that 'the function is the only pedagogically necessary and desirable object in these subjects [algebra, trigonometry, probability and statistics, pre-calculus and calculus]' (p. 2).

One challenge to their proposal is that they do not indicate what they mean by a function or the function concept. While they indicate the classes of function they consider in their conceptualization of the secondary school curriculum, in this piece, they do not help readers understand how their sense of the function concept relates to the formal, set-theoretic, definition of function prominent in the discipline, and explored in studies of teacher and student thinking like Even (1993) and Vinner (1983). In particular, for readers familiar with the New Math and experience of the difficulties students often have with abstract ideas as starting points, they do not indicate that they have a less formal 'relationship between co-varying quantities' notion of function (Chazan 2000, pp. 76–7; Confrey and Smith 1995) in mind, as the basis for their curricular developments.

A second way to describe approaches to school algebra: Approaches and instructional situations

So far, this chapter has focused on perspectives on the substantive structures of a discipline and their relationship to curricular approaches (only in the reference to the Yerushalmy and Chazan piece is there the beginning of an examination of the impact of a curricular approach on classroom interaction and work). In this section, I want to argue that the connection between curricular approach and student classroom work is a strong one.

The notion that curricular approaches and one's perspective on the fundamental objects of study has an impact on classroom work is fundamental to Vilma Mesa's argument in her examination of the material on functions in middle-grade textbooks from around the world (2004). Building on Balacheff's theory of conceptions (Balacheff and Gaudin 2010), Mesa makes the point that textbooks and curricula expect to create certain student conceptions in Balacheff's sense of the term.

Textbooks expect that students, when given problems to solve, will use particular operations and actions that involve specific representational tools, as well as criteria for determining which tools to use and when a problem has been solved (see also the chapter by Rezat and Straesser, this volume). Mesa creates quadruplets of values for actions and conceptualizes particular quadruplets of values that repeat in meaningful ways as practices related to functions that appear in the textbooks she examined.

Mesa's analysis of the practices of function promoted by textbooks is related to the argument in Chazan and Yerushalmy. For example, textbooks that conceptualize equations in two variables in the different ways outlined in Table 11.3 will expect different sorts of student work. In this vein, Mesa outlines how different textbooks can be described as seeking to create different student conceptions of the mathematical object 'function'. Mesa's view of the curricular interrelationship between tasks to solve and the work that students should do is brought closer to teaching by an argument made in Herbst and Chazan (2012) about the role of instructional situations in organizing relationships among the roles of the actors in the instructional triangle (teacher, students, content).

In particular, Herbst and Chazan (2012) argue that instructional exchanges lie at the heart of the work a teacher does in the instructional triangle: that is, the relationship between the teacher, student and the mathematical content to be learned. For them an 'instructional exchange . . . requires that a teacher engages in: (1) Deploying mathematical objects of study in the form of work for students to do and (2) Interpreting work (being) done by students in light of a mathematical object of study (we refer to this as cashing)' (Herbst and Chazan 2012, p. 606).

Thus, one way for a teacher to use a task is to assign it to students in order to have students do work that will allow the teacher to argue that the students have or have not learned what was to be taught. An instructional situation is a construct that describes, from the position of a researcher, how teachers manage instructional exchanges by outlining established norms for orchestrating the exchange of particular kinds of work for particular assessments of learning.

Thus, to follow the chain of the argument, the curricular determination of the mathematical objects of study brings with it a curriculum's desire to produce particular student conceptions. This desire can be seen if one analyses the nature of the tasks provided to students in a textbook. The teacher's role is to understand how particular student work will cash as evidence for the production of the desired student conceptions. In that sense, initial determinations of the fundamental objects of study, as mediated by the tasks present in a textbook, might also be described as determining sets of instructional situations that teachers will use to manage learning. Sets of instructional situations might be a complementary way of describing what is meant by a curricular approach to a content area. Determining the fundamental objects of study in this view influences the set of instructional situations that constitute a curricular approach to content.

Conclusion

In this chapter, I have proposed one aspect of what one might mean by 'approach' to a content area in school mathematics, what I have called a curricular approach. I have argued that the existence of ambiguity in mathematics itself about the nature of the objects that mathematicians study creates the possibility for multiple substantive structures of the discipline, and thus multiple curricular approaches to school subject-matter. I have then examined two ways of capturing what a curricular approach might be. These two ways of describing curricular approaches may not be in tension, but may in fact be complementary, though they may provide instructional designers with different notions of how to proceed. Following Schwartz and Yerushalmy, one might stipulate that a curricular approach to a content area involves identifying the fundamental objects of study for that area and the operations carried out on those mathematical objects. Alternatively, following Herbst and Chazan, one might conceptualize curricular approaches to a content area as built out of an ordering of instructional situations aimed at producing particular conceptions in students.

To return to the challenge of analysing differing approaches to school algebra, the notion of curricular approach that I have outlined earlier clearly does not capture all the ways in which approaches to algebra can differ. There can be many other aspects of what one might mean by an approach. One might mean how one addresses the syntactic structures of a discipline, or one might be interested in other dimensions outlined in the APPA Group and Sutherland (2004). Yet, in emphasizing the notion of a curricular approach to a content area, I want to make sure that we do not overlook the notion of the substantive structures of the curriculum as one aspect of what it means to take an approach to content to be taught in school.

This particular aspect of what one might mean by an approach to content allows one to ask the following curriculum development questions:

- Is it important or valuable for a school curriculum to invest in one perspective on the substantive structure of the discipline, or should school curricular move between different perspectives on the substantive structure of a discipline?
- When a school curriculum or a technological tool does move between different perspectives on the substantive structure of the discipline should this transition be discussed directly with students? Why or why not?
- Who determines what curricular approaches to algebra, for example, are used with students? What roles do mathematicians play in such decisions? Mathematics educators? Parents? Other stakeholders?
- Should curricular standards dictate an approach to a school subject or should that remain to the discretion of curriculum developers and teachers?

Notes

1. Earlier draft available for download from http://hdl.handle.net/2027.42/91281 [accessed on 15 May 2013].
2. The 2003 version can be downloaded from www.edu.haifa.ac.il/personal/michalyr/publications_articles.html [accessed on 15 May 2013].

Additional references

Bednarz, N., Kieran, C. and Lee, L., 1996. *Approaches to algebra: perspectives for research and teaching.* Dordrecht, Netherlands: Kluwer.

Byers, W., 2007. *How mathematicians think: using ambiguity, contradiction, and paradox to create mathematics.* Princeton: Princeton University.

Chazan, D., 2000. *Beyond formulas in mathematics and teaching: dynamics of the high school algebra classroom.* New York: Teachers College.

Confrey, J. and Smith, E., 1995. Splitting, covariation, and their role in the development of exponential functions. *Journal for Research in Mathematics Education*, 26 (1), 66–86.

Even, R., 1993. Subject-matter knowledge and pedagogical content knowledge: prospective secondary teachers and the function concept. *Journal for Research in Mathematics Education*, 24 (2), 94–116.

Herbst, P. and Chazan, D., 2011. Research on practical rationality: studying the justification of action in mathematics teaching. *Mathematics Enthusiast*, 8 (3), 405–62.

Kaput, J., 1995. Long term algebra reform: democratizing access to big ideas. In C. Lacampagne, W. Blair and J. Kaput, eds, *The algebra initiative colloquium*, Vol. 1. Washington: US Department of Education, 33–49.

Kilpatrick, J. and Izsak, A., 2008. A history of algebra in the school curriculum. In C. E. Greens and R. Rubenstein, eds, *Algebra and algebraic thinking in school mathematics. 70th Yearbook of the National Council of Teachers of Mathematics*. Reston, VA: NCTM, 3–18.

Labaree, D. F., 2003. The peculiar problems of preparing educational researchers. *Educational Researcher*, 32 (4), 13–22.

Schwab, J., 1978. Education and the structure of the disciplines. In I. Westbury and N. Wilkof, eds, *Science, curriculum, and liberal education: selected essays*. Chicago: University of Chicago.

Sutherland, R. and Rojano, T., 1993. A spreadsheet approach to solving algebra problems. *Journal of Mathematical Behavior*, 12, 353–83.

Sutherland, R., Rojano, T., Bell, A. and Lins, R., eds, 2001. *Perspectives on school algebra*. Dordrecht, Netherlands: Kluwer.

Thom, R., 1986. 'Modern' mathematics: an educational and philosophical error? In T. Tymoczko, ed., *New directions in the philosophy of mathematics*. Boston: Birkhauser, 67–78.

Thurston, W., 1994. On proof and progress in mathematics. *Bulletin of the American Mathematical Society*, 30 (2), 161–77.

Van der Waerden, B. L., 1985. *A history of algebra*. Berlin: Springer-Verlag.

Vinner, S., 1983. Concept definition, concept image and the notion of function. *International Journal of Mathematical Education in Science and Technology*, 14 (3), 293–305.

Further reading

The APPA Group and Sutherland, R., 2004. A toolkit for analysing approaches to algebra. In K. Stacey, H. Chick and M. Kendal, eds, *The future of the teaching and learning of algebra*: The 12th ICMI Study. Dordrecht, Netherlands: Kluwer, 71–96.

Balacheff, N. and Gaudin, N., 2010. Modeling students' conceptions: the case of function. *Research in Collegiate Mathematics Education*, 16, 183–211.

Usiskin, Z., 1988. Conceptions of school algebra and uses of variables. In A. E. Coxford and A. P. Schulte, eds, *The ideas of algebra*. Reston, VA: NCTM, 8–19.

Arithmetic 12

Julia Anghileri

Core readings

The Core readings addressed in this chapter are as follows:

Anghileri, J., Beishuizen, M. and van Putten, 2002. From informal strategies to structured procedures: mind the gap! *Educational Studies in Mathematics*, 49, 149–70.

Beishuizen, M. and Anghileri, J., 1998. Which mental strategies in the early number curriculum? A comparison of British ideas and Dutch views. *British Education Research Journal*, 24, 519–38.

Brown, M., Küchemann, D. and Hodgen, J., 2010. The struggle to achieve multiplicative reasoning 11–14. In M. Joubert and P. Andrews, eds, *Proceedings of the 7th British Congress for Mathematics Education* (BCME7), University of Manchester. Available at www.bsrlm.org.uk/IPs/ip30-1/BSRLM-IP-30-1-07.pdf [accessed on15 May 2013].

Carpenter, T. and Moser, J., 1984. The acquisition of addition and subtraction concepts in grades one through three. *Journal for Research in Mathematics Education*, 15 (3), 179–202.

Introduction

Many changes have taken place in arithmetic teaching over the past two generations. Most significant is the shift from formal procedures, which were mostly learned through drill and practice, to a focus on problem solving, independent thinking and the development of 'number sense'. Before the extensive use of modern technology, all 'calculators' were human, and it was important that standard procedures were adhered to so that calculations could be shared and records kept. In today's society all important calculations are done using technology, from fuel refills to wages and shopping. As a consequence, the calculation skills that are needed have changed, particularly for those who will make up the workforce of the future. Confidence is needed to *identify* the calculations inherent in a problem-solving situation, and to *decide upon* a suitable solution strategy that will *efficiently* solve the problem to an appropriate degree of accuracy.

Psychologists' views of the way children learn have also changed from a 'behaviourist' paradigm earlier in the twentieth century to the 'constructivist' belief that children construct their own knowledge and understanding (see the chapter by Lerman, this volume). Mathematics is learned most effectively as individuals make sense of their experiences, forming a network of connections: from early counting, through real-world situations, to use of symbols to represent and solve problems.

Research in arithmetic teaching has reflected the changing stances of psychologists and the different needs of society, undertaking investigations of the complexities inherent in the arithmetic operations, the ways learners think about calculations and their progression in understanding. The core readings for this chapter reflect these trends in research, starting with the Carpenter and Moser (1984) article analysing the meanings associated with addition and subtraction. This article illustrates a desire to uncover through research the diversity of meanings for the operations learned in the early years, and to identify progression in learning. Extensive research has subsequently been undertaken in the Netherlands, particularly at the Freudenthal Institute in Utrecht, and new approaches in arithmetic teaching have been implemented in Dutch schools, where a research-based curriculum has been developed. Beishuizen and Anghileri's (1998) article reflects much of this more recent thinking about arithmetic and investigates the approaches needed for effective calculation. The Dutch research-based approach is compared with requirements for the English curriculum which has some characteristics in common with many countries in the Western world. Anghileri et al.'s (2002) article reports a detailed study of pupils' methods for division calculations which reflect different teaching approaches in England and the Netherlands. Finally, Brown et al.'s (2010) study identifies the continuing problem of developing adequate understanding of multiplicative reasoning to support further mathematics learning.

As long ago as the 1930s, Brownell showed through his research that understanding – not mere repetition – is the basis for children's mathematics learning. In the United States he wrote textbooks based on meaningful arithmetic for Grades 1–8. Despite his research findings endorsing such an approach, more traditional methods for teaching standard algorithms through extensive practice persist even today.

Beishuizen and Anghileri's core reading describes how, more recently, success has been demonstrated with a holistic approach to number and the development of 'number sense' rather than the traditional algorithmic 'tens and units' approach which sets out calculations in columns. Many calculations can be done effectively using informal methods and jottings. In doing this, learners have the opportunity to make choices about the methods they use and there is scope for creativity. Consider the calculation 6067 – 5970. Undertaken using the traditional column method (try it now!) will involve such difficulties as 'taking' a larger number from a smaller one and subtraction from zero. Using number sense can lead to appreciation that both numbers are close to 6000, and this can result in an easy mental calculation. Central to working with numbers in such a flexible way is the development of a whole range of mental strategies, but the emphasis in the classroom on written methods can inhibit their use. A recent national assessment for 7-year-old children in England included the item: $176 - 49 = \square$. A report on the solutions noted that very few children used the fact that 49 is almost 50 to make the question accessible mentally: instead, they used more standard methods to subtract 40 and 9 (QCA 2004).

Change is slow to take place in the classroom, and textbooks struggle to move away from practice exercises. As a consequence there is persistent scope for further development of classroom approaches that encourage individuals to develop the confidence they need to identify appropriate strategies for different calculations and use number sense in problem solving. Existing practices are failing to make the improvements in arithmetic that are essential for further learning in mathematics as Brown et al.'s core reading will illustrate.

The role of counting

So how can we develop this number sense? It all begins with counting! 'Discovery of simple patterns and easy structures like abbreviated counting in steps of 2s, 5s and 10s, was conceived as an important emergent mathematising activity' (Beishuizen and Anghileri 1998). Most children develop confidence in counting – both forwards and backwards, and starting at any number. These different forms of counting can be a whole-class activity and can be extended later to counting in fractions (try counting in eighths and converting to halves and quarters as you count) or counting in decimals (try counting in 0.3s). That is not to say that counting is enough, and teachers need to know how to help children progress from counting to efficient calculating without jeopardizing understanding.

Progression in counting with whole numbers goes through stages as the operations of addition and subtraction are established. The classic studies of Carpenter and Moser reported in their core reading analyse in detail children's own methods for addition and subtraction, showing that counting skills are fundamental in this development of strategies. Children's solutions to simple addition and subtraction word problems were studied in a three-year longitudinal study that followed 88 children from Grades 1–3 (student age 6–8). The study showed that the children were able to solve the problems using a variety of modelling and counting strategies even before they received formal instruction in arithmetic. Four levels of problem-solving ability were found. At the first level, children solved addition problems by externally modelling them with physical objects. Modelling strategies were gradually replaced with more sophisticated strategies. Stages in learning addition include progression from *direct modelling*: 'counting all' using physical objects or fingers, through *counting strategies*; 'counting on from the first number' then 'counting on from the larger number', to *number fact strategies*; 'recalling number facts' and using them sometimes in combination with counting, then 'deriving new facts' from those that are known. Similarly, in the counting strategies for subtraction, Carpenter and Moser distinguish between *counting down from* and *counting up from given*. So that a calculation such as 8 – 5 may be calculated as '7, 6, 5, 4, 3' with the answer 3, or as '6, 7, 8' with the answer being the number counted between 5 and 8. These strategies may relate to the interpretation of subtraction as partition (take-away) or as comparison (difference between). Both of these methods will be seen as images on an *empty number line* in the next section. It becomes clear in Carpenter and Moser's article that addition and subtraction strategies are closely related, and that children's solution strategies will vary according to the context of a problem. At the highest level observed by the researchers the children solved each problem using number facts whatever the context.

Using imagery

Research in the Netherlands has shown that imagery plays an important role in understanding and analyses the development of representations for the calculation strategies identified earlier (Beishuizen and Anghileri 1998). Gains in performance were evident where an *empty number line* was used to illustrate and support mental methods. The abstract counting sequence, 1, 2, 3, . . ., is identified initially with beads on a bar or string that can be directly moved, and then with a numbered line to represent the beads. Addition and subtraction are associated first with the moving of beads, and represented later as jumps on the number line from one number to another. Thus 7 + 3 can be seen initially as 3 hops from 7 to 10 and then as a single jump of 3, modelling the number fact that 7 + 3 = 10 (see Figure 12.1).

Even at this stage the images show connections with subtraction, for example, 7 is a jump of 3 back from 10. When children are familiar with the sequence of numbers on the number line, they can begin to visualize them and work with an *empty number line* – a line on which all calibrations are absent.

Without the calibration, representation of a single jump of 3 is emphasized, and individuals are encouraged to use known facts rather than counting in ones. An empty number line provides an opportunity to support the child's thinking as an image can be drawn to represent a mental strategy. The actual size of the jump is irrelevant and may be used for calculating with small or large numbers, as can be illustrated for the calculation 6067 – 5970 discussed earlier in this chapter. Here an empty number line can be used to show the mental strategy of seeing how far each number is from the 'benchmark' 6000 (see Figure 12.2).

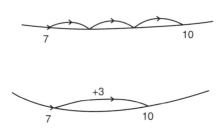

Figure 12.1 7 + 3 in hops, and in a single jump

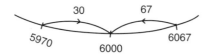

Figure 12.2 Calculating 6067 – 5970 on an empty number line

With an empty number line, rather than a calibrated one, the representation does not have to begin at zero and the size of jumps does not have to be in proportion to the intervals represented. Initially subtraction may be visualized as hopping back on the number line where 8 – 5 is seen as hopping back 5 steps from 8 to land on the number 3, modelling the 'counting down from' strategy of Carpenter and Moser. Alternatively, when seen as a single jump (of 3) from 5 to 8, this image is associated with subtraction using the 'counting up from given' strategy of Carpenter and Moser (see Figure 12.3).

Together with many different experiences, children come to recognize consistency in the results of counting and calculating, so that number facts are committed to memory, particularly those 'number bonds' that add to ten. This learning of number facts will be crucial in the development of strategies for dealing with larger numbers. The Dutch research shows that imagery can play an important role in learning number facts, and Dutch teachers represent number bonds of ten as 'hearts in love' for display around the classroom.

The use of a numbered line is not new, but the development of an uncalibrated *empty number line* is an innovation that research has shown to be very effective (Beishuizen and Anghileri 1998). Empty number lines are now evident in many classrooms and provide images to match the abstract strategies that children use (Murphy 2011). As indicated in the Beishuizen and Anghileri core reading, such images can provide access for the teacher into the thinking of individuals, revealing errors and misconceptions as well as identifying individuals who are effective in using known facts and efficient methods. They also provide opportunities for children to display their own methods rather than being reliant on the teacher to provide a method.

When children can locate numbers in relation to each other on an empty number line and identify benchmark numbers, such as the multiples of ten, they can show their thinking

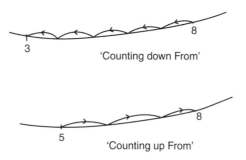

Figure 12.3 Two different strategies for calculating 8 – 5

for more complex calculations. For addition and subtraction of larger numbers the Dutch research makes a key distinction between 'sequence-tens' (N10) and 'separate tens' (1010) methods. The first relates to holistic counting-based methods (including the use of known facts) that can be represented with jumps on the number line: for example, 65 + 38 can be calculated by 'jumping' from 65 to 70 then adding 30 and finally an additional 3 to arrive at the number 103 so that 38 has been added as jumps on the number line. Subtraction, for example, 65 – 38 can be calculated by counting down 38 in convenient jumps from 65 to arrive at the number 27; or by comparison, and adding/counting on: 38 + 2 + 20 + 5 = 65, again giving the answer 27, this time represented on the number line as the size of the jump. By contrast, separate tens (1010) relates to calculation depending on place value, so that 65 – 38 starts with 5 – 8. This is 'not possible' so the calculation becomes 15 – 8 = 7 and 50 – 30 = 20, answer 27. This is most commonly represented in columns, perhaps headed 'tens' and 'units'. This method is the basis for the traditional algorithms for addition and subtraction that were taught almost exclusively in the past century. Dutch research found that guided learning 'emphasising pupils' (written) recording of their own solution methods from the beginning for the purpose of pupils' reflection and interaction in whole class discussion' (Beishuizen and Anghileri 1998, p. 523) enabled the gradual development of both cognitive and metacognitive strategies. An algorithmic approach with all pupils taught to use the same written methods can be demotivating for independent mathematical thinkers.

As well as straightforward addition and subtraction, problems can be presented with missing numbers, for example, 27 + __ = 65, and solution strategies are extended to this type. Beishuizen and Anghileri point out that 'in 1010 solutions to the problem 27 + __ = 65 many errors were found of the following type: 20 + 40 = 60, 7 – 2 = 5, 30 + 9 = 48'. While 'N10 solutions successfully used sequential anticipation (27 + 30 = 57, 57 + 8 = 65, answer 40 + 2 = 42)' (Beishuizen and Anghileri 1998, p. 524).

Written methods for addition and subtraction

Pupils are expected to learn efficient written methods for the four operations of arithmetic, but not at the expense of understanding. In the core reading, Beishuizen and Anghileri report Dutch research that exploits '*context situations* (that have been) deliberately designed and sequenced to invite specific informal strategies for calculating and then to stimulate abbreviation towards higher-level (and written) strategies' (p. 525). This didactic process of guided development is called *progressive mathematization*, which is 'accomplished not only through cognitive but also through metacognitive activation: monitoring strategy execution by written recording and reflection on strategy choice in whole class discussion' (p. 525). Learning that is accomplished through progressive mathematization is the keystone to the Dutch research-based Realistic Mathematics Education (RME) approach (Gravemeijer 1994). Based on the constructivist paradigm and using the notion of 'guided reinvention' the curriculum is planned using consistent models and images starting with real-world contexts. Beishuizen and Anghileri cite the 'bus model' (passengers getting on and off the bus) as a model for addition and subtraction.

Traditional approaches move quickly to symbolic representations with the learning of place value, and use of 1010 algorithms for addition and subtraction involving numbers arranged in columns, sometimes labelled 'tens' and 'units'. Calculation is done with the 'column value' rather than the 'quantity value' of the numbers. This distinction is explained by Thompson, who suggests a dual model for place value where, for example, the *quantity value* of 64 is 60 and 4 while the *column value* (sometimes called digit value) is 6 tens and 4 ones (Thompson 2003, p. 183). In the Dutch approach, and with the empty number line, such partitioning of numbers is not necessary in the early stages of learning and calculations are done with whole numbers. However, a Dutch study in 10 classes (student age 7–8) showed that after a good mastery of the holistic sequence-tens (N10) approach 'pupils easily adopted 1010 (separate-tens) as an alternative computation procedure'(Beishuizen and Anghileri 1998 p. 526).

In the traditional algorithms, rules have to be adhered to: for example, starting with the units when doing addition, subtraction and multiplication. Setting out the calculations in standard format and following specific rules can lead to mechanical application rather than a thinking approach that is understood. This can have the advantage of efficiency in calculating, but for some learners these very condensed written methods may become confused, with the learners unable to recall the rules and unable to reconstruct them when they are forgotten.

The mental strategies and number facts that are learned through counting and representation on an empty number line can form the basis for written methods that will support understanding. In the book *Issues in Teaching Numeracy in Primary Schools* (see the Further Reading list), a chapter by Meindert Beishuizen on the empty number line is followed by the chapter by Ian Thompson on written methods of calculation. Thompson explains standard column methods for addition and subtraction while acknowledging that 'there is a plethora of research evidence to suggest that neither young children, teenagers nor adults actually make use of these methods when performing calculations in the real world' (1999, p. 174). In written methods there is a development in the abbreviated format that can be achieved. Thompson outlines stages that reflect children's thinking and show a progression from mental calculations, initially horizontal and expanded: for example,

$$358 + 237 \rightarrow 358 + 200 \rightarrow 558 + 30 \rightarrow 588 + 7 \rightarrow 595$$

progressing to vertical expanded forms, and later to the abbreviated standard format in columns. This development will support children in recording a calculation without loss of

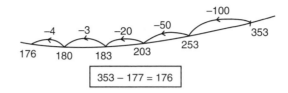

Figure 12.4 Calculating 352 − 177 on an empty number line

understanding of the underlying strategy. For subtraction, the abbreviated algorithm with the associated language of 'borrowing' or 'carrying' presents substantial difficulty for some children, and Thompson points out that informal methods can easily (and quickly) be modelled on an empty number line' (1999, p. 177).

For example, 353 − 177 (see Figure 12.4)

$$353 - 100 \rightarrow 253 - 50 \rightarrow 203 - 20 \rightarrow 183 - 3 \rightarrow 180 - 4 = 176$$

It becomes evident that children can be involved in decision making about the most appropriate strategy to use for any given calculation, and that they do not make the value judgement that the most abbreviated and complex method is necessarily the one that they should use.

Multiplicative reasoning

Although the operations of addition and multiplication are represented symbolically in a similar manner (5 + 3, 5 × 3) the progression from *additive thinking* to *multiplicative thinking* is significantly difficult. In their study of 11–14 year-olds in England, Brown et al. (2010) note that 'multiplicative reasoning is a key competence for many areas of employment and everyday life' and is 'the foundation of most mathematical applications and is relevant to all pupils' (p. 49). They warn that 'it is however a complex conceptual field' and their findings show that students in the lower secondary age range have a very weak grasp of important aspects of multiplicative reasoning and that 'understanding in this area has not improved since the 1970s. Relatively few students are achieving competence in the relevant areas of the Key Stage 3 [age 11–14 in England] framework' (p. 49).

This core reading reports one aspect of a four-year research project involving a large-scale survey of about 3,000 11–14 year-old students' understanding of algebra and multiplicative reasoning in England. This was followed by a collaborative research study with teacher-researchers using the results of the survey in classroom settings. The aim of the project was to examine how formative assessment (see the chapter by Hodgen and van den Heuvel-Panhuizen, this volume) can be used to improve attainment and attitudes. The focus of the study was the ratio/rate model for multiplicative reasoning as this was the most commonly taught in this age phase and was perceived to involve aspects of performance that students find difficult, and which form a major barrier to developing competence and confidence in functional applications.

In Brown et al.'s core reading, the main contexts of the ratio/rate application of multiplicative reasoning are explained as those where two or more values are being compared, and/ or where one value is being scaled up or down to give another. It is noted that the values being compared may be of essentially the same quantity and the comparison may be related to two or more different 'things', or to one 'thing' at two or more different times – the examples given are 'numbers of boys and girls' and 'changing numbers of boys'. Where the quantity is a discrete variable, or where the multiplying factor is a whole number or familiar fraction, this relationship is often expressed as a ratio $a{:}b$. Where the comparison is between two variables which refer to different quantities measured in different units, the relation is usually expressed as a rate a/b.

Brown et al.'s core reading reports the use of test items and attitude questionnaires first developed and used in a project in the 1970s, reported in the Concepts in Secondary Mathematics and Science (CSMS) study (Hart et al. 1981) and latterly used in 2008 and 2009 with a sample of approximately 3,000 students from 90 classes in 11 schools. Reporting preliminary results, 4 levels of competence are described from simple integer rates (like ×2 or ×3) to problems involving fractional quantities and ultimately (level 4) involving non-integer enlargement (e.g. 5:3) or problems set in a context involving scaling continuous quantities. Despite the fact that the higher levels are expected to be taught to students in this age group, the study concludes that 'under 20% of students are succeeding on this material'. The majority of students in the study, although competent at the lower levels, could not consistently manage anything in terms of rate and ratio other than reasoning involving whole number multiplication.

Foundations of multiplicative reasoning

In its simplest form, multiplication is seen as repeated addition and relates to a number triple that will be identified in different calculations. For example, 3, 5 and 15 are related by the calculations: $5 \times 3 = 15$, $3 \times 5 = 15$, $15 \div 3 = 5$, $15 \div 5 = 3$. Whereas the two numbers in addition are initially envisaged as objects to be combined, for multiplication one represents the multiplier that 'operates' on the other. Depending on how the calculation is read, as '5 multiplied by 3' or a '5 times 3', the interpretations relate to '5 + 5 + 5' or '3 + 3 + 3 + 3 + 3' respectively. The resultant total will be the same, but for any learner trying to visualize the calculation or relate it to actions, the ambiguity may lead to confusion which can erode an individual's confidence in thinking mathematically. Similar difficulties with language arise where expressions involving the division symbol can be interpreted in many ways. The expression '12 ÷ 3' can be read as '12 divided by 3', '12 shared by

3', '3 into 12' and the actions can relate to 12 objects shared into '3 lots of 4' or grouped into '4 lots of 3' (Anghileri 2005).

The language of division in schools as 'sharing' or 'shared by' rather than 'divide' is 'a long way from the notion of number required in order to, for example, find y when $6y = 7$' (Watson 2009, p. 17) and will have implications when written calculation methods are learned.

In the primary school, connections can be made explicit, with multiplication and division linked from the beginning as inverse operations. Initially, counting can be the foundation for learning the multiplicative triples as children seem to find number patterns, for example, counting in 2s or 5s, easy to remember and replicate. Building familiarity with such patterns can establish a 'sense' about different numbers that frequently appear and do not appear at all in counting patterns. The number 24 appears in the pattern of 2s, 3s, 4s, 6s, 8s and 12s while the number 23 does not appear in any counting pattern. This 'feel for numbers' or 'number sense' begins to mark differences in learners who make connections as they learn new facts and processes while other learners try to understand a mass of disconnected ideas.

The aspects of multiplication as repeated addition and division as sharing are most emphasized in the early curriculum and can make it harder for students to learn the connections inherent in multiplicative reasoning. Multiplicative reasoning involves both multiplication and division, not only as inverse operations but also as ratio and proportion ('five for every one of three', 'five times larger than three'). Division is fundamental for understanding the structure of fractions and rational numbers, for example that $\frac{3}{4}$ has the same value as $\frac{6}{8}$, and both represent the outcome of dividing 3 by 4. Familiarity with numbers and number patterns is the beginning of learning multiplication and division facts, but the rapid recall of related numbers is a necessary skill whose absence may handicap learners considerably in many areas of mathematics. Rote learning of multiplication tables is effective if connections are made and new facts can be derived from those that are known. Where learners find it difficult to commit unrelated facts to memory, it can be quicker to derive new ones, for example if $7 \times 7 = 49$ is known then 8×7 can be found. Multiplicative thinking involves linking facts like this and extending understanding, for example,

$$70 \times 7 = 490 \text{ and } 7 \times 700 = 4900, \quad 500 \div 7 = (490 + 10) \div 7$$

Division by 10 or 100 will provide a link between fractions and decimals with $\frac{1}{10}$ and $\frac{1}{100}$ represented as 0.1 and 0.01 respectively. Understanding this relationship will enable learners to work flexibly between the two different forms and make sensible decisions about the most effective use of notation.

The operation of division can also be used to show how a progression can be achieved from understanding the meaning of the operation to efficiency in calculating: this progression is the focus of the core reading by Anghileri et al. (2002). This study compares cohorts of English (N = 276) and Dutch (N = 259) students regarding their ability to solve a range of division problems. Students were tested at two points in the school year before and after explicit teaching of written division methods. At the time, the English pupils used the traditional algorithm almost exclusively, while the Dutch students were taught a 'chunking' method (explained in the following text). The findings showed that the Dutch cohort displayed their understanding of division and tackled the calculations very much more effectively than the English cohort, many of whom showed considerable confusion.

The traditional algorithm involves working with digits (column value) rather than real number values (quantity value), so that the written calculation (displayed $7\overline{)98}$ in England, like a 'bus shelter', with variants in other countries) would begin with '7s into 9' and not '7s into 90'. The remainder '2' is then 'joined' with the 8 (there are variations in how this is displayed) to make 28, where the 2 now represents 20. The understanding needed to know when to use 2 and when to use 20 can confuse some learners. Many also find difficulty in deciding when to write a zero in the answer: for example, in an item involving dividing 1256 by 6, use of the traditional algorithm begins with 6 divided into 1 (which does not require a zero) but omission of the later zero (when 6 is divided into 5) results in the answer 29 (instead of 209), an error made by many of the English participants in the study. The Dutch chunking method which has been successfully adopted in many English schools uses whole number values throughout, and involves successively removing multiples of 7 in progressively more efficient chunks.

To illustrate the methods found in the study:

Calculating 98 ÷ 7 by subtracting chunks of 14 (see Figure 12.5).

```
7 ) 98
     14   2×
    ───
     84
     14   2×
    ───
     70
     14   2×
    ───
     56
     14   2×
    ───
     42
     14   2×
    ───
     28
     14   2×
    ───
     14
     14   2×
    ───
     00
```

Figure 12.5 Dividing 98 by 7 by 'chunking' (first version)

```
7 ) 98
     70    10×
     ──
     28
     28    2×
     ──
     00
```

Figure 12.6 Dividing 98 by 7 by 'chunking' (second version)

Calculating 98 ÷ 7 by subtracting larger chunks s(see Figure 12.6)

It can be seen that the second example (Figure 12.6) closely matches a way of thinking about the calculation mentally with the number 98 recognized as 70 + 28. The traditional English algorithm, on the other hand, depends on the use of digit (column) values rather than real (quantity) values and does not easily fit with a mental calculation (Anghileri 2001). Chunking is unlikely to be quite as efficient as the traditional algorithm, but it has the benefit that the individual will make a choice of chunks to be taken, thus retaining ownership of the method and working to a degree of efficiency that corresponds to the level of understanding of the student at that point in time.

Conclusion

From these core readings it becomes clear that there are complexities that warrant further investigation both in the meanings of arithmetic operations and in the ways that children think about them. Further research is needed so that teachers can support children in becoming familiar with numbers and number operations, and confident and effective in using and applying them.

Further reading

Anghileri, J., 2005. *Teaching number sense* (2nd edn). London: Continuum.

—, 2007. Developing number sense: progression in the middle years. London: Continuum.

Thompson, I., 2003. *Enhancing primary mathematics teaching*. Buckingham: Open University Press.

—, 2010. *Issues in teaching numeracy in primary schools* (2nd edn). Buckingham: Open University Press.

Additional references

Anghileri, J., 2001. Development of division strategies for Year 5 pupils in ten English schools. *British Education Research Journal*, 27 (1), 85–103.

Gravemeijer, K. P. E., 1994. Educational development and developmental research in mathematics education. *Journal for Research in Mathematics Education*, 25, 443–71.

Hart, K., Brown, M. L., Küchemann, D. E., Kerslake, D., Ruddock, G. and McCartney, M., eds, 1981. *Children's understanding of mathematics: 11–16*. London: John Murray.

Murphy, C., 2011. Comparing the use of the empty number line in England and the Netherlands. *British Education Research Journal*, 37 (1), 147–61.

Nunes, T., Bryant, P. and Watson, A., 2009. *Key understandings in mathematics learning*. London: Nuffield Foundation. Available at www.nuffieldfoundation.org [accessed on 14 November 2011].

QCA, 2004. *Implications for teaching and learning from the 2004 tests: Key Stage 2 Mathematics*. London: Qualifications and Curriculum Authority.

Thompson, I., 1999. *Issues in teaching numeracy in primary schools*. Buckingham: Open University Press.

Watson, A., 2009. Paper 6: algebraic reasoning. In T. Nunes, P. Bryant and A. Watson, eds, *Key understandings in mathematics learning*. London: Nuffield Foundation. Available at www.nuffieldfoundation.org [accessed on 14 November 2011].

Geometry 13

Angel Gutiérrez

Core readings

The Core readings addressed in this chapter are:

Gutiérrez, A., 1996. Visualization in 3-dimensional geometry: in search of a framework. In L. Puig and A. Gutiérrez, eds, *Proceedings of the 20th Conference of the International Group for the Psychology of Mathematics Education*, Vol. 1. Valencia, Spain: PME, 3–19. Available at www.uv.es/angel.gutierrez/archivos1/textospdf/Gut96c.pdf [accessed on 18 May 2013].

Gutiérrez, A. and Jaime, A., 1998. On the assessment of the van Hiele levels of reasoning. *Focus on Learning Problems in Mathematics*, 20 (2/3), 27–46. Available at www.uv.es/angel.gutierrez/archivos1/textospdf/GutJai98.pdf [accessed on 16 May 2013].

Presmeg, N. C., 1986. Visualization in high school mathematics. *For the Learning of Mathematics*, 6 (3), 42–6.

Vinner, S., 1991. The role of definitions in the teaching and learning of mathematics. In D. Tall, ed., *Advanced mathematical thinking*. Dordrecht, Netherlands: Kluwer, 65–81.

Introduction

Traditionally, geometry has been a 'poor relation' in school mathematics curricula, and textbooks and teachers have tended to reduce the content taught to some basic definitions, properties and formulae. In recent years, research and teaching experience has shown that some difficulties encountered by students when learning other areas of mathematics could be overcome if students had deeper knowledge of geometry and geometric reasoning. As a consequence, teachers are becoming aware of the importance of geometry in school curricula, and researchers are working on providing teachers with knowledge and tools that could help them improve their practice. This makes research in geometry education an important field of research with many interesting directions. Gutiérrez and Boero (2006) and Battista (2007) provide overviews of the current state-of-the-art, and propose questions for further research.

In such a context, this chapter introduces readers to some essential elements of research in geometry education, and prepares the ground for them to undertake research in this field. The chapter is divided into three sections, devoted to three theoretical frameworks which are relevant for research on different aspects of geometry teaching and learning at any educational level.

Teachers should be aware of the visual abilities and skills that students use when drawing or seeing pictures, drawings or diagrams; this is particularly critical when learning three-dimensional geometry. Therefore, the first section of the chapter introduces readers to the main characteristics of a useful theoretical framework that identifies and analyses the elements of visualization used by students when solving geometric problems.

The second section describes the constructs defined by Shlomo Vinner to explain the processes of learning mathematical concepts in geometrically rich contexts. Vinner's model describes students' conceptions of mathematical concepts, and helps teachers and researchers to better understand students' learning processes, outcomes and errors, as well as to design effective teaching materials.

The third section presents the van Hiele model of geometrical reasoning. This influential model has proved to be very useful for describing and analysing students' mathematical reasoning when they are studying geometric content, and it is widely used in mathematics education. In fact, it is the framework most often used to organize the teaching of geometry, from national curricula (for instance, the NCTM Principles and Standards in the United States, and the Singapore National Curriculum) to the design of classroom activities. The van Hiele model is also very useful for providing teachers and researchers with accurate data for the assessment of students' geometrical reasoning.

Spatial visualization in geometry

Visual thinking is necessary in any area of mathematics, at all levels, and especially in geometric contexts, and it is very important for students to develop their visualization skills. Therefore, a relevant research question involves characterizing students' mental visual activity at different school grades. The development of dynamic geometry environments, and other software able to graphically represent mathematical concepts taught at any school level, has opened a new research field (see the chapter by Ruthven, this volume).

Visual thinking is also useful in many other disciplines (e.g. in medicine, in order to use Computed Axial Tomography and other three-dimensional-image techniques; in geography, for map reading; in chemistry, for modelling complex molecules; in architecture and engineering; etc.) and in everyday activities (to anticipate trajectories when driving;

to estimate object sizes, etc.). This wide range of applications has resulted in a lack of coordination or agreement among researchers from different specialities, so it is easy to find discrepancies in the use of terms or their meanings in the literature (see the core reading Gutiérrez 1996 for a deeper discussion on this issue). As an illustration, cognitive psychologists tend to define 'mental image' as a quasi-picture created in the mind from memory, whereas mathematics educators give a wider meaning to this same term, as we will see later.

Several approaches for analysing visualization in school mathematics can be found in the mathematics education literature. I shall present here an approach, from the core reading by Presmeg. This approach was first proposed in the 1980s, and is still useful to researchers and teachers. In any geometric activity, we can differentiate between external actions and internal, mental actions. External actions obtain information from outside, produce outcomes and communicate with others. By contrast, mental actions consist of processing external information to transform it into internal data, analysing internal data to generate new internal information, and converting internal information and results into external outcomes.

When the mental actions are based on the visualization of geometric objects, researchers have differentiated three components integrating those actions:

1. The *mental objects* handled. Presmeg (1986) called these objects *mental images*. She observed teachers and students, and identified several types of mental images: concrete pictorial images, pattern images, memory images of formulae, kinaesthetic images and dynamic images.
2. The *mental processes* that transform external or mental information into mental images, and vice versa. The process of creation of mental images occurs when students look at pictures in the textbook, on the blackboard, computer screen, and so on, when they read or hear a text and represent the information graphically in their mind, and also when students transform other mental images. Bishop (1983) called this process *visual processing* (VP) of information.

   After having created mental images, students may analyse them, retrieving information needed to solve the problem they are working on, and exteriorize the information by using appropriate language and graphical representations. Bishop (1983) called this process *interpretation of figural information* (IFI).
3. Students need to have learned some *visualization abilities* in order to perform the above-mentioned mental visual processes while solving a problem, in the same way as a person should have learned some manual abilities to use a screwdriver or a hammer in order to join two pieces of wood. Del Grande (1990) compiled a list of mental visualization abilities necessary to solve geometric problems. Abilities like figure-ground perception, perceptual constancy, mental rotation, perception of spatial positions or spatial relationships, visual discrimination, visual memory, and others are necessary to solve geometry problems, especially in three-dimensional geometry. See Del Grande (1990) for details.

From the point of view of research and teaching, the most important of the components mentioned above are the mental images. Presmeg (1986) introduced the different types of mental images she identified in her research experiments and included a description of each image, with characteristic examples of students using them to solve mathematics problems. The scope of Presmeg's article extends beyond geometry within school mathematics, and certain types of images are more often used in some areas of mathematics than in others.

In each of the core readings summarized in the previous paragraphs, the authors introduce one element that is relevant to understanding how individuals use visualization, but an integration of the three components was necessary. Gutiérrez (1996) presented the integration of visualization processes, images and abilities into a theoretical framework, with examples of students' outcomes to complete the description of the framework and facilitate its understanding. The diagram (Figure 13.1), adapted from Gutiérrez (1996), summarizes the elements of mathematical visualization used to solve a problem of geometry.

We can exemplify and apply this diagram practically. What comes to your mind after reading the word 'pyramid'? Most probably this external input has prompted you to create the mental image of a square-based pyramid lying on its (horizontal) base (IFI to a concrete pictorial image). Now, make your mental pyramid rotate to lie on one of its triangular faces. This is a different mental image, generated from the previous one (IFI + VP to a dynamic image). Finally, draw the pyramid you have in your mind (VP to an external representation). Different readers may have used different visualization abilities for the same process in this task, but most likely perceptual constancy, mental rotation, perception of spatial positions or visual memory have been used by some readers.

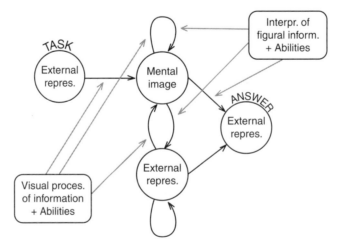

Figure 13.1 Elements of mathematical visualization used to solve a problem of geometry

The learning of basic geometric concepts

The experience of both researchers and teachers shows that most students feel more confident when they learn new mathematical concepts represented in specific examples than when students are just presented with a definition, often in their textbook (Watson and Mason 2005). An interesting research activity is to analyse students' learning and understanding of mathematical concepts when they are taught using examples and non-examples.

A student is asked for the definition of a regular polygon. He replies: *A regular polygon is a polygon having all its sides equal and all its angles equal* – that is, the standard definition. Now the student is given some geometric figures and he is asked to select the regular polygons. One of the figures that he selects is a rectangle. When the researcher asks the student why this rectangle is a regular polygon, he replies: *Because it has four equal angles.*

Another student is asked for the definition of a square. She replies: *A square is a quadrilateral having four equal sides and four right angles* – that is, again, the standard definition. Now the student is given some drawings of quadrilaterals and she is asked to mark the squares. One of the polygons she does not mark is represented in Figure 13.2. When the researcher asks the student why this quadrilateral is not a square, she replies: *Because it is not in the correct position.*

Both answers, which many teachers will recognize, appear similar because both students can repeat the definition: however, they differ in the following respect. The first student understands the meaning of having all the sides equal, and he is able to discriminate between polygons having, or not having, this property; he can also correctly manage the property of having all the angles equal. But he does not understand that both properties have to be true at the same time for a polygon to be regular.

The second student can identify squares only when they are in the standard position, that is, resting on a horizontal base. She does not understand the definition of square and, in fact, she does not use it to classify the quadrilaterals but uses the prototypical *image* of square that she has seen in textbooks and the blackboard as the target against which to match the drawings in the exercise.

Figure 13.2 Is it a square?

A powerful framework that explains these two students' behaviours was proposed by Vinner (1991), as follows. The information that students receive in their mathematics classes and outside school is of two types:

- Graphical: this includes pictures, drawings, physical objects, and so on that students see in text-books, blackboards, and elsewhere. It works like a collection of photos.
- Verbal: this includes definitions, theorems, formulas, and so on that students read in textbooks or hear from teachers or other persons. It works like a collection of newspaper cut-outs.

Neuropsychologists tell us that the human brain stores verbal and graphical information in different places. Vinner represented those places in the memory as two boxes: the graphical box is called *concept image* and the verbal box is called *concept definition* (Figure 13.3).

Figure 13.3 Concept image and concept definition as two connected boxes

Teachers should aim to enable students to *connect* the two boxes.

Typically, when students are introduced to a geometric concept, they populate their concept definition and concept image 'boxes' with the contents learned, but students are not always taught how to establish relationships between them. As a consequence, when students feel that the question formulated by the teacher asks for a definition, property, formula, and so on, they access their concept definition and, when students feel that the question asks them to identify or reproduce a shape they resort to their concept image.

In the example of identification of squares, the student did not establish a relationship between her definition and her concept image of a square. Furthermore, her concept image was limited to prototypical images – squares with a horizontal base – so she decided to reject the 'diamond' shape because it was not similar to any other held in her concept image of a square.

Vinner's model of acquisition of mathematical concepts offers a resolution to such learning difficulties. Vinner (1991) is an extended compilation of previous publications by this researcher and other colleagues in which he presents the different components of the model in detail and provides many examples. The chapter by Vinner also discusses different patterns of students' behaviours depending on their concept definitions, concept images and the relationships between them that students are able to manage.

Vinner suggests starting teaching a new concept with a carefully organized set of examples and non-examples, to help students learn the concept in the same way as everyday concepts are learned, that is, by comparing examples and non-examples, and identifying discriminating properties as follows:

- the comparison of examples and non-examples should highlight the properties of the examples which are not present in the non-examples, that is, the necessary properties of the concept;
- comparison of two different examples should indicate a property of one example which is not present in the other example, that is, a non-necessary property of the concept;
- the necessary properties identified should enable students to formulate a definition of the concept, and to generate links between this definition and their concept images.

Figure 13.4 presents the way a Spanish textbook introduces the concept of polyhedron in Grade 2 (student age 13–14) of the secondary school (Colera et al. 1997). This is a quite simple but effective illustration of the use of examples and non-examples in typical geometry teaching. An application of Vinner's model is the following procedure of designing a sequence of examples and non-examples to teach a certain geometric concept, based on the following steps (Hershkowitz 1990):

- Decide on the definition of the concept to be taught.
- Select the necessary properties of the concept that students should discover.
- Select the non-necessary properties that students often select erroneously in the identification of a shape as an example or a non-example. Non-necessary attributes such as shape, position, number of sides or faces, and so on are often accepted as necessary properties by students.
- For each necessary property, draw an example and a non-example differing in this property.
- For each non-necessary property, draw two examples differing in this property.

Figure 13.5 shows the result of applying these steps to the concept of a right prism.

Vinner's model may also be used as a research framework to evaluate teachers' and students' understanding. Hershkowitz et al. (1987) and Gutiérrez and Jaime (1999) present findings of research based on this model. Watson and Mason (2005) elaborated on Vinner's

OBJECTS IN SPACE: POLYHEDRA

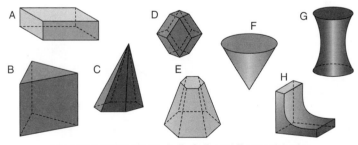

Among the solids above, A, B, C, D, and E are polyhedra.

A geometric solid is called a **polyhedron** when its faces are polygons.

Figure 13.4 Introducing the concept of polyhedron (Colera et al. 1997)

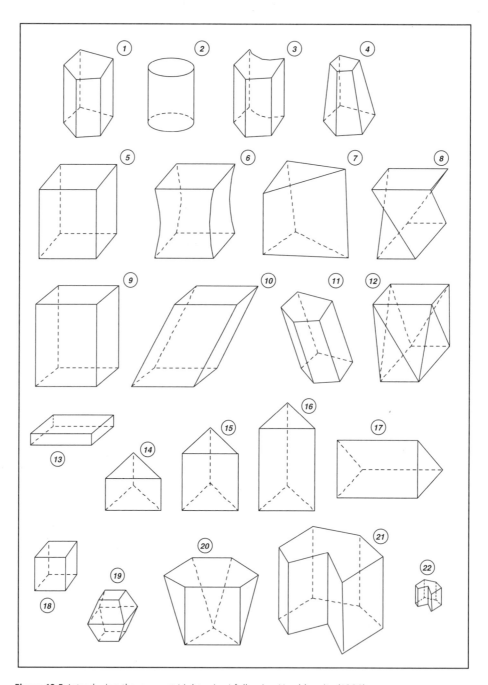

Figure 13.5 Introducing the concept 'right prism' following Hershkowitz (1990)

concept image to define students' *example spaces* as 'small pool[s] of ideas that simply appear in response to particular tasks in particular situations' from which examples produced by students arise. Vinner's model is still widely used by other researchers, for example, Gilboa et al. (2011), and several articles in the *Educational Studies in Mathematics* special issue 69 (2) (2008).

The van Hiele model of students' geometrical reasoning

People studying mathematics, from kindergarten children to professional mathematicians, exhibit different modes of mathematical reasoning. The *van Hiele model of geometrical reasoning* characterizes those modes (or *levels*) of reasoning in geometrical contexts. Furthermore, the van Hiele model provides guidelines for teachers to plan their lessons and to help their pupils develop their reasoning. The guidelines to teachers are known as *the phases of learning*. Due to space limitation, I will focus on the use of the levels as a framework to evaluate students' geometrical thinking. A more comprehensive study of the van Hiele model from a research perspective should begin with Clements and Battista (1992) and Battista (2007).

The main characteristics of the van Hiele levels follow. The core reading Gutiérrez and Jaime (1998) gives a more detailed account.

Level 1: Students recognize geometric concepts by their physical appearance, and in a global way, without explicitly distinguishing their mathematical components or properties.

Level 2: Students recognize the mathematical components and properties of geometric concepts. They are able to verify conjectures through empirical reasoning and generalization. Students can only manage basic logical relationships between mathematical properties.

Level 3: Students can manage any logical relationship. They are able to prove conjectures using informal deductive reasoning. Students can understand simple formal proofs, but they cannot construct them themselves.

Level 4: Students understand the need for rigorous reasoning and they can write formal deductive proofs. They understand the function of axioms, hypotheses, definitions, and so on.

Level 5: Students are able to manage different axiomatic systems, and they can analyse and compare properties of geometric objects in two axiomatic systems (for instance, Euclidean geometry and spherical geometry).

The first researchers using the van Hiele model considered – in keeping with the van Hieles' early writings – that a given student always performed at *the same* level; consequently, the assessment procedures tried to elucidate *which* level of reasoning students had attained (Burger and Shaughnessy 1986; Fuys et al. 1988; Usiskin 1982). However, these authors were unable to assign a level of reasoning to a significant number of subjects in their experiments due to contradictory results because some students 'failed' the questions focusing on one level and 'succeeded' in the questions focusing on a higher level, and other students gave answers that showed a mixture of levels of reasoning.

For instance, a Spanish student in Grade 3 of the secondary school (student age 14–15) was given a sheet with drawings of several quadrilaterals, and was asked to mark squares (C), rectangles (E) and rhombuses (O); after having marked the shapes (Figure 13.6), the student was asked to explain what he had paid attention to when making his classification of the quadrilaterals. Some of his answers were:

> For squares: [I paid attention] *to its equal and parallel sides, and the angle of 90°* (a level 2 answer).
>
> For rectangles: *its long shape with 4 parallel sides making 4 angles of 90°* (an answer mainly at level 2 but with aspects of level 1).
>
> For rhombuses: *its four sides, 2 slanted parallel sides and 2 right parallel sides* (a level 1 answer; the intended meaning of the terms 'slanted' and 'right' is unclear).
>
> Is shape 1 a square? *Yes. Because of its 4 parallel sides, and its width and short shape* (answer mainly at level 1, but partly at level 2).
>
> Is shape 5 a rectangle? *No, because its sides do not form 90° angles* (a level 2 answer).

The van Hiele levels have some core characteristics that ought to be taken into account when using them to assess students' geometrical reasoning, or to design teaching materials, as follows:

- The levels are *sequential*: levels are ordered, so that progression from one level is always to the next level.
- The levels are *local*: showing a level of reasoning in a certain topic of geometry does not necessarily imply showing the same level in a different topic. Geometrical reasoning is highly dependent on knowledge of mathematical content, so students and teachers may be reasoning at a high level in one geometrical topic but at a low level in another geometrical topic that they are just beginning to study. Several researchers have administered similar questionnaires based on different geometric topics to sample groups of students or teachers, and all of them have reported that the levels of reasoning in most participants depended on the topics (Clements and Battista 1992, p. 429).

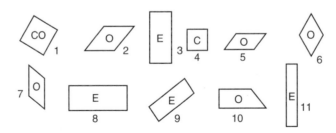

Figure 13.6 A student's classification of some quadrilateral drawings

For instance, Gutiérrez and Jaime (1988, cited in Clements and Battista 1992) administered two tests to a group of 232 pre-service primary school teachers, one test based on plane shapes and the other on solids. They found that only 10 per cent of the students showed the same level of reasoning in both tests; 80 per cent of the students showed levels 2 or 3 in plane geometry, and 9 per cent of the participants showed levels 2 or 3 in solid geometry.

- Each level has a characteristic *language*: students at different levels may give different meanings to the same term, for instance to 'proof'. For example, suppose that a secondary school teacher asks his pupils to deduce the formula for the sum of the interior angles of an *n*-sided polygon. Students calculate the sums of several polygons (triangle, quadrilateral, pentagon, . . .) and they induce the formula *Sum of angles = 180(n–2)*. To prove that their formula is correct, the students show that it works for some polygons (*n* = 3, 4, 5, . . .). The teacher rejects the students' argument, and asks them for a 'general' proof, but the students do not understand why a deductive proof is necessary when (they reason) the examples clearly prove that the formula works. The reason for this didactical obstacle is that students are reasoning at level 2, so 'to prove' the formula means, for them, to check it in specific cases, while the teacher expects a level 3 proof, so for him 'to prove' the formula means to make a deductive abstract argument. As Pierre van Hiele (1959/1984, p. 246) wrote, 'two people who reason at two different levels cannot understand each other.'

Clements and Battista (1992) give a more detailed description of the core characteristics of the van Hiele levels, and present an analytic review of the relevant research literature.

Gutiérrez and Jaime (1998) and Gutiérrez et al. (1991) presented a comprehensive methodology for the assessment of individuals' levels of geometrical reasoning, based on an original approach to the structure of the levels. Their approach has proved to be useful for researchers (Battista 2007, p. 848) and overcomes earlier difficulties in applying the van Hiele theory. Gutiérrez and Jaime (1998) described and exemplified a technique for the design of questionnaires for the assessment of van Hiele levels, using multilevel questions and multiprocess super-items (these ideas are explained later): this approach optimizes the questionnaire efficiency, in terms of number of items and administration time. The work by Gutiérrez et al. (1991) presented a new conception for the assessment of the levels of reasoning based on the *continuity* of the levels and the possibility to measure the transition between levels.

According to Gutiérrez and Jaime (1998, p. 29), mathematics is a complex activity, integrated by five mathematical processes – recognition and description, use of definitions, formulation of definitions, classification and proof (see the chapter by Stylianides, this volume). Thus mathematical reasoning is a multiple activity that, in practice, depends on the mathematical processes required to solve a problem (see the chapter by Verschaffel et al., this volume). The acquisition of a van Hiele level implies the mastery of all the five processes of reasoning associated with the mathematical processes, so that the determination of a person's level of geometrical reasoning has to take into consideration the acquisition of each process of reasoning. Table 13.1, adapted from Gutiérrez and Jaime (1998, p. 32), summarizes the characteristics of each process of reasoning as practised in each van Hiele level.

Table 13.1 Distinctive attributes of the processes of reasoning in the van Hiele levels

	Level 1	Level 2	Level 3	Level 4
Recognition and description	Physical attributes	Mathematical properties	–	–
Use of definitions	–	Only definitions with simple structure	Any definition	Accept several equivalent definitions
Formulation of definitions	List of physical properties	List of mathematical properties	Set of necessary and sufficient properties	Can prove the equivalence of definitions
Classification	Exclusive, based on physical attributes	Either exclusive or inclusive, based on mathematical attributes	Move among inclusive and exclusive when definitions are changed	–
Proof	–	Empirical verification in examples	Informal deductive proofs	Formal mathematical proofs

Most primary and secondary school mathematics curricula pay more attention to some mathematical processes than to others; for instance, in the 1970s and 1980s, the curricula in those countries adopting the 'new mathematics' approach (for instance, United States and Spain, among many others) restricted experimental tasks (levels 1–2) in favour of extensive use of deductive proofs of properties (levels 3–4), while in the 1990s, deductive proofs were removed from their curricula and more emphasis was placed on the empirical verification of properties (level 2). Consequently, it should not be surprising to find that students are mastering some processes of reasoning at a certain level while they are still using other processes of reasoning at a lower level.

When designing a reliable test to evaluate students' levels of reasoning, it is necessary to ensure that each van Hiele level and each process of reasoning are evaluated – that is, each cell in Table 13.1 is evaluated. However, the use of multilevel questions and multiprocess super-items can help researchers to design short but still reliable tests, as follows. On the one hand, students' reasoning is not indicated by the fact of correctly having solved some problems, but by the way they have solved them. Different students may solve the same problem using different levels of reasoning; for instance, a proof problem may be solved by empirically checking the conjecture in one example, or a few examples (level 2), or by formulating a deductive argument in an informal (level 3) or formal (level 4) way. Similarly, a description of a geometric object may be physical (level 1) or mathematical (level 2). In the same way, the solution of a *multilevel* problem item may require the use of several mathematical processes. So, it is not necessary to include a different problem in the test in order to assess each level and process. On the other hand, a set of related questions and/or problems is more efficient than a set of independent questions and/or problems since related questions make it easier to graduate different difficulties or complexities. Then, as suggested by Gutiérrez and Jaime (1998), we can use *super-items* – sets of related questions having a common core – to discriminate the use of different van Hiele levels depending on the questions in the super-item answered by each student. In the core reading, Gutiérrez and Jaime (1998) give examples of eight super-items. Finally, since the levels of reasoning expected vary at different grades, it is more efficient to design different tests for students in different school grades.

These techniques allow the development of tests that reliably assess students' degrees of acquisition of the van Hiele levels and can be administered in a reasonable amount of time, typically 1 hour in class. Gutiérrez and Jaime (1998) presented a longitudinal study where a set of eight super-items was used to design three related tests to evaluate a sample of Spanish students from Grade 6 (student age 11–12, primary school) to Grade 12 (student age 17–18, end of secondary school).

Conclusion

In this chapter, I have introduced three theoretical frameworks that form part of the essential underpinning for research in geometry education. This chapter has set out the main features of each framework, as a starting point for more detailed reading of the core readings and the references indicated below.

It is worth mentioning that the three theories introduced here are compatible and complementary to each other. The information about a student's behaviour (with regard to reasoning, learning or representation) gained from one of the theoretical frameworks can be expected to warrant and reinforce information about their behaviour with respect to the other frameworks. For instance, knowing the kind of visual images and abilities students use can give clues about the type of concept image they are able to create, and their level of reasoning.

The frameworks introduced here are among the most important elements of research in geometry education, but they are not the only ones. Other important topics include research on the teaching and learning of proof, on the use of dynamic geometry software in primary and secondary school classrooms, on the view of geometry classrooms as communities of practice, and research on the teaching and learning of specific geometry topics. These research areas are addressed in other chapters of this book, and also in edited handbooks such as Gutiérrez and Boero (2006) and Lester (2007).

Further reading

Battista, M. T., 2007. The development of geometrical and spatial thinking. In F. K. Lester, ed., *Second handbook of research on mathematics teaching and learning*. Reston, VA: NCTM, 843–908.

Clements, D. H. and Battista, M. T., 1992. Geometry and spatial reasoning. In D. A. Grouws, ed., *Handbook of research on mathematics teaching and learning*. New York: MacMillan, 420–64.

Del Grande, J., 1990. Spatial sense. *Arithmetic Teacher*, 37 (6), 14–20.

Gutiérrez, A., Jaime, A. and Fortuny, J. M., 1991. An alternative paradigm to evaluate the acquisition of the Van Hiele levels. *Journal for Research in Mathematics Education*, 22 (3), 237–51.

Hershkowitz, R., 1990. Psychological aspects of learning geometry. In P. Nesher and J. Kilpatrick, eds, *Mathematics and cognition*. Cambridge: Cambridge University Press, 70–95.

Hershkowitz, R., Bruckheimer, M. and Vinner, S., 1987. Activities with teachers based on cognitive research. In M. M. Lindquist, ed., *Learning and teaching geometry, K-12*. Reston, VA: NCTM, 222–35.

Additional references

Bishop, A. J., 1983. Spatial abilities and mathematical thinking. In M. Zweng et al., eds, *Proceedings of the 4th International Congress in Mathematics Education* (ICME). Boston, MA: Birkhauser, 176–8.

Burger, W. F. and Shaughnessy, J. M., 1986. Characterizing the van Hiele levels of development in geometry. *Journal for Research in Mathematics Education*, 17 (1), 31–48.

Colera, J., Gaztelu, I., de Guzmán, M. and García, J. E., 1997. *Matemáticas, 2º de ESO [Mathematics, Secondary School Grade 2]*. Madrid, Spain: Anaya.

Fuys, D., Geddes, D. and Tischler, R., 1988. The van Hiele model of thinking in geometry among adolescents. *Journal for Research in Mathematics Education Monograph*, 3.

Gilboa, N., Dreyfus, T. and Kidron, I., 2011. A construction of a mathematical definition – the case of parabola. In B. Ubuz, ed., *Proceedings of the 35th Conference of the International Group for the Psychology of Mathematics Education*, Vol. 2. Ankara, Turkey: PME, 425–32.

Gutiérrez, A. and Boero, P., eds, 2006. *Handbook of research on the Psychology of Mathematics Education*. Rotterdam, Netherlands: Sense.

Gutiérrez, A. and Jaime, A., 1999. Preservice primary teachers' understanding of the concept of altitude of a triangle. *Journal of Mathematics Teacher Education*, 2 (3), 253–75.

Lester, F. K., ed., 2007. *Second handbook of research on mathematics teaching and learning*. Reston, VA: NCTM.

Usiskin, Z., 1982. *Van Hiele levels and achievement in secondary school geometry*. Columbus, OH: ERIC. Available at www.eric.ed.gov/PDFS/ED220288.pdf [accessed on 16 May 2013].

van Hiele, P. M., 1959/1984. The child's thought in geometry. In D. Fuys, D. Geddes and R. W. Tischler, eds, 1984. *English translation of selected writings of Dina van Hiele-Geldof and Pierre M. van Hiele*. Columbus, OH: ERIC, 243–52. Available at www.eric.ed.gov/PDFS/ED287697.pdf [accessed on 16 May 2013].

Watson, A. and Mason, J., 2005. *Mathematics as a constructive activity: learners generating examples*. Mahwah, NJ: Lawrence Erlbaum.

Probability 14

Dave Pratt

Core readings

The Core readings addressed in this chapter are as follows:

Fischbein, E. and Gazit, A., 1984. Does the teaching of probability improve probabilistic intuitions? An exploratory research study. *Educational Studies in Mathematics*, 15 (1), 1–24.

Piaget, J. and Inhelder, B., 1951. *The origin of the idea of chance in children* (trans. L. Leake, P. Burrell and H. D. Fischbein). New York: Norton. [In particular, Chapter 10. Conclusion: Chance, probability, and operations.]

Pratt, D. and Noss, R., 2002. The micro-evolution of mathematical knowledge: the case of randomness. *Journal of the Learning Sciences*, 11 (4), 453–88.

Tversky, A. and Kahneman, D., 1974. Judgement under uncertainty: heuristics and biases. *Science*, 185, 1124–31.

Introduction

In this chapter, the core readings are used, first, to describe and explain the current orthodoxy regarding the challenge inherent in teaching and learning probability and, second, to propose new approaches, which to some extent undermine that orthodoxy.

Why is probability hard?

Although there are calls for the teaching of statistics to be embedded in disciplines which use statistics as a tool for analysing data, there is a widespread consensus that an appreciation of probability is a key aspect of statistical literacy but part of the mathematics curriculum.

Even so, it has proved problematic to decide the most effective age at which to introduce probability. Probability began to appear in the curriculum and textbooks in many countries in the 1980s but was often later withdrawn for young children (6–11 year-olds). In the United Kingdom, for example, probability is almost now non-existent in the primary curriculum. Perhaps, this is evidence that the teaching and learning of probability is especially difficult. Indeed, Threlfall (2004) has argued that probability tasks in school cannot challenge everyday notions of chance, and are more suitable for 11–16 year-olds, when such tasks can be supported by a more formal approach. There is then a perception that probability is hard, and this view is not only based on experience of teaching the topic but on a number of epistemological, psychological and pedagogical arguments, four of which are outlined in the following sections.

A confusing epistemology

Probability as a measure of likelihood is computed in different ways according to the circumstances of the situation. Although some circumstances admit triangulation because several methods of computation can all be applied in the same situation, students can be confused when the same concept, probability, is associated with a multitude of different approaches, generating insecurity about what probability *is*.

As an illustration, consider how mathematics teachers are used to talking to students about the probability of a head on a coin or a six on a die. In this situation, there is a clear sample space in which it is possible to set out the values of a random variable (1, 2, 3, 4, 5 and 6 in the case of a cubical die) and attach an associated probability distribution ($\frac{1}{6}$ for each, based on the symmetry of the die). Such an approach is often referred to as 'classical'. Students are encouraged to calculate the probability of an event by counting how many of the equally likely discrete cases in the sample space contribute to the event and divide by the number of cases in the overall sample space.

Teachers also regularly conduct experiments in which a trial is carried out many times. For example, a drawing pin might be thrown to count the frequency of occurrences in which it falls on its head as opposed to on its side. A drawing pin might be chosen because it is asymmetric and so cannot be treated in the classical fashion. The teacher's intention is generally to examine the relative frequency of occurrences with which the drawing pin lands on its head. A second step would be to demonstrate that this relative frequency tends towards a limit, which is taken to be the 'true' probability. Sometimes referred to as the 'experimental probability', the relative frequency can in some situations be shown to be close to the classical probability. So, the die example would allow triangulation of the two methods of computing the probability. Without doubt, some students will remain confused by the fact that the relative frequency does not in fact exactly equal the classical probability.

Most situations in everyday life do not permit either a classical or experimental calculation of probability. Estimations of likelihood are often judgement calls. Ironically most curricula introduce probability as a measure on a scale between 0 and 1 and students are invited to judge the likelihood of events such as the headteacher walking into the classroom in the next 5 minutes. Curricula subsequently tend to ignore subjective probability though students will meet it in everyday conversation and media discussion.

Statisticians continue to argue about the most appropriate approach, but mostly they live with this ambiguity. For learners, it might present a considerable obstacle and Wilensky (1997) has reported 'epistemological anxiety' (see the chapter by Törner, this volume) among higher education students when challenged with apparently paradoxical problems in probability. The reader might experience epistemological anxiety by trying to think through what weather forecasters mean when they state for example, that the probability of rain at 10.00 a.m. tomorrow in London is 70 per cent. Which method of computing probability is being used here? This question will be revisited in the conclusion to this chapter.

The use of inappropriate heuristics to make judgements of chance

Seminal work into how people make judgements of chance was carried out in the 1970s and 1980s by Kahneman and Tversky, who catalogued the heuristics used in a series of psychological experiments. By 'heuristic', they refer to an intuitive method for making quick judgements. The core reading (Tversky and Kahneman 1974) summarizes research on two of the most widely reported heuristics, 'representativeness' and 'availability'.

The representativeness heuristic
According to Kahneman and Tversky, this heuristic is used when there is a need to assess the likelihood that an event belongs to a given category or results from a particular process. Here is one research item (Tversky and Kahneman 1983, p. 297):

> Linda is 31 years old, single, outspoken and very bright. She majored in philosophy. As a student she was deeply concerned with issues of discrimination and social justice, and also participated in anti-nuclear demonstrations.
>
> Which of the following two statements about Linda is the more probable:
>
> (i) Linda is a bank teller, or
> (ii) Linda is a bank teller who is active in the feminist movement.

Arguing that the given pen portrait resembles someone who is in the feminist movement, many respondents in Tversky and Kahneman's study chose option (ii). Of course, more careful thought would lead to option (i) because everyone who is both a bank teller and a feminist is in any case a bank teller. Thus option (i) must be more frequent than option (ii). In this and similar examples, Kahneman and Tversky have argued that the representativeness heuristic leads to a wrong answer because, in cases of a logical conjunction, there can be a mismatch between frequency and resemblance.

A second example illustrates the use of the representativeness heuristic when the event results from a specific process. Imagine that a gambler playing roulette has seen the ball land on a red number for six throws in a row and is contemplating whether to bet that the next ball will land on a red or a black number. Many respondents in Kahneman and Tversky's research chose black, which is an example of 'negative recency'. Kahneman and Tversky have argued that this is because the gambler believes that the outcomes should resemble the sample space. In the sample space, red and black are equally likely and so people believe that the imbalance between the set of results and the sample space needs to be redressed. They respond such that the results resemble more closely the sample space. The tendency towards negative recency is sometimes referred to as 'the gambler's fallacy'. The failure of the representativeness heuristic to come to the correct solution is because the expected resemblance between the generating process and the next outcome falsely assumes that the next outcome is dependent on what has already happened.

The availability heuristic

The core reading (Tversky and Kahneman 1974) also refers to the availability heuristic. According to Kahneman and Tversky, this heuristic is applied by testing how easy it is to recall instances of the event whose likelihood is being judged. Consider whether availability accounts for some people's aversion to flying, even though statistics show very clearly that it is a relatively safe way to travel, compared, say, with driving a motor vehicle. When aeroplanes crash it is headline news because there are simultaneously many victims. By contrast, deaths and injuries from car accidents are spread out and less newsworthy. Evoking memories of instances of an event is based largely on salience or significance and less on frequency and so can lead to errors in judgement of chance.

There have been many criticisms of Kahneman and Tversky's work based on one or more of the following assertions: (1) the work is atheoretical and so conclusions are difficult to interpret; (2) the test items are designed to 'trick' the subjects; (3) methods which allow little time and limited access to tools do not promote reasoned responses; (4) human fallibility is an inevitable conclusion when you test people in areas that extend beyond their domain of knowledge or capability. Nevertheless, their body of work still stands as some of the most careful and rigorous psychological research of how people make judgements of chance. Whereas Kahneman and Tversky's research set out to describe how people make judgements of chance, the aim of teachers of mathematics is somewhat different. Teachers seek to intervene and might hope that heuristical thinking will improve. Thus, the research question for those in mathematics education may focus on how heuristical thinking might be enhanced. The pessimistic view for mathematics education would be that Kahneman and Tversky have catalogued human fallibility that is somehow hardwired into our genetic make-up. If that view is correct there is little that can be done. A more optimistic view would be that there are pedagogical approaches, perhaps not yet invented, that might intervene in the learning process.

The equiprobability bias

Other research has also recorded human fallibility. Lecoutre (1992) conducted an experiment to study the tendency for people to assume that outcomes are equally likely, a misconception that she labelled the 'equiprobability bias'. Lecoutre offered her subjects a bag containing three sweets, two of which were orange and one lemon. Subjects were asked whether, if choosing blindly, it was more likely that they would choose an orange sweet or a lemon sweet. The response would often be that it was not possible to say or that they were equally likely. Lecoutre then provided three shapes, two were triangles and one was a square, chosen so that the triangle could fit exactly on one edge of the square. A house shape could be made by sitting the triangle, as a roof, on top of the square. When selecting two of the three pieces, there are two choices that could make a house (a square plus one of the two triangles) and one choice that would not make a house (two triangles). There is then a degree of isomorphism about the mathematics in the sweets and shapes tasks except that the subjects could see and handle the shapes. The choice of shapes might be based on logical argument. People were more successful in obtaining a correct solution to the combinatoric problem when handling the shapes than the mathematically similar random choice problem when blindly choosing a sweet from the bag. Lecoutre argued that the chance element added to the difficulty of the task as people tended to regard the answer as 'just a matter of luck, 50–50, it could be one or the other'. Furthermore, her studies and other follow-up research have pointed to a resistance to modification of the equiprobability bias.

The outcome approach

Another study (Konold 1989) proposed that many people tend to focus on what actually happened in practice rather than on the strategic value of the approach that led to that outcome. For example, in games playing, it is common to be satisfied if the result was successful, although in the long term the winners will be those who attend to the strategy of the game rather than to a result that may merely have arisen through good fortune. When people focus primarily on outcomes, they are also likely to see little value in weighing the odds and are likely to respond in a way similar to Lecoutre's subjects in dismissing the situation as '50–50, just a matter of luck'.

The plethora of research on human fallibility is usually couched in terms of misconceptions, often accompanied by a pedagogical inference of a need to remove or overcome those misconceptions and replace them with correct ideas. Smith et al. (1993) argued persuasively that this is an anti-constructivist position in the sense that new conceptions must be built from current knowledge; correct ideas cannot simply replace misconceptions. From this perspective, the pedagogic challenge is to consider so-called misconceptions as perhaps naïve conceptions that may offer in some cases an element of truth that could be nurtured through astute teaching. More sophisticated knowledge might emerge, not through replacement, but by designing experiences that support the recognition of the limitations in the current understanding. Often these limitations relate either to knowledge being overgeneralized so that the scope of the understanding has not yet been recognized, or undergeneralized because the power of the idea has not yet been revealed (Pratt and Noss 2002).

The late onset of formal operations in cognitive development

It is reasonable to ask how these heuristics and naïve conceptions emerge and, according to the research referred to in the section on 'The use of inappropriate heuristics to make judgements of chance', continue to be the dominant way of making sense of a stochastic world. (Here, the word 'stochastic' is intended to refer to situations which involve uncertainty, including the topics commonly referred to as 'probability' and 'statistics'.) The core readings include a chapter from the seminal work on the origins of the idea of chance (Piaget and Inhelder 1951) which offers a third reason for probability being 'hard' to learn. Attention is drawn to three critical paragraphs in this final chapter of the book that capture the authors' analysis of how the idea of chance emerges.

Consider the opening paragraph of Chapter 10:

> Logical and arithmetical operations constitute systems of actions interrelated in a rigorous way and always reversible, this reversible aspect rendering deduction possible. Transformations occurring by chance, on the contrary, are not interrelated in a rigorous way and the most probable systems that they form are essentially irreversible. (p. 212)

Here, Piaget and Inhelder begin in the first sentence by iterating one of the properties of operational thinking. In Piaget's theory, operational thinking is one of the developing organism's milestone achievements, and the mind continues to assimilate knowledge through the application of that operational thinking. Operational thinking makes possible deductions about the causal relationship between two factors. The second sentence argues that there is a key difference when considering chance: given the outcome, the source of the effect is indeterminate. Their experiments with children using random mixtures demonstrated the confusion that resulted when there was no sense of how such a mixture might have been generated and indeed how different mixtures might have emerged from the same starting position.

Now consider the next key paragraph:

> As soon as chance is discovered as indeterminate relationships not composable by operative methods and, contrary to all the operations, irreversible, the mind seeks to assimilate this unexpected obstacle encountered on the road to developing deduction. (p. 230)

Piaget's notion of equilibrium is at play here. According to his theory, the mind seeks to accommodate radically new ideas, if they cannot be ignored, by fundamentally restructuring its organization. The mind aims to strike a balance, to seek an equilibrium, between a state of flux, brought about by such accommodation, and a sort of stasis, in which the mind is not open to new ideas. In Piaget's thesis, chance mounts a fundamental challenge to operational thinking, one that is slow to be resolved (and for many students may never be properly accommodated). Perhaps, it is in this vacuum that heuristics and naïve conceptions are constructed as an intuitive means of coping with uncertainty.

Later in the same paragraph, Piaget and Inhelder signal how, at least for some, the challenge is indeed resolved:

> If chance for a moment makes reason useless, sooner or later reason reacts by interpreting chance, and the only way of doing this is to treat it as if it were, in part at least, composable and reversible, that is, as if one could try to determine it in spite of everything. (p. 231)

They refer to the *invention* of probability. In this sense, probability is constructed by the mind in order to operationalize chance. The laws of probability systematize chance by providing a mathematical formulation, an algebra that can be applied to uncertainty. Chance comes to be understood through the notion of a random variable, whose outcomes are associated with probabilities that obey well-defined rules and create a probability distribution.

Such an achievement, however, in Piaget's theoretical framework must be a late construction. A full appreciation of probability depends fundamentally on knowledge about proportion and combinatorics, each of which is dependent on multiplicative reasoning, as well as randomness. If the operationalization of chance takes so long, it is perhaps not surprising that psychologists report relatively naïve intuitive thinking, interpretable as psychological heuristics with built-in bias. The suggestion, based on Piaget and Inhelder's work, that probability is difficult because it is a late stage of development could be seen as in opposition to the fourth explanation, which is discussed next.

Naïve intuitions are allowed to wither

Whereas Piaget's studies focused on operational thinking, Fischbein based his research on the notion of intuition. In the core reading, Fischbein and Gazit (1984) describe an intuition as a 'global, synthetic, non-explicitly justified evaluation or prediction' (p. 2). Fischbein (1975) has elsewhere written extensively about intuitive thought and distinguishes between primary and secondary intuitions, the latter being scientific in the sense that they are schooled through a carefully planned process. The core reading tests the hypothesis that improved probabilistic intuitions will be observable as a result of a carefully designed teaching intervention.

Fischbein's ideas about intuitive probabilistic thinking stem from a startling observation reported in 1975. As a result of experiments conducted with preschoolers, he claimed that even such young children have intuitions for relative frequency and this would not be predicted by Piaget and Inhelder's analysis. His key conclusion from that observation is that naïve intuitions for chance are not supported by schools because the curriculum reinforces the deterministic at the expense of developing more sophisticated ways of thinking about the stochastic. According to Fischbein, learning about probability is difficult because at earlier ages naïve intuitions for chance are allowed to wither.

Fischbein (1975) argued for a new curriculum in which chance experiments would be used to facilitate the development of secondary intuitions building on the early primary intuitions. The experiment reported in the core reading is his response to his own challenge. It is clear that the experiment had mixed outcomes. There was relatively little success resulting from the teaching of Grade 5 children (age 11–12), yet most Grade 6 and the vast majority of Grade 7 children seemed to benefit. Fischbein and Gazit concluded that a systematic teaching programme on probability should be introduced at Grades 6 or 7. Perhaps, this is some recognition that development of operational thinking is needed before it is possible to support the primary intuitions observed in preschool. Nevertheless, Fischbein and Gazit remained optimistic, proposing that improved versions of the teaching programme would overcome the difficulties and obstacles observed during the 1984 study.

The study was not conducted as design research, that is to say research in which a product is iteratively designed in the light of trials with participants with the aim of developing not only the product but also theoretical explanations for the participants' activity. Such an approach to the development of a sequence of teaching tasks might have teased out in a more nuanced way the relationship between the teaching programme and intuitive thinking. One of the key difficulties in developing primary intuitions for chance is its ephemeral and transient nature. People engage with situations that are uncertain; they take an action and observe the outcome. It is not normal in everyday practice to focus on strategy (hence, Konold's outcome approach discussed earlier), nor on aggregation, since most events are observed only once or repeated at such an interval that the collation of such experience is unlikely. The teaching approach in the core reading attempted to resolve this by artificially focusing attention on the aggregation of results and the underlying mathematical formalisms.

Since 1984, there has been substantial research into how digital technology might provide exactly the sort of feedback that would inevitably have been lacking in the teaching programme used in the core reading. The following example illustrates the pedagogic response afforded by digital technology to the perception that probability is hard to teach and learn.

The ChanceMaker study

Technology certainly provides no magic solutions and is often misused in teaching and learning mathematics. All the more reason to look carefully at what sort of opportunities might be offered by digital technology to respond to the four sources of difficulty outlined in the section, 'Why is probability hard?' The ChanceMaker study took place in the 1990s. At the time, almost all of the stochastic research focused on how people, including children, were mistaken. In line with Smith et al.'s (1993) take on misconceptions, Pratt set out to uncover, through a design research methodology, the meanings for chance that children of age 10–11 years already held, and to explore how careful design of digital tools might perturb and perhaps enhance those meanings.

In the core reading, Pratt and Noss (2002) report that these children used expert-like meanings to make sense of short-term behaviour of simulated coins, spinners and dice. These 'local' meanings drew on observation of the unpredictability, irregularity and uncontrollability of the simulated devices (referred to as 'gadgets') in deciding whether the gadgets behaved randomly. Children also referred to the fairness of the gadget as a property of randomness. Significantly, the children did not, prior to using the gadgets or in the early stage of their use, articulate differential meanings for randomness in the long term. Interestingly, such global meanings might stand at least partially in opposition to local meanings since they might draw on the predictability and regularity of long-term relative frequency.

The ChanceMaker domain of stochastic abstraction was iteratively designed to explore how global meanings might be triggered. The final version provided a range of gadgets, a coin, a spinner and a die to name three, which were animated to act much like their material equivalents. As a result, it was hoped that meanings developed from everyday life might be triggered when trying to make sense of the simulated versions. Some of the gadgets were preprogrammed to 'misbehave'. For example, the die in Figure 14.1 was more likely to generate a 6 than would a material standard die. The children were challenged to identify which gadgets were programmed correctly. When they had identified a gadget, such as the die, which they thought was not working properly, they were challenged to mend the gadget. At this stage, the gadget was opened up to reveal the tools in Figure 14.1.

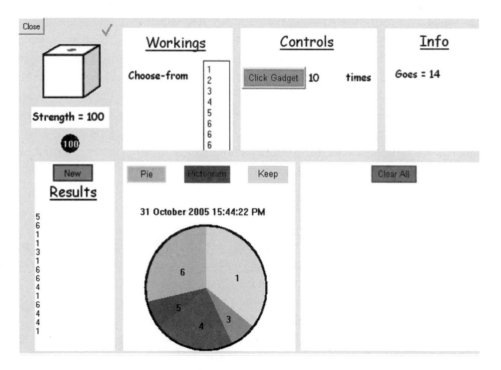

Figure 14.1 The tools inside the die gadget

The tools include the facility to repeat quickly many trials, list results and display them in graphical form. A key aspect of the design is the 'workings' box. In Figure 14.1, the workings box indicates that the die is more likely to generate a 6 than any other outcome. However, to read the workings box in that way demands some knowledge about the relationship between a probability and a data distribution. To the children in the study, the workings box simply provided a mechanism for controlling the configuration of the die. They could edit the workings box, for example, by reducing the number of 6s to just one.

The children used the software in pairs during lengthy clinical interviews in which the research probed the children's understanding of the behaviour of the gadgets. When they edited the workings box of the die so that it contained only one 6, they would typically be confused when the resulting pie chart did not look 'fair', that is to say when the sectors were far from uniformly spaced. The idea that fairness was an indicator of randomness seemed to transfer from the appearance of the gadget to the appearance of the pie chart. Of course, the pie chart would be unlikely to appear uniform even when the workings box had been adjusted, unless the trial was repeated many times.

The need to repeat the experiment many times was not obvious but gradually the children began to articulate the notion that 'the more times you throw the die, the more even is its pie chart'. Fischbein might have called this a secondary intuition. Pratt and Noss refer to it as a situated abstraction, an expression that captures generalized behaviour in a specific situation. In a way, this situated abstraction can be seen as a humble version of the Law of Large Numbers, which (briefly) states that, in a repeated sequence of independent trials in which the probability of one outcome, called a 'success', is constant, the relative frequency of successes tends to a limit as the number of trials increases. Later, a second situated abstraction would typically emerge, 'the more frequent an outcome in the workings box, the larger its sector in the pie chart'. This situated abstraction focuses on the distributional aspect as represented by the workings box. Some children combined both situated abstractions by recognizing that the larger sectors would only predictably appear when the trial was conducted many times. These situated abstractions would initially be very focused in the particular gadget but gradually extended across gadgets.

Conclusion

The ChanceMaker study implies rethinking the notion that teaching and learning probability is hard. In this concluding section, each of the four postulated reasons for that notion (discussed earlier) is revisited in the light of the ChanceMaker study.

The role of digital technology has promoted a modelling perspective on the nature of probability. In the ChanceMaker study, students were able to create their own probability distribution, in the unconventional form of a workings box. In a sense they were creating a model of a material coin, spinner or die. Running the model generated data. A modelling perspective goes some way to unifying the *differing epistemological perspectives* since it reflects the notion that although a mathematical formulation might be explored for its own sake, as soon as it is applied to behaviour in the world beyond mathematics, that choice reflects a modelling perspective. The parameters of the model might be based sometimes on the symmetry of the situation, sometimes on known long-term behaviour and sometimes on subjective judgement. In the digital setting, the consequences of those choices can be explored and examined over the long term, which is usually impractical in the material world. The modelling approach is being widely adopted in educational software (see, for example, the modelling tools in Tinkerplots 2 www.keypress.com/x26233. xml [accessed on 15 May 2013]). When probability is seen as a modelling tool, it somehow becomes more acceptable that different choices might be made as to how to measure chance. Earlier, the question was posed about how forecasters might compute probabilities of certain weather conditions. One solution might be to imagine the immense computing facilities used to track weather and how complex models are designed of weather systems. Running those models might sometimes result in a prediction of rain and other times not. So, one way to think about the weather forecaster's probability is that it is the proportion of times that their models predict rain given the current weather data entered into that model.

On the second reason for the difficulty of probability, the theoretical underpinning of the ChanceMaker study positions *heuristics and naïve thinking* as resources for teaching. The meanings that the children held for short-term behaviour were largely correct, but the children did not appreciate that these meanings were limited in scope. In that sense the meanings were overgeneralized. Once they identified in the feedback, not usually available in everyday settings, that these meanings could not explain the behaviour of the gadgets, a search for alternative explanations began. The surprise that the pie chart was not uniform led to the need to find circumstances in which it was. It turned out that fairness was only achieved when the number of trials was high, and only then when the workings box was also uniform. The construction of these situated abstractions seemed to depend on the opportunity to generate many results without undue calculation overload. It also needed the facility to make personal conjectures and to test these out before refining situated abstractions that seemed to have strong powers of explanation. Certainly, the ChanceMaker study interprets the research on heuristics as a description of unschooled intuitive thinking and supports the notion that digital technology can be exploited by providing artificial experiences that are not typical in the everyday.

Such situated abstractions are not formal ways of thinking but they might represent routes towards formalized approaches to probability. In that sense, the ChanceMaker study offers an example of the sort of chance experiments envisaged by Fischbein, by exploiting the affordances of digital technology. Such experiments might counteract the *withering of naïve intuitions* though they might need to begin rather early in the curriculum and perhaps before Grade 6 as suggested by Fischbein when using approaches that were not enhanced by digital technology.

There is no suggestion that a formal understanding of probability is anything other than hard, depending as it does on a range of other mathematical concepts, which are also known obstacles for children. A formal appreciation of probability is likely to be a *late development* as suggested by Piaget. Nevertheless, there is evidence that the use of a modelling perspective to probability aligned with the careful use of the affordances of digital technology can act as an intuitive grounding to facilitate successful engagement with the conventional formalizations of probability.

Further reading

Fischbein, E., 1975. *The intuitive sources of probabilistic thinking in children*. Dordrecht, Netherlands: Reidel.

Konold, C., 1989. Informal conceptions of probability. *Cognition and Instruction*, 6, 59–98.

Konold, C., Harradine, A. and Kazak, S., 2007. Understanding distributions by modeling them. *International Journal of Computers and Mathematical Learning*, 12, 217–30.

Lecoutre, M. P., 1992. Cognitive models and problem spaces in 'purely random' situations. *Educational Studies in Mathematics*, 23, 589–93.

Wilensky, U., 1997. What is normal anyway? Therapy for epistemological anxiety. *Educational Studies in Mathematics*, 33, 171–202.

Additional references

Smith, J. P., diSessa, A. A. and Rochelle, J., 1993. Misconceptions reconceived: a constructivist analysis of knowledge in transition. *Journal of Learning Sciences*, 3 (2), 115–63.

Threlfall, J., 2004. Uncertainty in mathematics teaching: the National Curriculum experiment in teaching probability to primary pupils. *Cambridge Journal of Education*, 34 (3), 297–314.

Tversky, A. and Kahneman, D., 1983. Extensional versus intuitive reasoning: the conjunction fallacy in probability judgement. *Psychological Review*, 90, 293–315.

Part III
Comparative Mathematics Education

European Mathematics Curricula and Classroom Practices

Paul Andrews

15

Core readings

The Core readings addressed in this chapter are:

Kaiser, G., 2002. Educational philosophies and their influence on mathematics education: an ethnographic study in English and German mathematics classrooms. *ZDM – The International Journal on Mathematics Education*, 34 (6), 241–57.

Haggarty, L. and Pepin, B., 2002. An investigation of mathematics textbooks and their use in English, French and German classrooms: who gets an opportunity to learn what? *British Educational Research Journal*, 28 (4), 567–90.

Wilson, L., Andrew, C. and Below, J., 2006. A comparison of teacher/pupil interaction within mathematics lessons in St Petersburg, Russia and the North-East of England. *British Educational Research Journal*, 32 (3), 411–41.

Andrews, P., 2011. The cultural location of teachers' mathematical knowledge: another hidden variable in mathematics education research? In T. Rowland and K. Ruthven, eds, *Mathematical knowledge in teaching*. New York: Springer, 99–118.

Introduction

Increasingly research is showing that mathematics and its teaching vary from one system to another, not least because education reflects culturally normative values about what is good, right and desirable in a society (Schwartz 1999, p. 25). If the purpose of education is to induct learners into those beliefs and practices that history has shown to be effective for the maintenance of a society (Hofstede 1986; Triandis and Suh 2002), then that society will present a particular, culturally determined, perspective on mathematics.

The first three core readings discussed in this chapter examine the cultural construction of school mathematics in England, France, Germany and Russia, countries that have influenced greatly curricular traditions around the world (Cummings 1999). This discussion is prefaced by a brief socio-historical commentary on those four curricular traditions, which acknowledges that all curricula are founded on a system's conception of an ideal person (Cummings 1999), represents a form of social regulation (Popkewitz 1997) and are substantially more than the documentary presentation of the knowledge and skills students are expected to learn. The final core reading, in considering the curriculum intersection of curriculum and classroom practice in two other European systems of interest to the mathematics education researcher, Flanders and Hungary, presents a culturally based theorization of teacher knowledge (see the chapter by Rowland, this volume) that helps explain further the issues raised in the first three core readings.

A socio-historical commentary of education in England, France, Germany and Russia

English education, in its emphasis on Protestant values and the importance of sport in the development of a healthy mind and body (Cummings 1999), so highlights personal morality and experiential knowledge over rationality (Pepin 1999) that 'the chapel and the playing field were in many ways more important . . . than the classroom' (Lauwerys 1959, p. 288). In drawing on the English public school's liberal arts tradition, and its rejection of science and engineering, it offers an education appropriate for gentlemen (Holmes and Mclean 1989) and, although modern emphases on employment (see the chapter by Ernest, this volume) have compromised this tradition in mass education, 'its usefulness in the business of earning a living is rejected quite decisively' (Lauwerys 1959, p. 289). Thus, the English tradition accords with Kamens et al.'s (1996) description of an arts and humanities curriculum predicated on the maintenance of both an intellectual elite and an established high culture.

French education draws on Enlightenment principles that education should not only be separated from superstition but include all human knowledge in ways that emphasize rationality (Cummings 1999; Holmes and McLean 1989) and that not only are truth and goodness closely related but also that if it is not rational then it is not education (Lauwerys 1959). Post-revolutionary principles of égalité and laïcité underpin a curriculum focused on the removal of social inequalities and the expectation that moral issues will be addressed at home (Pepin 1999). In sum, the French tradition resonates closely with classical curricula whereby an 'intellectually demanding and character-enhancing' experience produces 'well-rounded generalists rather than highly trained specialists' to form a political and social elite whose responsibility is the maintenance of the natural social order (Kamens et al. 1996, p. 119).

Falling somewhere between the English and the French traditions, German education, rooted in Lutheran notions of justification by faith (Lauwerys 1959), emphasizes both an encyclopaedic perspective on knowledge and personal piety (Cummings 1999; Prange 2004). Drawing on the humanistic tradition, or bildung, it emphasizes a 'spiritual awareness of the inwardness of the world of men and of things' (Lauwerys 1959, p. 290). Based on an underlying belief that every occupation has dignity, the tripartite structure of German schools, with its equal privileging of academic and practical knowledge, poses no barrier to higher education (Pepin 1999). In sum, the German tradition can be seen as resonant with the comprehensive curriculum that aims not only to allow all children, irrespective of background, similar opportunities to learn and achieve but also 'to produce competent citizens and productive workers rather than technical specialists' who are endowed with 'certain rights and duties' (Kamens et al. 1996, p. 120).

Finally, Russian education draws on soviet principles of egalitarianism and locates vocationalism and an encyclopaedic model of knowledge within a socialist moral philosophy (Cummings 1999). Described as polytechnicalist (Holmes and McLean 1989), it reflects a 'desire to use education as an instrument for changing the conventional attitude to work', with not only manual labour to be 'as highly considered as intellectual or clerical work' but also every subject 'considered from the point of view of the help which it is capable of giving to the . . . builder of a socialist society' (Lauwerys 1959, p. 291). Such a tradition, alongside emphases on industrial and military growth, fit well with notions of mathematics and science curricula, which developed to facilitate a rapid growth from an agrarian to an industrial society (Kamens et al. 1996).

Inevitably such descriptions are prone to revision. For example, Russian education, while retaining elements of its soviet legacy, is undergoing change as part of its shift towards a market economy. These changes have included a decentralization of responsibilities, reforms to curriculum and assessment (Mitter 2003) and the introduction of parental choice (Laczik 2006). In similar vein, post-war reforms in France have addressed, in particular, concerns with respect to a 'scientific and technical lag' (Resnik 2007, p.157). However, despite such ongoing changes sufficient remains of the above traditions to facilitate not only our understanding of research reports located in those countries but also our abilities to evaluate the veracity of claims made. The remainder of this chapter, therefore, is given to examining how researchers have characterized different aspects of mathematics in these countries.

Mathematics teaching in England and Germany

Kaiser's article is atypical and, despite the rather strained English, exemplary. Unlike most comparative studies of mathematics teaching she pays considerable attention to framing her ethnography within a historical analysis of the two countries' curricular traditions. To do this she draws, in the first instance, on McLean (1990) and presents summaries, not dissimilar to those discussed, of the English, French and German traditions. It is interesting, in this respect, that she tends to accept without comment McLean's analyses of the English and French traditions although she makes explicit reference to elements of his account of the German with which she disagrees. Had she been French, would she have critiqued McLean's analysis of the French system and accepted his summary of the German? Following this general introduction she offers detailed accounts of the English, continuing to draw on McLean, and the German, drawing extensively on Blankertz 1982). Both summaries are extensive and helpful in alerting the reader to the origins of the two systems' philosophical and pedagogical traditions. In so doing she highlights English emphases on morality, individualism, specialism and the privileging of inductive rather than deductive knowledge, and German emphases on virtue, the importance of deep and connected knowledge and the equal privileging of all forms of legitimate human activity. However, it was a little disappointing that each review drew, essentially, on a single piece of writing, not least because the Lauwerys (1959) article addresses both particularly well.

In describing her project Kaiser offers an extensive discussion of the theoretical underpinnings of ethnography in educational research. In so doing not only does she make an interesting and valuable contribution to the methodology of comparative education research but also highlights three key considerations; the long-term presence of the researcher in the field, flexibility of data collection and analysis, and detailed field notes. This is followed, drawing on more than 300 observed lessons, by her analysis of the two systems' didactic traditions as reflected in lessons taught primarily to students in Grades 8–10. Acknowledging the impossibility of ethnography yielding generalizable outcomes she locates her analysis in the sociological tradition of the ideal type developed in the early years of the twentieth century by Max Weber. This seeks to stress recurrent patterns of behaviour in the construction of a model that reflects some sense of the typicality of the phenomenon under scrutiny. However, the word 'ideal' does not connote any moral evaluation but frames the ordering of the social world.

Through her ideal types she shows well how the different socio-cultural underpinnings of the two systems play out in classrooms. For example, in German mathematics teaching 'theoretical mathematical considerations are of great importance' while English mathematics teaching privileges a 'pragmatic understanding of theory' (p. 249). In Germany, mathematics is taught in an order defined by the structure of the subject with large thematic fields taught independently of each other, while in England a spiral curriculum enables topics, typically taught over a small number of lessons, to be introduced at an elementary level, picked up again later and taught independently of any obvious sense of structure. In German lessons, new topics or methods are given high priority and introduced by means of class discussions and often illustrated by real-world examples, while in England they have a low importance and are often 'given by the teacher just as information or in the style of a recipe' (p. 250) or inductively through investigation. The role of proof in German mathematics, while important, varies according to school type. In England, formal proof is rare with theorems warranted by experiment, example or teacher assertion. German lessons are progressed by high expectations of students' correct and confident execution of algorithms, with clear expectations that each is undertaken in well-defined and predetermined ways. In English lessons 'rules and standard algorithms (are) of minor importance' (p. 252). Priority is given to students' own solutions rather than systematically introduced approaches. German teachers place great importance on precise mathematical language in all official discourse, while English teachers view such matters as of minor importance. German teachers exploit real-world problems rarely, and when they do they tend to be artificial examples used in the introduction of new concepts or methods. English teachers place a high importance on such problems, particularly in respect of applying mathematics to extra-mathematical problems. Such descriptions, even if not typical of all lessons, resonate with the literature's summaries of the two traditions and confirm how culture influences in largely hidden ways classroom participants' enacting of their roles.

Textbooks and the teaching of angle in England, France and Germany

Haggarty and Pepin focus on the nature and use of text books (see the chapter by Rezat and Straesser, this volume) in the teaching of lower secondary mathematics in England, France and Germany. In introducing the topic they highlight not only the importance of text books in the construction of children's mathematical competence but also the role of culture in determining both a textbook's content and the manner of its use. Their literature review alerts readers to different analytical frameworks, as in Van Dormolen's (1986) didactical analysis, Schmidt et al.'s (1997) topic complexity analysis and Dowling's (1996) sociological analysis, reminding us that textbooks are neither value-free in their authorship nor independent of the teacher in the manner of their use. This latter point leads to an extensive summary, framed against five subheadings, of how textbooks are used in classrooms. The first of these, the authority of the textbook, is particularly interesting in its offering three distinctive perspectives on authority: authority as reflected in a book's presentation of societally valorized knowledge, authority as reflected in teachers' acquisition of author status by dint of how they use the texts and authority as reflected in teachers' mediation of a text's content.

Research methods are discussed briefly and the reader reminded that qualitative research does not seek to generalize but facilitate understanding. However, they indicate that their analysis 'uses a schedule which draws on the range of ideas in the literature' but say nothing with respect to its precise content or the 'comprehensive set of questions' (p. 574) that underpin it. Also, nothing is offered to indicate the means by which data were analysed. Despite such criticisms, their analyses confirm the extent not only to which culture influences textbook content and use but also the robustness of the curricular traditions described earlier.

Examining textbooks, focused on students in Grades 6–8, through the framing lens of angle they found that French texts were comprehensive and cognitively challenging. They incorporate extensive explanatory text, sufficient for students to 'do the questions . . . without additional support' (p. 576), with technical vocabulary used throughout. Exercises included opportunities for students to speculate and links to other topic areas. The German texts were differentiated according to school type although, fundamentally, few differences were found. They attempted to establish links 'between everyday situations and what pupils are to learn' (p. 578). Detailed explanatory text is included and technical vocabulary is used consistently. 'Pupils are not required to speculate and most questions require low-level applications of the skill.' English texts were 'less densely packed and contain fewer examples than textbooks in either France or Germany' (p. 579). They incorporate no explanatory text, thereby ensuring some teacher mediation, and little emphasis on technical vocabulary. Exercises included opportunities for students to estimate before measuring, although questions 'are of a low level' with 'no obvious scope for extending them' (p. 582). In the two books analysed only one question was put in context.

French teachers used textbooks primarily for exercises, preferring to devise their own topic presentations, although students were encouraged to learn how to use the book as a resource for their learning. The mixed ability nature of French classes meant that all students 'were given the same questions to do' and 'exposed to the same cognitive and language demands as each other' (583), although teachers spent time with individuals if they thought they needed additional support. While all German teachers used textbooks to plan their teaching, classroom use varied according to school type. Gymnasium teachers used them less than Hauptschule teachers although typically any use was as a source of exercises. Teachers in the former tended to make assumptions about the maturity of their students and adopted more discursive approaches to teaching than their Hauptschule colleagues, who tended to assume that their students would not be 'able to cope with too many deviations from the straightforward mathematical algorithms' (p. 584) or word problems. English teachers used textbooks regularly as both a source of exercises and ideas for presentation. All 'considered that it would be impossible to use the same textbook with all pupils in a year group' (p. 584) and spoke of the need for different ability students to be offered different types of problem, not least because of lower ability students' linguistic deficiencies and their need for 'plenty of straightforward questions practising particular skills or techniques'. In reality, few English pupils experienced an 'opportunity to develop their reading and comprehension skills in mathematics'.

Teacher–pupil interactions in the mathematics classrooms of Russia and England

The article by Wilson et al. focuses on teacher–pupil interactions in primary mathematics classrooms in St Petersburg, Russia and the North East England. Their descriptions of their locations were deliberate as, with all case-study research, a small number of schools researched in one location should not be construed as representative of the schools generally. Their article is framed against curriculum reform in both countries. In England, reform has encouraged teachers to introduce regular whole-class teaching into a tradition largely dominated by individual work, while in Russia, somewhat ironically, reform has focused on making more individual a tradition based on whole-class work. In framing their study, no allusion was made to the socio-historical underpinnings of the two countries' didactic traditions.

They present their methods clearly and, in so doing, highlight well how several recurrent issues in comparative mathematics education research were addressed. For example, five consecutive days of mathematics lessons were observed in a range of year groups in two primary schools in each country, which 'enabled observers to record the story of the mathematical experience of each class during the week and counteracted the possible effect of observation of a single atypical lesson with any one class' (p. 413). Typically lessons were observed by two English and one English-speaking Russian researcher and three forms of data were collected. These derived from a semi-structured observation schedule designed to produce 'a time-related description of specific features of the lesson at each stage' (p. 413), a lesson narrative, constructed in real time, to record 'as fully as possible the events of the lesson in chronological order', and an interaction map used to record the location of any pupil involved in an interaction with the teacher and whether it was private or public. With regard to the interactions, attempts were made to 'record the duration of each interaction' although, as they concede, this proved difficult.

Their analyses highlight some interesting patterns in the ways that interactions played out in project lessons. On the one hand, English lessons, typically, were structured around four or five sections. Within that structure they comprised large numbers of private interactions, which were typically located between introductory sections of public interaction and closing sections of public interaction, highlighting the increasing prevalence of the three-part lesson recommended by the English authorities. Mixed periods of interaction were rare. Russian lessons, on the other hand, comprised relatively few private periods of private interaction. Solely public interactions were seen to dominate, 'occasionally punctuated by . . . a mixture of public and private exchanges' (p. 421). Russian public interactions were found to be longer than the English. Indeed, the limited evidence available indicated that around 30 per cent of Russian public interactions lasted more than 3 seconds and a further 12 per cent that lasted more than 10 seconds. In contrast, of the English around 7 per cent lasted longer than 3 seconds and only 3 per cent lasted longer than 10.

In both countries the typical public interaction involved two elements, the teacher initiates and the class responds. However, the manner of these class responses varied. Russian teachers expected students to 'focus on repetition of rules and procedures whereas English teachers concentrated on counting and chanting number sequences'. That is, the Russian responses focused on the general concepts or algorithms underlying the question while the English focused on the particular numerical operations necessary to address it.

When compared with their earlier study (Wilson et al. 2001), the data reported in this article confirm an increase in private interactions in the Russian classrooms and public interactions in the English, in line with reform objectives in both countries. Importantly, when a Russian student responds in a public interaction, he or she 'appears to do so on behalf of the class as a whole and is expected to articulate the standard answer; the rest of the class is expected to participate by silently rehearsing the same answer while listening' (p. 431). When an English pupil responds, he or she may be reporting a method unfamiliar to other pupils. This means not only that students may not be able to 'predict the response and collectively mentally rehearse the procedure' but also that 'they are required to make sense of . . . a procedure which may not resonate with the method they have themselves chosen' (p. 431).

The intersection of mathematics curricula and teaching in Flanders and Hungary

The final core reading is framed against recent categorizations of teachers' mathematical knowledge for teaching (MKT) that is, Andrews argues, typically construed as an individual rather than a cultural construction. He outlines a tripartite curricular framework for analysing teachers' mathematical knowledge that explicitly acknowledges 'the cultural discourse in which mathematics teaching and learning occur' (p. 100). According to Andrews, teachers work within an intended curriculum, as conceived by the second international mathematics study (Garden 1987), reflecting the knowledge and skills privileged by the system in which teachers operate. They work within a received curriculum, amenable only to inference, reflecting the hidden and culturally derived beliefs and practices teachers acquire by dint of being who they are. Finally, they work within an idealized curriculum, which is articulable, reflecting individual teachers' personal and experientially informed beliefs. Having proposed the framework, he shows, through an analysis of a sequence of lessons taught on linear equations in each of Hungary and Flanders, how the tripartite curriculum plays out. In so doing, he summarizes the two systems' curricula's statements with respect to linear equations, highlighting both differences and similarities in the ways in which the topic is framed. In respect of differences the Flemish curriculum comprises a general statement for each grade, while the Hungarian comprises detailed statements for each grade alongside indications as to solution processes. In terms of similarities both highlight the solution of equations of the first degree and, more generally, locate the topic in a systemic desire to encourage students to translate text into equations for solving. In addition, he frames his analyses of the two sequences against literature on linear equations and, in particular, the distinction between arithmetic equations and algebraic equations (Filloy and Rojano 1989; Kieran 1992).

The two sequences of lessons, taught by Pauline in Flanders and Eva in Hungary, derived from a larger project involving four case-study teachers from each of England, Finland, Flanders, Hungary and Spain. Andrews reports on the ways in which videotaped data were collected and, with respect to quantitative analyses, discusses briefly the application of a coding schedule developed during a year of live observations in the year prior to data collection. This comprised seven generic and inferable mathematical learning outcomes and ten generic and inferable didactic strategies. He reports that on differences and similarities in the codes applied to the lessons of the two countries under scrutiny. In general, Hungarian teachers privileged higher-order learning outcomes and exploited didactic strategies commensurate with those outcomes more frequently than their Flemish colleagues.

Andrews then presents qualitative analyses of the two teachers' lesson sequences. He highlights how they both exploited realistic word problems in their teaching; deferred introducing analytical solutions, which were based on the balance scale, until they presented their students with algebraic equations; frequently invited their students to solve algebraic equations involving brackets, negatives and fraction coefficients. However, their exploitation of word problems varied considerably, with only a single example in Pauline's sequence and many in Eva's. The extent to which they sustained the balance varied, with Pauline mentioning it in passing while Eva sustained it through several examples, including drawing it on the board. Pauline spent much time in three of her five lessons on exercises in which students worked individually while Eva never asked her students to work on more than one question before sharing publicly the solutions obtained. Finally, he discusses each teacher's teaching against the tripartite curriculum. For example, he writes that Eva's teaching showed a clear adherence to Hungarian intended curricular expectations, both in terms of the content expected of Grade 7 students and her exploitation of non-routine problems. Second, the explicit manner in which she exploited and sustained the balance, her 'invocation of brackets, negatives and fractions' accorded with 'earlier findings that Hungarian teachers operate with the general rather than the particular', and her close adherence 'to a previously observed cycle of problem posing, solving and sharing' (p. 114) all indicated a close adherence to a well-established received curriculum. However, her use of word problems, which earlier observers of Hungarian teaching had noted as a rarity, alluded to a particular idealized curriculum.

Conclusion

I began this chapter by examining the distinctive socio-historically derived characteristics of the English, French, German and Russian educational traditions. It is my conjecture, supported by the evidence of the first three articles examined, that these traditions permeate all aspects of mathematics teaching. Whether one is examining the text books available for teachers to use, the classroom interactions of teachers and students, or the forms of mathematics privileged in different classrooms, the evidence suggests that all are prone to largely hidden cultural influences that make the mathematics classrooms of one country unique. For example, the first three articles highlight an intellectually impoverished English mathematics that permeates both text books (Haggarty and Pepin 2002) and classroom expectations (Kaiser 2002) and which is exacerbated by the idiosyncratic ways in which classroom interactions, located in a tradition of individualism, play out (Wilson et al. 2006). Such traditions contrast greatly with the evidence from the other three key systems – whether the mathematical formalism of German classrooms (Kaiser 2002), the intellectual rigour of French textbooks (Haggarty and Pepin) or the well-rehearsed collective interactions of Russian classroom (Wilson et al. 2006). In short, the differing mathematics education traditions highlighted in the first three articles are clearly manifestations of cultural expectations with respect to the ideal person. In this respect, whether one's particular cultural lenses lead one to feel more comfortable with one system's perspectives than another's is not the issue; all three systems clearly operate a distinctive control over what children are expected to learn and how they learn it.

The fourth paper, while not located in analyses of the four major traditions, attempts to explain how much of what teachers do in their classrooms is so culturally embedded as to be hidden and beneath teachers' immediate articulation. Indeed, Andrews would argue that the interactions of the idealized, received and intended curricula confirm the extent to which teachers are products of the cultures in which they are raised and work. Such interactions structure not only the ways in which textbooks are produced but also the ways in which they are used; they underpin the ways in which individual teachers, as members of a particular collective, structure the classroom interactions characteristic of a system.

All four core readings confirm that mathematics and its teaching are elements of a collective psychological conditioning (Triandis and Suh 2002) or collective mental programming of a particular group of people (Hofstede 1986). Of course, there are those who challenge the extent to which mathematics teachers' work is culturally determined on the basis that teachers' core teaching practices show little cross-national variation (LeTendre et al. 2001). However, Andrews (2009) has argued that similarity of broad categories of didactical strategy, for example, explaining, are inevitable and that characteristic differences lie in other practices such as the use of high-level questioning or the public sharing of student ideas.

Further reading

Andrews, P., 2007. Mathematics teacher typologies or nationally located patterns of behaviour? *International Journal of Educational Research*, 46 (5), 306–18.

Aubrey, C., Tancig, S., Magajna, L. and Kavkler, M., 2000. The development of numeracy in England and Slovenia. *Education 3–13*, 28 (3), 13–23.

Wolf, A. and Steedman, H., 1998. Basic competence in mathematics: Swedish and English 16 year olds. *Comparative Education*, 34 (3), 241–59.

Additional references

Andrews, P., 2009. Mathematics teachers' didactic strategies: examining the comparative potential of low inference generic descriptors. *Comparative Education Review*, 53 (4), 559–81.

Cummings, W., 1999. The Institutions of education: compare, compare, compare! *Comparative Education Review*, 43 (4), 413–37.

Dowling, P., 1996. A sociological analysis of school mathematics texts. *Educational Studies in Mathematics*, 31, 389–415.

Filloy, E. and Rojano, T., 1989. Solving equations: the transition from arithmetic to algebra. *For the Learning of Mathematics*, 9 (2), 19–25.

Garden, R., 1987. The second IEA Mathematics Study. *Comparative Education Review*, 31 (1), 47–68.

Hofstede, G., 1986. Cultural differences in teaching and learning. *International Journal of Intercultural Relations*, 10, 301–20.

Holmes, B. and McLean, M., 1989. *The curriculum: a comparative perspective*. London: Unwin Hyman.

Kamens, D., Meyer, J. and Benavot, A., 1996. Worldwide patterns in academic secondary education curricula. *Comparative Education Review*, 40 (2), 116–38.

Kieran, C., 1992. The learning and teaching of school algebra. In D. Grouws, ed., *Handbook of research on mathematics teaching and learning*. New York: Macmillan, 390–419.

Laczik, A., 2006. Comparing Hungary and Russia: methodological implications of a qualitative research project. *Research in Comparative and International Education*, 1 (2), 136–45.

Lauwerys, J., 1959. The philosophical approach to comparative education. *International Review of Education*, 5 (3), 281–98.

LeTendre, G. K., Baker, D. P., Akiba, M., Goesling, B. and Wiseman, A., 2001. Teachers' work: institutional isomorphism and cultural variation in the U.S. Germany, and Japan. *Educational Researcher*, 30 (6), 3–15.

McLean, M., 1990. *Britain and a single market Europe*. London: Kogan Page.

Mitter, W., 2003. A decade of transformation: educational policies in Central and Eastern Europe. *International Review of Education*, 49 (1/2), 75–96.

Pepin, B., 1999. The influence of national cultural traditions on pedagogy: classroom practices in England, France and Germany. In J. Leach and B. Moon, eds, *Learners and pedagogy*. London: Paul Chapman, 122–35.

Popkewitz, T. S., 1997. The production of reason and power: curriculum history and intellectual traditions. *Journal of Curriculum Studies*, 29 (2), 131–64.

Prange, K., 2004. Bildung: a paradigm regained? *European Educational Research Journal*, 3 (2), 501–9.

Resnik, J., 2007. The democratisation of the education system in France after the Second World War: a neo-Weberian glocal approach to education reforms. *British Journal of Educational Studies*, 55 (2), 155–81.

Schmidt, W., McKnight, C., Valverde, G., Houang, R. and Wiley, D., 1997. *Many visions, many aims: a cross-national investigation of curricular intentions in school mathematics*. Dordrecht, Netherlands: Kluwer.

Schwartz, S., 1999. A theory of cultural values and some implications for work. *Applied Psychology*, 48 (1), 23–47.

Triandis, H. and Suh, E., 2002. Cultural influences on personality. *Annual Review of Psychology*, 53, 133–60.

Van Dormolen, J., 1986. Textual analysis. In B. Christiansen, A. G. Howson and M. Otte, eds, *Perspectives on mathematics education*. Dordrecht, Netherlands: Reidel, 141–71.

Wilson, L., Andrew, C. and Sourikova, S., 2001. Shape and structure in primary mathematics lessons: a comparative study in the north-east of England and St Petersburg, Russia-some implications for the daily mathematics lesson. *British Educational Research Journal*, 27 (1), 30–58.

Teaching and Learning Mathematics in Chinese Culture

Ngai-Ying Wong

Core readings

The Core readings addressed in this chapter are as follows:

Wong, N. Y., 2004. The CHC learner's phenomenon: its implications on mathematics education. In L. Fan, N. Y. Wong, J. Cai and S. Li, eds, *How Chinese learn mathematics: perspectives from insiders*. Singapore: World Scientific, 503–34.

Cai, J. and Wang, T., 2010. Conceptions of effective mathematics teaching within a cultural context: perspectives of teachers from China and the United States. *Journal of Mathematics Teacher Education*, 13, 297–309.

Huang, R. and Li, Y., 2009. Pursuing excellence in mathematics classroom instruction through exemplary lesson development in China: a case study. *ZDM – The International Journal on Mathematics Education*, 41, 279–96.

Wong, N. Y., Lam, C. C., Sun, X. and Chan, A. M. Y., 2009. From 'exploring the middle zone' to 'constructing a bridge': experimenting in the spiral *bianshi* mathematics curriculum. *International Journal of Science and Mathematics Education*, 7 (2), 363–82.

Introduction

In recent decades, the consistently high mathematics achievement of Far Eastern students has caught the attentions of sociologists, educationalists and psychologists (Watkins and Biggs 1996, 2001). In particular, it is frequently perceived that the Chinese learning environment stresses recitation and memorization; that classes are large, filled with passive learners and led by authoritative teachers. Such settings are in sharp contrast to those highlighted in the Western literature as conducive to learning. This is especially true when learning is not measured by the number of facts memorized but qualitative aspects (Biggs 1991) such as understanding and the active building of new knowledge (NCTM 2000). Some, for example, Huang and Leung (2006), even speak of 'myth' and 'paradox' to describe the Chinese learners' phenomenon. In this chapter, I aim to examine the myth and highlight those Chinese mathematics classroom practices that may contribute to the betterment of teaching and learning.

However, when reading research papers about the Chinese it is important to be aware of key aspects of the underlying context, not least of which is the assumption that Chinese learners, whether in China itself, its special administrative regions like Hong Kong, or other countries, share the same cultural origin – Confucianism. Many aspects of Chinese culture derive from the traditions of Confucianism, which developed from the teachings of the Chinese philosopher Confucius (551–479 BC), who lived in a rather chaotic period of the country's history. Confucius saw the importance of education in restoring law and order, and believed that everyone, talented or not, is educable. Under this belief, diligence, obedience and untiring practice are some of the features of learning. Since Confucianism echoed the Chinese agricultural tradition and the wish for state control of emperors, it became part of mainstream Chinese culture.

In the following, drawing on the first core reading, I present a basic picture of the Chinese learner. Second, drawing on the second core reading, I discuss the underlying beliefs held by Chinese students and teachers. The third core reading frames a discussion of the general characteristics of the Chinese mathematics classroom. Finally, based on the fourth core reading, a teaching mode common to the Chinese mathematics classroom will be introduced.

'Chinese-ness' – characteristics of the Chinese learner

The first core reading (Wong 2004) summarizes much literature on the topic, including theoretical dispositions and empirical accounts, which has attempted to portray the typical Chinese learner. On the one hand, the Chinese learner is frequently perceived as disciplined and achievement-oriented, someone who attributes success to effort and possesses a strong belief that 'practice makes perfect'. In brief, the image associated with the Chinese learner is one of working harder rather than being smarter (section 2 in the first core reading). On the other hand, contemporary empirical studies indicate that the Chinese privilege deep learning and genuine understanding. It is reported in section 3 of the first core reading that explanations of this apparent paradox can be found in various empirical studies showing the importance of memorization and repetition to Chinese learners. These issues are discussed in the following sections.

Wong's (2004) study, which investigated 'the essence of being Chinese', noted that Confucianism is not the only cultural root of the Chinese. Other ideologies such as Daoism (or Taoism) and Buddhism are also influential. Also, China is a very large country comprising 56 ethnic groups. For instance, a large number of Muslims reside in north-western China and the influence of Confucianism there is minimal. What is more, Confucianism evolved across time and Confucianism today may not necessarily accord with the beliefs that Confucius (or early Confucians) held. In reality, as in any country, what takes effect is always a mix of different cultures, and these cultures are further manipulated by other forces such as utilitarianism (like climbing up the social ladder through high-stakes examinations) and the wills of those in power, including in earlier times the emperor (see Wong et al. (2012) for more details). In other words, it is quite impossible that the modern-day Chinese are products of a single cultural tradition. Likewise, one should not assume that there is 'the' Chinese way of teaching (whether in mathematics or in other subjects). Nevertheless, teaching and learning are often influenced by culturally located beliefs. Therefore the next section examines various Chinese beliefs about how mathematics should be learned and taught.

Effective mathematics teaching in the eyes of Chinese teachers

It is widely accepted that teachers' beliefs impact teaching and shape both students' *lived space* and *outcome space*, including cognitive and affective learning outcomes as well as their own beliefs (Wong et al. 2002). Such 'beliefs' typically focus on mathematics, its learning and teaching. The second core reading (Cai and Wang 2010) reported on a systematic investigation of these beliefs held by Chinese mathematics teachers, which included how they view the characteristics of an effective mathematics lesson and an effective mathematics teacher.

The study involved a cross-national comparison of mathematics teachers in Australia, the Chinese mainland, Hong Kong and the United States, the full account of which can be found in Cai et al. (2009). The second core reading comprised the China–US element of the study, through which one is able to present an East–West contrast and a salient picture of how Chinese teachers view effective mathematics teaching. In the study, in-depth semi-structured interviews were conducted with 9 and 11 expert mathematics teachers in the Chinese mainland and the United States, respectively. All aspects of their beliefs about mathematics, its learning and teaching, were solicited. It was found, not surprisingly, that teachers' views on effective mathematics teaching are closely associated with their view on the nature of mathematics. Chinese teachers encourage students' mathematical understanding by connecting pieces of abstract knowledge. They consider memorization as preceding understanding because memorization can serve as an intermediate step towards conceptual understanding. Furthermore, Chinese respondents see effective teaching as teacher-led instruction with a coherent structure. The issue of teacher-led versus student-centred instruction will be further discussed later.

The results of this study echoed earlier studies on teachers' perspectives on mathematics (Wong 2002) showing that teachers regard mathematics as logical, widely applicable to daily life, and involving thinking and the manipulation of numbers and symbols. Importantly, they believed that a major goal of mathematics teaching is the development of a mathematical way of thinking.

By way of contrast, and further highlighting the cultural heterogeneity of the Chinese people, the study from which the second core reading derived also examined Hong Kong teachers' beliefs. For these teachers, effective mathematics teaching sets a path for students to go from the concrete to the abstract, and helps them to acquire an ability to apply mathematical rules flexibly (even when the context is changed). To achieve these, well-organized practice can serve as a scaffold leading from basic to higher-order thinking skills (Wong 2006). The details of this will be elaborated in the last section.

Thus far, I have shown how teachers' beliefs affect their teaching. It is important, also, to consider how teaching takes place. Zhang and Wong (2010) report a study of the relationship between Chinese teachers' beliefs and their teaching under the categorization proposed by Ernest (1989): see also the chapter by Ernest, this volume. It was found that when Platonic-instrumentalists approach a lesson, memorization is emphasized: they regard teaching as a course to help students memorize important facts and skills so that they can avoid making mistakes in solving mathematics problems; they believe that teachers need to pay attention to the norms of teaching and to the consistency of content in the class. By contrast, the problem-solving oriented teachers consider how mathematical concepts relate to students' experiences when preparing a lesson. To them, teaching is a course to help students experience the procedure and thinking process of problem solving: whether the answer is right or wrong is secondary. This shows that teachers' beliefs greatly affect classroom teaching, although their depth of professional knowledge is another important factor affecting classroom teaching.

All these studies result in a general scenario of what effective classroom learning and teaching in the Chinese context looks like. An effective (mathematics) teacher possesses rich mathematics knowledge and teaching experience, prepares the lesson well, and has a reflective and flexible mind. The teacher uses various methods to explain the content clearly and provides well-structured exercises. Although teaching is apparently teacher-led, the teacher still puts effort into making it student-centred by facilitating teacher–student interactions. Questioning, a way to solicit student feedback, should not only help the teacher understand whether students really understand but also keep students engaged and the class in order. There are two facets of the goal of teaching in the eyes of teachers, the generic one and the specific one. On the one hand, teachers are resolved to meet the requirements of the mathematics curriculum (and examination). They aim to help students develop their mathematical concepts and problem-solving abilities. On the other hand, they realize that non-mathematics-specific educational goals (e.g. being observant and being equipped with analytical skills and creativity) have to be addressed. In the eyes of these teachers, these goals can be accomplished by, besides doing mathematics itself, providing student–teacher interactive classroom activities as mentioned. Students are brought up in this *lived space* shaped by the teacher that generates students' learning outcomes, including students' beliefs about mathematics and mathematics learning.

The role of practice: Repetitive learning versus learning by rote

I have examined Chinese mathematics teachers' beliefs and identified the importance of practice and how it is utilized in the classroom. This section, therefore, links the first two core readings, which focus more on cultural contexts and beliefs, and the last two core readings, which focus on the reality in the Chinese mathematics classroom.

The first core reading summarizes the academic discourse on the Chinese learner in the context of mathematics. As the phenomenon unfolds, one key issue is whether the Chinese lean too much towards procedural knowledge. Much has been researched and discussed on the distinctions and interrelationships among memorization, practice, repetitive learning and learning by rote.

In a study, reviewed in the first core reading, Marton et al. (1997) identified a relationship between memorization and understanding among Chinese learners that is uncommon among their Western counterparts. In other words, memorization is not necessarily detrimental to understanding. Moreover, there are many ways of interpreting *memorization* and *practice*. How teachers view this differently has been discussed earlier and in the second core reading. Rote-memorization and getting something memorized, for instance, can have very different meanings (Wong 2009). It is natural that one has to get something (e.g. formulas) memorized in the course of learning, whether in mathematics or in other subjects. This is not something wrong and there are many more means of remembering than mere recitation, and practice is one.

Again, as mentioned in the first core reading, repetition may also be viewed differently. Revisiting the earlier findings of Marton and Booth (1997) and Bowden and Marton (1998) leads to the conclusion that a way of experiencing a phenomenon can be characterized in terms of those aspects of the phenomenon that are discerned and kept in focal awareness by the learner. Thus, discernment is an essential element of learning, and variation is crucial to bringing about discernment. Marton often uses a metaphor to show this: if the world had only one colour, *green*, the concept of *colour* could not exist; in order to discern the concept of *colour*, the learner is exposed to different colours (green, red, blue, etc.). The same is true of mathematical concepts. For example, scalene triangles, non-equilateral isosceles triangles, large and small triangles, triangles with different colours and triangles made from different materials are shown to students to discern the concept of equilateral triangles so that they realize that length (equal sides) is the key issue (critical aspect) of the concept, while position, colour and material are not. Since variation is the key to understanding, repetition is indispensable. The crux of the matter is whether systematic variation can be built into the repetition.

On the other hand, Star (2005) proposed the notion of deep procedures, which were further echoed by a series of studies by Rittle-Johnson and Star (2007) (see also Wong 2009). These studies showed that comparison is an effective means to enhance mathematical understanding. Thus, repetition may not be as meaningless and mechanical as it seems. The example given in Star (2005, p. 409) was the solution of a series of linear equations: (1) $2(x + 1) + 3(x + 1) = 10$; (2) $2(x + 1) + 3(x + 1) = 11$; and (3) $2(x + 1) + 3(x + 2) = 10$. This is a typical example of purposeful repetitive practice with variation (an extensive discussion can be found the last section of this chapter), which helps explain why the Chinese learner, while seeming to rely on learning by rote, has the potential for deep learning (Biggs 1994).

A typical Chinese mathematics lesson

Although it is has been noted earlier that teaching practices vary across the vast country of China, characteristics of a typical Chinese mathematics lesson can still be identified. The third core reading presents a portrait of the typical Chinese mathematics lesson. In summarizing an earlier study (Leung 1995), which was based on the analyses of around 200 mathematics lessons in Beijing, London and Hong Kong, it presents the Chinese mathematics lesson as comprising four phases. These are '(1) revising work that students had learnt in the previous lesson; (2) introducing and developing the topic of the lessons; (3) demonstrating and discussing classroom exercises on the black board; and (4) summarizing and assigning homework' (Huang and Li 2009, p. 298). Such features resonated with the earlier work of the Third International Mathematics and Science 1999 Video Study (Hiebert et al. 2003) and remain 'widely in place in China although variations in the pattern of teaching can be noted' (Huang and Li 2009, p. 398). Thus, despite possibilities of variation in practice in, say, rural areas of the country (Ma et al. 2004; Wong et al. 2012), the available evidence offers a generally accurate picture of what is happening in the Chinese mathematics classroom, a conjecture supported by the rather centralized Chinese teacher education system. However, contrary to popular conceptions of Chinese teaching, it is interesting to note that 'there are some student-centered features within a tightly teacher-controlled class' (Huang and Li 2009, p. 398). That is, there may not be a dichotomy between teacher-led and student-centred learning, as first proposed by Ausubel (1963). In this respect Wong (2004) has proposed the possibility of a *teacher-led yet student-centred* mode of teaching, whereby the lesson 'script' is well prepared by a teacher who leads students through it (*teacher-led*) but adjusts it spontaneously in accordance with students' reactions (*student-centred*).

The third core reading does not just describe salient features of the Chinese mathematics lesson; in fact, the theme of the reading was to highlight how teachers promote excellence in learning through the ways in which they manage four key characteristics of Chinese teaching. First, comprehensive and feasible teaching objectives are carefully set; second, core concepts (sometimes including *difficult points*) are identified; third, students are guided to form, develop and consolidate the mathematical concept progressively (by variation); and finally, teachers adapt their teaching by collecting students' feedback. Such practices offer an explanation as to why Chinese mathematics students, typically construed as learning by rote, are successful, with a deep mathematical understanding (deep procedures). In this respect, other articles mentioned in the third core reading offer further evidence in support of our rich understanding of what a Chinese mathematics lesson looks like. Not least among this is the role of student discipline, attentiveness and respect of classroom routines, which are emphasized in the Chinese upbringing. Without these, the so-called Chinese way of classroom instruction could not be conducted effectively (Wong 2008).

Bridging the gap between basic skills and higher-order abilities

The preceding sections give a general impression that basic skills are stressed in China. This is attained through an abundance of practices. However, Chinese teachers also want to build a bridge between basic skills and higher-order abilities (Wong 2008). As mentioned in the third core reading, this is done by first diagnosing key and difficult points of the topic. Such diagnoses may involve analyses of the teaching material as well as previous student work. Clinical interviews with students may also be included in the process. Accordingly, a well-structured lesson can be developed gradually, and hopefully, deep procedural knowledge (as well as mathematical concepts) will be developed via the systematic introduction of variation. Teaching with variation, or *bianshi*, has been practised in China for half a century and has recently led to the now familiar Western pedagogy of variation (Gu et al. 2004; Runesson 1999). It is widely believed that this is one of the reasons underpinning Chinese mathematics teaching effectiveness (Huang and Leung 2006). The fourth core reading offers a comprehensive account of its development, design and implementation and the results of some of the experimentation studies.

At the early stage of its development two notions of *bianshi*, conceptual and procedural, were proposed, related to what are known as *bianshi* problems. In brief, after students handle a *source problem* (e.g. solving $x + 5 = 6$), the teacher offers a series of problems, which include the changing of the numbers involved (e.g. solving $x + 2.5 = 1.7, 3x + 8 = 6, 3x + \frac{1}{2} = 3.5$), the changing of the form of presentation (e.g. solving $y + 8 = 9, (x + 7) + 5 = 6, 2x + 8 = x - 9$), the changing of representations (from arithmetic to geometric), and the changing of contexts (various word problems). Most importantly, the general rules and patterns (the unvaried) are synthesized through comparisons of these varied problems. Such approaches resemble closely the work of Star and Rittle-Johnson discussed earlier.

The spiral *bianshi* mathematics curriculum

The fourth core reading (Wong et al. 2009) describes in detail the *bianshi* mathematics curriculum design. First, the authors expand *bianshi* problems into four basic categories in accordance with the nature of mathematics learning. There are inductive *bianshi* problems, which teachers use to help students derive rules and concepts through the inspection of a number of realistic situations. These rules are consolidated by a systematic introduction of variations into mathematical tasks. Yet, at this point, no new rules and concepts are introduced; learners broaden the scope of their knowledge by means of a variety of broadening *bianshi* problems. At a certain point, by further varying the types of mathematical tasks, the learner is exposed to more mathematical skills and concepts. Such tasks reflect deepening *bianshi* problems. Finally, drawing on notions of realistic mathematics, students' mathematical knowledge is exploited through application *bianshi* problems. This process goes round and round, deepening with each loop. The curriculum thus designed is called a spiral *bianshi* curriculum. Illustrations of each of these forms of *bianshi* are offered in the fourth core reading.

For example, the topic of speed and its *bianshi*-related presentation is elaborated in the fourth core reading. Different rates such as birth rates and website hit rates were inspected to invoke the concept of speed (inductive *bianshi*). After familiarizing the student with the concept through some standard problems, students were challenged with problems involving a shift from integers to decimals and fractions and more varied units, like m, km, cm; sec, min, hr. This is the broadening *bianshi*. The problem types were then gradually changed from those that presented 'Speed = Distance ÷ Time' to those that where 'Distance = Speed × Time' and 'Time = Distance ÷ Speed'. This is the deepening *bianshi*. Students are then asked to apply all these to a vast number of situations, such as the average speed of someone with a slower speed midway, someone catching up with another one who started earlier, and so on.

It should be noted that these curricula should not be designed in a vacuum. In line with what was described, the prior analyses of core and difficult points are crucial. This requires the diagnosis of student learning, especially for the identification of difficult points. Afterwards, one builds a scaffolding with a series of problems (in which variation is systematically introduced) to help students cross the learning hurdle.

As mentioned earlier, *bianshi* teaching has been practised in the Chinese mainland for decades. It was not until recently that its effectiveness was investigated systematically in Hong Kong. This is precisely the theme of the fourth core reading. The framework of the spiral *bianshi* curricula has been utilized to develop curriculum plans and teaching materials for a number of topics in primary as well as secondary mathematics. They were tried out and the effectiveness evaluated in a treatment-reference group, pre-test/post-test experimental design. The results were encouraging in that the idea of the *bianshi* curriculum works well in different areas, including topics in algebra, geometry and data handling.

Conclusion

It is hoped that a picture of mathematics teaching and learning in China has been clearly delineated. Its cultural assumptions, rationale and how these underlying ideas are put into practice have also been described. This was done through the first two core readings, which offered a background of Chinese culture and empirical studies on beliefs among Chinese mathematics teachers and students. The typical classroom practice was described, in broad brush strokes, in the third reading. In particular, the idea of *teacher-led yet student-centred* mathematics teaching challenged conventional dichotomies of classroom practice and led to a discussion of the *bianshi* curriculum, which has been widely practised in China for decades. All these offer potential explanations for the high mathematics achievement of Chinese students. However, as has been repeatedly emphasized, China is a vast country, and one can never be certain how widely such methods are practised. For example, there is evidence that one may find a different picture in rural areas (Ma et al. 2004). Nevertheless, an understanding of these practices might inspire us to improve our mathematics teaching.

As a final remark, it is well known that teaching and learning traditions that work well in one culture may not necessarily work well in another (Watkins and Biggs 2001). It has already been pointed out that each practice has its cultural assumptions and, importantly, as suggested by an old Chinese maxim, 'stones from other hills can be used to polish the jade'.[1] In other words, practices from countries other than one's own can serve as nutrients for the improvement of practice at home, but there is no point in just transplanting other practices. It is hoped that understanding what is happening in the Chinese mathematics classroom may facilitate such reflection on teaching and learning that practice will be improved elsewhere.

Acknowledgement

The author would like to thank his daughter Shirley for her valuable comments.

Note

1. Taken from 'Call of the Cranes, Minor Odes of the Kingdom' in the *Book of Ancient Poetry*.

Further reading

Cai, J., Kaiser, G., Perry, B. and Wong, N. Y., eds, 2009. *Effective mathematics teaching from teachers' perspectives: national and cross-national studies.* Rotterdam, Netherlands: Sense.

Watkins, D. A. and Biggs, J. B., eds, 1996. *The Chinese learner: cultural, psychological and contextual influences.* Hong Kong: Comparative Education Research Centre, University of Hong Kong; Victoria, Australia: Australian Council for Educational Research.

Wong, N. Y., Marton, F., Wong, K. and Lam, C. C., 2002. The lived space of mathematics learning. *Journal of Mathematical Behavior,* 21, 25–47.

Wong, N. Y., Wong, W. Y. and Wong, E. W. Y., 2012. What do Chinese value in (mathematics) education? *ZDM – The International Journal on Mathematics Education,* 44 (1), 9–19.

Additional references

Ausubel, D. P., 1963. *The psychology of meaningful verbal learning.* New York: Grune and Stratton.

Biggs, J. B., 1991. *Teaching for learning: the view from cognitive psychology.* Hawthorn, Victoria, Australia: Australian Council for Educational Research.

—, 1994. What are effective schools? Lessons from East and West. *Australian Educational Researcher,* 21, 19–39.

Bowden, J. and Marton, F., 1998. *The university of learning.* London: Kogan Page.

Ernest, P., 1989. The impact of beliefs on the teaching of mathematics. In P. Ernest, ed., *Mathematics teaching: the state of the art.* New York: Falmer, 249–54.

Gu, L., Marton, F. and Huang, R., 2004. Teaching with variation: a Chinese way of promoting effective mathematics learning. In L. Fan, N. Y. Wong, J. Cai and S. Li, eds, *How Chinese learn mathematics: perspectives from insiders.* Singapore: World Scientific, 309–47.

Hiebert, J., Gallimore, R., Garnier, H., Bogard Givvin, K., Hollingsworth, H., Jacobs, J., et al., 2003. *Teaching mathematics in seven countries: results from the TIMSS 1999 video study.* Washington: National Center for Educational Statistics.

Huang, R. and Leung, K. S. F., 2006. Cracking the paradox of Chinese learners: looking into the mathematics classrooms in Hong Kong and Shanghai. In L. Fan, N. Y. Wong, J. Cai and S. Li, eds, *How Chinese learn mathematics: perspectives from insiders.* Singapore: World Scientific, 348–81.

Leung, F. K. S., 1995. The mathematics classroom in Beijing, Hong Kong and London. *Educational Studies in Mathematics,* 29, 297–325.

Ma, Y., Zhao, D. and Tuo, Z., 2004. Differences within communities: how is mathematics taught in rural and urban regions in mainland China? In L. Fan, N. Y. Wong, J. Cai and S. Li, eds, *How Chinese learn mathematics: perspectives from insiders.* Singapore: World Scientific, 413–42.

Marton, F. and Booth, S., 1997. *Learning and awareness.* Mahwah, NJ: Lawrence Erlbaum.

Marton, F., Watkins, D. A. and Tang, C., 1997. Discontinuities and continuities in the experience of learning: an interview study of high-school students in Hong Kong. *Learning and Instruction,* 7, 21–48.

National Council of Teachers of Mathematics (NCTM), 2000. *Principles and standards for school mathematics.* Reston, VA: NCTM.

Rittle-Johnson, B. and Star, J. R., 2007. Does comparing solution methods facilitate conceptual and procedural knowledge? An experimental study on learning to solve equations. *Journal of Educational Psychology,* 99 (1), 561–74.

Runesson, U., 1999. *Variationens pedagogik: skilda sätt att behandla ett matematiskt innehåll* [*The pedagogy of variation: different ways of handling a mathematics topic*]. Doctoral dissertation. Sweden: Göteborgs Universitet.

Star, J. R., 2005. Reconceptualizing procedural knowledge. *Journal for Research in Mathematics Education*, 36 (5), 404–11.

Watkins, D. A. and Biggs, J. B., eds, 2001. *Teaching the Chinese learner: psychological and pedagogical perspectives*. Hong Kong: Comparative Education Research Centre, University of Hong Kong.

Wong, N. Y., 2002. Conceptions of doing and learning mathematics among Chinese. *Journal of Intercultural Studies*, 23 (2), 211–29.

—, 2006. From 'entering the Way' to 'exiting the Way': in search of a bridge to span 'basic skills' and 'process abilities'. In F. K. S. Leung, G.-D. Graf and F. J. Lopez-Real, eds, *Mathematics education in different cultural traditions: the 13th ICMI Study*. New York: Springer, 111–28.

—, 2008. Confucian heritage culture learner's phenomenon: from 'exploring the middle zone' to 'constructing a bridge'. *ZDM – The International Journal on Mathematics Education*, 40, 973–81.

—, 2009. Exemplary mathematics lessons: what lessons we can learn from them? *ZDM – The International Journal on Mathematics Education*, 41, 379–84.

Zhang, Q. P. and Wong, N. Y., 2010. Mathematics teachers' professional knowledge, beliefs and their implications on their teaching. In Y. Shimizu, Y. Sekiguchi and K. Hino, eds, *Proceedings of the 5th East Asia Regional Conference on Mathematics Education*, Vol. 2. Tokyo, Japan: Japan Society of Mathematics Education, 849–56.

Classroom Culture and Mathematics Learning

Eva Jablonka

17

Core readings

The core readings addressed in this chapter are as follows:

Bauersfeld, H., 1980. Hidden dimensions in the so-called reality of a mathematics classroom. *Educational Studies in Mathematics*, 11 (1), 23–41.

Yackel, E. and Cobb, P., 1996. Sociomathematical norms, argumentation and autonomy in mathematics. *Journal for Research in Mathematics Education*, 27 (4), 458–77.

Lubienski, S., 2000. Problem solving as a means toward mathematics for all: an exploratory look through a class lens. *Journal for Research in Mathematics Education*, 31 (4), 454–82.

Gellert, U. and Jablonka, E., 2009. 'I am not talking about reality': word problems and the intricacies of producing legitimate text. In L. Verschaffel, B. Van Dooren and S. Mukhopadhyay, eds, *Words and worlds: modelling verbal descriptions of situations*. Rotterdam, Netherlands: Sense, 39–53.

Introduction

Alongside emergent new theories that treat cognition as culturally situated and learning as a social process, mathematical reasoning and thinking have come to be seen as inseparable from the socio-cultural contexts in which they develop. These socio-cultural theories do not describe mathematics learning in terms of individuals' acquisition of knowledge, but as their participation in, or movement through, various mathematical practices, in which they learn to participate successfully. Consequently, a number of researchers have viewed classrooms as the socio-cultural context of mathematical reasoning and thinking at school.

In mathematics classrooms, the meanings that teachers and students ascribe to objects and activities are established and modified in an interactive process. Thus, as Bauersfeld

(1980) reminds us, the dynamics of classroom life have to be acknowledged if we are to understand success and failure in learning mathematics. In this respect, Yackel and Cobb (1996), starting from a cognitive perspective derived from constructivism, found a need to broaden their perspective when trying to understand classroom events. Drawing on the work of several German mathematics educators, including Bauersfeld, they developed a micro-sociological approach, based on interactionism, to the analysis of mathematical activity. From this perspective, as outlined by Bauersfeld, the development of individuals' reasoning and sense-making processes cannot be separated from their participation in the interactive constitution of taken-as-shared mathematical meanings in the classroom.

However, to understand how students' participation in mathematics classroom practice develops and is sustained we need to go beyond notions of locally produced taken-as-shared mathematical meanings. For example, not all students are equally skilled in interpreting the cues by the teacher that legitimate what counts as an appropriate contribution to a mathematical discussion. In this respect Lubienski's (2000) investigation into her own classroom, as a teacher in a problem-centred curriculum development project, shows that such differences have social rather than individual bases. Finally, drawing on theories of recontextualization, Gellert and Jablonka (2009) show how students' difficulties may be linked to the ways in which the discontinuity between school mathematics and practical everyday knowledge is embodied in classroom communication.

Through an examination of these core readings, this chapter discusses how students' access to mathematical knowledge is shaped by classroom culture. A key issue that emerges from the core readings is that the choice of theoretical vantage point for investigating what is going on 'below the surface' informs greatly our understanding of the mathematics classroom.

The constitutive role of classroom interaction

In 1979, Heinrich Bauersfeld, one of the pioneers of mathematics education research in Germany, gave an invited address to the annual meeting of the National Council of Teachers of Mathematics (NCTM) in Boston (documented in Bauersfeld 1980). He spoke about 'hidden dimensions in the so-called reality of a mathematics classroom' and provided good reasons for researching these dimensions. Whether what is going on 'below the surface' in mathematics classrooms remains not only hidden to the students and teachers, but also to the researcher, is a matter of methodology and theorizing. Bauersfeld suggests that ethnomethodology and linguistics are promising theoretical vantage points for researching the hidden dimensions of mathematics classrooms. While promoting the study of the interactive constitution of shared meanings in classrooms, Bauersfeld also reminds the reader to consider the impact of institutional settings. Institutions 'constitute norms and roles', 'develop rituals in actions and in meanings', 'tend to seclusion and self-sufficiency' and 'even produce their own content – in this case, school mathematics' (pp. 35–6).

Bauersfeld suggests that theoretical sophistication is necessary if research is to inform classroom practice. Through a review of influential theory in neighbouring fields, he argues for viewing human interaction as constitutive for the social generation of mathematical knowledge and for individuals' constructions in the social context of the classroom. Bauersfeld draws on two doctoral dissertations from the University of Illinois showing how classroom interaction plays a constitutive role in students' development of mathematical meanings, namely Stanley Erlwanger (1975) and George Bernard Shirk (1972). While Erlwanger's case study of Benny's conceptions of fractions became rather well known, Shirk's work did not. In his article, Bauersfeld demonstrates the constitutive role of interaction through his reanalysis of transcripts from one of Shirk's geometry lessons and shows how both teacher and students act according to their particular subjective realities. They work at 'cross purposes', both convinced they understand the situation (Bauersfeld 1980, p. 30).

The unfamiliar approach to geometry represented in the lesson belongs to a reform curriculum that became known as 'New Math' in the United States initiated by economic arguments that stressed the competitive advantage of a nation with a mathematically skilled workforce (after the Sputnik satellite had been successfully launched by the Soviet Union). New Mathematics was intended to be a uniform mathematics curriculum that would provide access to scientific knowledge for all students. However, as can be seen in the analysis, the way the new geometry curriculum was enacted in Shirk's classroom failed to afford an introduction for all the students to a form of motion geometry based on definitions of 'slides', 'flips', and 'turns' and their corresponding icons (e.g. 'slide arrows' and 'turn arrows').

In the episode, after presenting an image of two intersecting lines, the teacher obviously expected a statement such as 'intersecting lines cannot be parallel because one cannot draw a slide arrow that would move the lines together'. However, Kevin appeared to interpret his teacher's question, 'Can you draw a slide arrow that'll go from one of these lines to the other?' as an invitation to devise new forms of slide arrows, and not as a theoretical question asking for a statement about the impossibility of doing so. Consequently, students began drawing 'wrong versions' of slide arrows. While Shirk reconstructs the teacher's and students' utterances merely as an externalization of their conceptual frameworks, in his reinterpretation Bauersfeld stresses that the meanings are interactively constructed, through mutually related expectations and interpretations that change in the course of the conversation.

In his theoretical considerations, Bauersfeld points out that the mathematical problems (tasks) and concepts are functions of the situation and not stable. Further, the construction of meanings cannot be ascribed to one single participant, and there is no causality in the development of meanings. Still, the meanings developed by the participants are not to be seen as completely unpredictable and arbitrary. There are still 'rules', but these are 'rules about the constituting of situations and meanings rather than rules about the situations and meanings themselves' (p. 33). The participants' turns are not only reactions to the preceding moves of the other side but depend on more general interpretations of the situation and one's own role in it. These interpretations are used 'as an index from which he [the speaker] forms his utterances and from which he decides his "choice of grammar"' (p. 34).

Since Bauersfeld's address, many researchers in mathematics education have come to investigate 'the hidden dimensions in the so-called reality of a mathematics classroom'. An essential question is how the students' understandings of the hidden rules afford or constrain their access to mathematical knowledge. The most prominent theories employed to achieve this goal include Symbolic Interactionism and phenomenology, in particular ethnomethodology, as well as theories that are concerned with social reproduction through schooling, such as those of Pierre Bourdieu and Basil Bernstein.

Negotiation of mathematical meanings in inquiry classrooms

Yackel and Cobb (1996) start with an interest in developing research-based instructional designs. In their article, they expand their earlier work on 'classroom social norms' through a focus on the changing character of the 'sociomathematical norms' when the construction of new mathematical knowledge is at issue. Empirical data are episodes from a second-grade classroom that followed an inquiry approach. In their analysis, Yackel and Cobb focus on the processes by which sociomathematical norms are interactively constructed and how these norms regulate mathematical argumentation. Through their investigation, they attempt to account not only for how students develop specific mathematical beliefs and values that are consistent with the reform movement's emphasis on mathematical inquiry but also how students develop 'a mathematical disposition'. Similar to Bauersfeld, they use their empirical data as illustrations for their theoretical considerations.

In Yackel and Cobb's terminology, 'classroom social norms' are general norms that can apply to any subject and are not unique to mathematics. As the authors are interested in project classrooms that adopt an inquiry approach, they document and analyse how teachers develop and sustain social norms that afford this approach, such as explanation, justification and argumentation (e.g. Yackel et al. 1991). 'Sociomathematical norms' are normative aspects of mathematics discussion specific to regulating students' mathematical activity. For example, normative understandings of what counts as a mathematically different, mathematically sophisticated, mathematically efficient and mathematically elegant solution, and what counts as an acceptable mathematical explanation.

In their article, Yackel and Cobb reconstruct the establishment of the norms of 'mathematical difference' and 'mathematical sophistication' and discuss how these regulate mathematical argumentation and thereby influence the learning opportunities for the students and their teacher. They also look at the interactive construction of what counts as an acceptable mathematical explanation or justification. In the classroom, there is also a taken-as-shared sense of *when* it is appropriate to contribute to a discussion and not only *how*.

Yackel and Cobb notice a reflexive dynamic in the development of new sociomathematical norms. The current perceived general norms regulate the students' mathematical argumentation, but these norms in turn are only established through single events of mathematical argumentation. In general, this relationship between singular meanings and the context in which these meanings are established is referred to as 'reflexivity' by ethnomethodologists. Voigt (1994) gives an example from primary mathematics instruction: When first-graders come to the classroom, they might be confronted with objects they know from their everyday context, such as apples or coloured wooden blocks. Then the participants in the classroom get used to ascribing mathematical signs and meanings to configurations of these objects. At the same time it becomes clearer to the participants, how the context of a mathematics classroom constrains possible meanings, that is, what mathematical activity is supposed to be about. Through such a reflexive process, the context of school mathematics is continually constituted.

Yackel and Cobb are optimistic about the potential of an inquiry approach, stating that establishing 'a community of validators' in an inquiry mathematics classroom encourages the 'devolution of responsibility', which in turn affords the growth of intellectual autonomy (p. 473). A question that is not asked here concerns the implicitness of both the classroom social norms and the sociomathematical norms. The teacher in the inquiry classroom seems to face a paradoxical situation. Obviously, the overall norms to be established were there from the outset, in the form of a characterization of a project classroom following an inquiry mathematics tradition. One of these norms is that children should feel obliged to try to develop personally meaningful solutions that they can explain and justify in a legitimate way. But as has been elaborated by means of the construct of 'reflexivity', what counts as legitimate is only in the making and it can only be inferred from instances. While the researchers can infer the norms from observing patterns and regularities in interaction, the students might not all be equally skilled in guessing what is to be considered the essential thing in a mathematical argumentation according to the emerging norms. The teacher's comments and evaluations that aim at establishing a new sociomathematical norm might be subtle and indirect, as can bee seen in the transcript from the episode about 'different' solutions. Are all students equally skilled in interpreting the teacher's hints? This is the question Lubienski (2000) investigates.

Unequal negotiation of meanings?

Lubienski (2000) is interested in how a school mathematics reform launched by the NCTM with a focus on problem solving might affect different students. The pedagogy advocated in the reform shows similar features as the one employed in the classrooms studied by Yackel and Cobb. Lubienski sees student preferences for a specific mathematical pedagogy not as originating in individual differences (in achievement and temperament) but in differences in their social class culture. That is, the differences have a social rather than an individual base. She argues for the importance of studying class-related equity issues because success in mathematics education is potentially rewarding in terms of social and economic status. In addition to other barriers, changing mathematics curricula and pedagogy might remove or add barriers for lower class students.

From most students' points of view, if they were struggling with the new pedagogy and content, something other than the mathematics posed the difficulties. Two aspects of the mathematical problems as advocated in the reform were their openness and their contextualized nature. In Lubienski's study it turned out that these two aspects favoured students with higher socio-economic status (SES). Several other features of classroom interaction that adopted the 'sociomathematical and classroom social norms' of the reform also made a difference. Some of the differences were linked to favourable study habits and dispositions, such as perseverance, intellectual curiosity and self-confidence.

Another main differentiating factor was the implicitness of the criteria for what counts as an appropriate mathematical investigation. The tasks in the curriculum project in Lubienski's class were designed so that in the course of their investigations, as well as through follow-up questions and the teacher's scaffolding, the students should encounter important mathematical ideas. The contextualization in real-world contexts served as a means towards this end. That is, it is not the problem context that is of interest, but the potential for generalizing mathematical structures and methods. Homework problems were mathematically similar, but contextualized differently. The problems seemed to be quite diverse in terms of their 'size'. The amount of time required to solve them could vary from several minutes to several days. Altogether, these features of the problems make it very hard to infer criteria for what counts as accepted mathematical activity. Lubienski (pp. 469–70) offers an extended example of an approach to a problem about sharing pizza, an approach heavily influenced by practical concerns as it was typical of many of the lower SES students (see also the discussion of Cooper and Dunne's work in the chapter by Lerman, this volume). The problem was meant to help students learn to create and compare ratios. From the question, 'If you like the two groups of friends equally well, which table would you join and why?', it is not possible to determine the criteria for a legitimate solution. What type of response is expected and how is one supposed to articulate one's ideas? As far as contextualized problems are concerned, Gellert and Jablonka (2009) explore these difficulties.

Lubienski's results indicate that the higher SES students could see themselves more in the role as creators of mathematical knowledge ('figuring out the rules'), whereas the lower SES students did not. The two groups of students also positioned themselves differently in relation to the knowledge. The lower SES students talked in the third person about the curriculum ('what they want us to learn').

These were not unexpected findings. In a study in Victoria, Australia, Teese (2000) also found that the inquiry curriculum of the 'investigative project 1992' disadvantaged working-class girls. Indeed, about 40 per cent of the female working-class students, who had been successful in their earlier traditional setting, received the lowest possible grade or could not even master the minimum criteria for getting a grade (p. 171). In her seminal investigation, Anyon (1981) found differences in the general conception of knowledge, and in particular of mathematical knowledge, in relation to differences in school cultures. Her case study of five New Jersey elementary schools in contrasting social class settings showed that while there were similarities in curriculum topics and materials, there were differences in the way the curriculum was enacted within the schools. These differences corresponded with different views about knowledge. In the working-class schools, knowledge was perceived by the children as being about given facts and right answers. In the middle-class school, it was seen as resource for qualification, and in the affluent professional school, knowledge was linked to having ideas and to thinking. In Lubienski's class the students also seemed to hold different views, as reflected in their preferences, even if they were experiencing a similar enacted curriculum.

The problem of recontextualization

Gellert and Jablonka discuss the problems students face with word problems from a theoretical perspective that employs notions from Basil Bernstein's theory of pedagogic discourse and related sociological research. They see mathematical classroom practices and their associated activities (such as solving word problems) as an outcome of a 'recontextualisation of discourses'. Recontextualization is a key notion in Bernstein's theory, where a pedagogic discourse is *defined* 'by the fact that it recontextualises a practice by moving it from its original site in order to use it for a different purpose' (Gellert and Jablonka 2009, p. 42). When recontextualizing knowledge into the school mathematics curriculum, decisions are taken about what areas of knowledge are selected, how these areas are related to or separated from each other, and also how they relate to other domains inside as well as outside school. Particularly primary and lower secondary school curricula often intend to connect school mathematical knowledge to the local and particular of everyday knowledge. The recontextualization of everyday activities in school mathematics brings about a new focus and a change of perspective. There are certain aspects to be sought after while others have to be dismissed, and a decision has to be made about what is considered significant and what is accidental. New meanings and new relationships between meanings are established and at the same time new forms of expressions are introduced as well as new rules for elaborating their internal coherence.

Employing a categorization by Dowling (1998), Gellert and Jablonka describe word problems as located in an intermediary domain, between everyday discourse and school mathematical discourse. As with the two pizza-tables problem discussed in Lubienski's study, many such word problems aim to offer a route into the esoteric domain of mathematics, but this purpose may remain largely hidden to many students. However, there are also curricula, as shown by Dowling (1998), that more or less deprive students of any esoteric domain activities. For these students, school mathematics is restricted to public domain activities, in which they get 'stuck'. According to Dowling's analysis, this pedagogy is implicitly aimed at students' identification with manual occupations or the prolongation of domestic activities. He calls this 'the myth of participation'.

For other students, mathematics curricula sketch routes from the public domain to the esoteric domain, as, for example, the reform curriculum in Lubienski's class. The students were meant to develop mathematical knowledge that is transferable across the different contexts represented in the problems. From the students' point of view, this means that weakly institutionalized expressions (everyday language in the problem statements) need to be transformed into strongly institutionalized expressions (mathematical terms and symbols), as the reference of these expressions shifts towards strongly institutionalized school mathematical meanings. In the pizza-table problem, for example, friends and pizzas have to be translated into ratios between whole numbers, and by this translation, the reference context can be changed from eating pizzas to rational number arithmetic. But the transformations of expression and reference context do not necessarily coincide. According to Gellert and Jablonka (2009) there is no straightforward step from public to esoteric domain text. They describe the transformation in terms of a transition from horizontal to vertical discourse, two constructs that also stem from Bernstein's theory.

> For the students, the shift from weakly institutionalised to strongly institutionalised expressions and contents translates into intricacies of adequate participation in the mathematics classroom, that is, of producing legitimate text. (p. 48)

In a transcript from a German classroom, where they solve a problem about farmers exchanging parts of their property, as well as in the formulation of a problem about a rower rowing downstream and upstream discussed in a Hong Kong classroom, Gellert and Jablonka look at hints from which the students might have guessed on which knowledge domain one is supposed to draw when solving the problems. Looking again at the pizza-table problem from Lubienski's class, it becomes obvious that it is of help to know the mathematical area to which the problem is related. This area is stated in the title of the figure, 'Figure 1. Problem from trial version of Comparing and Scaling' (Lubienski 2000, p. 569), but not in the problem as given to the students. Some higher SES students seemed to be more skilled in understanding at least the hint that the problem is to be approached through the gaze of school mathematics. One such clue is, for example, the strange pattern-like drawing of the tables, pizzas and people. The everyday experience of sharing turned out to be only partly helpful or even distracting for the students.

According to Dowling (1998), the suggestion that mathematics would be directly helpful in solving problems from the everyday domain, also constitutes a myth, the 'myth of reference'. This myth is distributed through a curriculum that uses contextualized problems as a starting point for mathematical abstractions, usually a curriculum for students aiming at non-manual professions. But in contrast to the 'myth of participation', this myth is overcome as soon as the students engage in mathematical explorations and make mathematical generalizations (and thus leave the problem context behind as irrelevant). In Lubienski's classroom, the students faced the same curriculum, but still learned different lessons. Only higher SES students seemed to have acquired the rules behind the game, namely that the contextualized problems are meant to lead to mathematical generalizations. Gellert and Jablonka see the problem linked to the implicitness of the criteria:

> We interpret the students' difficulties when solving word problems, which serve as a pedagogic device aiming at providing a route from the public to the esoteric domain, as a consequence of the implicitness of the recontextualisation principle in classroom discourse. (Gellert and Jablonka, p. 51)

In Lubienski's class, the implicitness of the principle differentiated between students in line with their socio-economic status and gender. Male students and high SES students were favoured. This suggests they must have acquired the rules of the game very quickly or elsewhere. When looking at the transcript from the episode about 'slide arrows' in Bauersfeld's article, one sees that the possibility of 'misreading' a task as located in everyday discourse is not limited to contextualized problems. As there is no shared frame of reference from the outset, the teacher's initial question or task is necessarily ambivalent in order to make the interactive construction of new knowledge possible. Only retrospectively the official solution reduces the ambivalence of the question (e.g. one has to use 'slide arrows' in the answer). Paradoxically, the institutionalized solution constitutes the meaning of the task of which it is a consequence (cf. 'reflexivity', referred to in the section 'Negotiation of mathematical meanings in inquiry classrooms'). Consequently, if one does not want to reduce mathematics to its purely technical and algorithmic features, the tension between implicitness and explicitness cannot be resolved just by simply stating the criteria. It is an issue of research to explore different scaffolding strategies of teachers that do not reproduce a stratification of achievement within the classroom.

Researching hidden dimensions

Norms of classroom practice as (emerging) conventions

The 'sociomathematical' and 'social' norms (Yackel and Cobb 1996) embody expectations and values that are supposed to be shared by the group about what is an appropriate contribution to the practice. These norms can be reconstructed from an observers' point of view by the fact that most participants show some signs of having adopted the expected actions at some stage. The reconstruction resembles an ethnographer's reconstruction of the 'folk-ways'. Such an interpretation of classroom practice will be a hermeneutic, immanent one. But it is not done by the participants who are involved, except, perhaps, in the case of a breakdown of the smooth flow of coordinated actions. The 'didactical contract' (Brousseau 1980), and some of the 'meta-discursive rules' (e.g. Sfard 2001) refer to these types of norms. As it is in Yackel and Cobb's article, the focus in studies of classroom practice is often on the changing character of the norms when the construction of new mathematical knowledge is at issue. Teachers and students in mathematics classrooms turn out to be in the possession of unconscious practices or routines that help them to structure the process of constituting knowledge that eventually counts as shared knowledge. The notion of routine here refers to the fact that these interaction patterns are unconsciously accomplished, have the function of reducing the complexity of the situation and yield a harmonizing effect (Voigt 1994). However, successful participation in these routines does not imply that all students share the mathematical meanings the teacher intended to constitute. The students might only have developed the competencies of how to participate in the interaction. They might spend much effort in finding out the implicit rules of the 'didactical contract', which is constituted through mutual expectations and interpretations of 'specific habits' of the teacher by the students and vice versa (Brousseau 1980, p. 180). This description of the didactical contract is reminiscent of the description of interpretative procedures described by ethnomethodology (see Bauersfeld 1980).

Hidden principles related to a wider social context

Teachers and students are not free to redefine the practice of school mathematics in their negotiation of meanings; there are principles in operation that guarantee continuity of classroom practices. Teachers have an obligation to deliver the intended curriculum and reach a result that is defined by curriculum documents and assessment practices. Teaching is the mediation of the institutional culture by local personnel. Patterns of classroom interaction are not only accomplished at the initiative of the participants in a single classroom, but also functional in terms of the goals of the institution. One of these goals is channelling different groups of students into different career pipelines. The question of who the students are (in terms of educational career and academic achievement, social and economic background, immigrant status, etc.) and whether they understand the (hidden) agenda behind the teacher's instructions or questions, is neither a focus of Bauersfeld's discussion, nor is it taken up by Yackel and Cobb. This is partly due to the theoretical frameworks chosen by these researchers.

For analysing classrooms in relation to the institutional context, a layer of interpretation has to be introduced that goes beyond both the reconstruction of the participants' interpretations (and the individual students' learning) and the reconstruction of classroom norms. The participants' ways of acting is then interpreted by using information and theories, which the participants are not aware of. This is to reveal the social function of what happens in classrooms, caused by factors to which the students and teachers have no access. It is to reconstruct those principles that function in covert ways and serve the interest of power in the social system, independently of the actors' intentions. Conceptualization and investigation of these principles draws on structuralist and critical theories.

Lubienski's and Gellert and Jablonka's articles deal with issues and principles that account for social reproduction. Lubienski's study shows that the recontextualization of domestic practices in school mathematics in the context of an inquiry mathematics classroom can serve as a means of stratification of achievement. Bernstein's notion of recontextualization draws attention to the fact that what he calls 'instructional discourse' (cf. the 'sociomathematical norms') is inevitably shaped by the 'regulative discourse' (cf. the 'social norms') that operates in the institutional context. Different recontextualization principles create different 'sociomathematical' and 'social' norms, which in turn might facilitate or restrict access for different social groups to specific forms of mathematical practices and discourses.

Teese's (2000) study also includes a curriculum analyses. He draws on the work of Bourdieu and argues that the potential for discriminating between groups with different social backgrounds is already built into the curriculum. The mathematics curriculum, which increases cognitive demand with each grade, calls increasingly on embedded scholastic attitudes and behaviours. As such, students' success depends on personal characteristics, such as personal organization, study habits, concentration and self-reliance in the face of difficulties.

Many of the features of the curriculum and pedagogy in the classrooms studied by Yackel and Cobb as well as by Lubienski resemble what Bernstein (1996) called an 'invisible pedagogy'. Bernstein's theoretical considerations 'predict' that low SES students prefer stronger teacher control and more explicit directions, and also that they would experience more difficulties with having to move from descriptions of everyday situations to exploring mathematical structures that could be used to describe these and solve problems.

Conclusion

Classroom research challenges simple assumptions about mathematics teaching and learning, but also offers possibilities to develop sophisticated ways of analysis of classroom data that help disentangle different aspects and avoid all too simple descriptions of what works in classrooms. Cross-cultural classroom studies have the potential to identify different ways in which teachers overcome similar problems.

Further reading

Barwell, R., ed., 2009. *Multilingualism in mathematics classrooms*. Bristol: Multilingual Matters.

Clarke, D., Emanuelsson, J., Jablonka, E. and Mok, I., eds, 2006. *Making connections: comparing mathematics classrooms around the world*. Rotterdam, Netherlands: Sense.

Cobb, P. and Bauersfeld H., eds, 1995. *The emergence of mathematical meaning. Interaction in classroom cultures*. Hillsdale, NJ: Lawrence Erlbaum.

Jablonka, E. and Gellert, U., 2012. Potentials, pitfalls and discriminations: curriculum conceptions revisited. In O. Skovsmose and B. Greer, eds, *Opening the cage: critique and politics of mathematics education*. Rotterdam, Netherlands: Sense, 287–308.

Krummheuer, G., 2011. Representation of the notion 'learning-as-participation' in everyday situations of mathematics classes. *ZDM – The International Journal on Mathematics Education*, 43 (1), 81–90.

Additional references

Anyon, J., 1981. Social class and school knowledge. *Curriculum Inquiry*, 11 (1), 3–42.

Bernstein, B., 1996. *Pedagogy, symbolic control and identity: theory, research, critique. Vol. 5: Class, codes and control*. London: Taylor and Francis.

Brousseau, G., 1980. L'échec et le contrat. *Recherches*, 41, 177–82.

Dowling, P., 1998. *The sociology of mathematics education: mathematical myths/pedagogical texts*. London: Falmer Press.

Erlwanger, S. H., 1975. *Case studies of children's conceptions of mathematics*. Doctoral dissertation. Urbana-Champaign: University of Illinois. (Reprinted in *Journal of Children's Mathematical Behavior*, 1, 157–281.)

Sfard, A., 2001. There is more to discourse than meets the ears: looking at thinking as communicating to learn more about mathematical learning. *Educational Studies in Mathematics*, 46, 13–57.

Shirk, G. B., 1972. *An examination of conceptual frameworks of beginning mathematics teachers*. Unpublished doctoral dissertation. Urbana-Champaign: University of Illinois.

Teese, R., 2000. *Academic success and social power. Examinations and inequality*. Melbourne: Melbourne University Press.

Voigt, J., 1994. Negotiation of mathematical meaning and learning mathematics. *Educational Studies in Mathematics*, 26, 275–98.

Yackel, E., Cobb, P. and Wood, T., 1991. Small-group interactions as a source of learning opportunities in second-grade mathematics. *Journal for Research in Mathematics Education*, 22, 390–408.

Index